D0997453

EXTREME
RAMBLING

To the four women who made this possible:
Jenny, Margaret, Nava and Susan.

MARK THOMAS
EXTREME RAMBLING

EBURY
PRESS

First published in 2011 by Ebury Press, an imprint of Ebury Publishing
This edition published 2012

The Random House Group Limited Reg. No. 954009

Addresses for companies within the Random House Group can be found at
www.randomhouse.co.uk

A CIP catalogue record for this book is available from the British Library

Penguin Random House is committed to a sustainable future for
our business, our readers and our planet. This book is made from
Forest Stewardship Council® certified paper.

Printed and bound in Great Britain by Clays Ltd, St Ives plc

Designed and set by seagulls.net

ISBN 9780091927813

To buy books by your favourite authors and register for offers visit
www.randomhouse.co.uk

contents

ISRAEL AND THE WEST BANK

- - - 1949 ARMISTICE GREEN LINE
- BARRIER CONSTRUCTED
- PLANNED ROUTE

Kilometers
0   5   10   20

MEDITERRANEAN SEA

ZUBUBA

AL JALAMA

BISAN

WEST BANK

TOXIC

TULKARM

ZOO

ARAB AR RAMADIN

QALQILIYA

SALFIT

JORDAN RIVER

JORDAN

TEL AVIV

BEN GORION AIRPORT

NI'LIN
RAMALLAH

MAKKABIM

JERICHO

EAST JERUSALEM

JERUSALEM

ISRAEL

BETHLEHEM

HEBRON

IDHNA

DEAD SEA

AT TUWANI

read this now!

Epiphanies simply are not what they used to be. They used to involve being blinded by spiteful gods or screaming in overflowing bathtubs, but on my road to Jerusalem there was no great road-to-Damascus moment. When I decided to walk the length of the Israeli Barrier (the 'Wall'), to use its concrete and wire as a route map across the West Bank, the dawning was slow and gradual. The light bulb that went on over my head was an environmentally friendly one, so there was a prolonged period of darkness eventually followed by a dim yellow light that appeared slightly sickly.

While the notion to hike the West Bank arrived gently and without fuss one afternoon in 2009 the transformation of the idea into an obsession was rapid and total. I even gave it a name: 'Walking the Wall'. Time in the diary was set aside for 'Walking the Wall', my computer had a budget file for 'Walking the Wall', a map was stuck on the wall under the title 'Walking the Wall', but, most of all, I talked to a lot of people about 'Walking the Wall'.

The first person whose advice I sought was a friend from teenage years called Tony. Talking to him first was essential, as he might live in Stoke Newington and have the usual worries about work and children but he regularly goes on holiday to North Korea. In fact, he recently took his fifteen-year-old son to the Mongolian plains for a month to live off yak butter, and hunt with eagles. With a track record like that, he was exactly the person to discuss walking in a territory under military occupation: if *he* had said that the idea was ludicrous I would simply have called the whole thing off.

Unsurprisingly, Tony approves as we chat over a Formica table in a Charing Cross Road deli. Wearing three days' worth of stubble, he slouches over a cappuccino, skimming the froth off with a teaspoon and slurping chocolate powder.

'How long is it?' he asks.

'The wall? Quite long.'

Tony fires a look through his glasses at me that suggested any serious traveller would know how long their journey was going to be.

'Hundreds of miles,' I stammer, 'at least ... but not silly hundreds.'

'Not thousands, then.'

'No, not thousands, no.'

'That *would* be silly,' he says wryly.

'These hundreds are very reasonable.'

'Walkable hundreds?'

'Oh, very.'

Tony stirs his coffee, before mischievously asking, 'Do you think you'll find out how long it is before you go, or would you rather it was a surprise?'

Stung by my lack of knowledge, I found five simple facts that I wish I had known in the café. I commend these facts to you, and recommend that these are the ones you retain:

1) The Israeli Barrier already virtually encircles the West Bank; when finished it will surround the Palestinian territory and its population completely.

2) Currently 415 kilometres of the Wall's planned 723 kilometres[1] have been erected since the decision to build it was taken in 2002.

3) The length of the finished Barrier will be over twice as long as the boundary of the West Bank, which is only 315 kilometres long (some readers are currently thinking, 'Why is the Barrier twice as long as the thing it is going round?' The rest of you need to keep up. The answer is that the Barrier snakes in and out of the

West Bank, all the while taking in Palestinian land. The West Bank has, in fact, lost nearly ten per cent of its land, which is now on the other side of the Wall – the Israeli side).

4) This is a simple and good fact to use: the route the Barrier takes is illegal. It was found to be illegal by the International Court of Justice in 2004. The ruling said: 'The wall … and its associated regime are contrary to international law.'*

5) The last fact is that the boundary of the West Bank is called the Green Line.[2] It is internationally recognised and forms the basis for the International Court of Justice's ruling that the Barrier's route, which crosses over the Green Line, is illegal. Israel has consistently refused to recognise the Line, although strangely it comes in handy for demarcating the extent of Israeli law and the start of military law in the Occupied Territories (the West Bank). Just remember that Green Line = boundary and you'll be fine.

Just as I expected Tony to react sympathetically, some of my family, I suspected, might not. My mum lives in a bungalow in Bournemouth and has her thermostat set two degrees below care-home level. She is a devoted and wonderful woman who happens to read the *Daily Mail* and would have been happier if all the clothes I took had had nametags with the words, 'Mark Thomas – Hostage' sewn into them. By the time I left for the airport she had essentially written her television appeal for my release, and was looking forward to meeting Terry Waite.

Others (friends, colleagues and people who had been in the same room as a Muslim in the last ten years) managed to discuss the trip without mentioning the words, 'Al-Qaeda', 'gaffer tape'

---

* *'Legal Consequences of the Construction of a Wall in the Occupied Palestinian Territory'*

and 'diet of hummus for five years'. But no matter what their perspective, everyone I spoke to about 'Walking the Wall' did offer advice on the journey, usually concerning the walking aspect of it. A neighbour and geography teacher cheerily suggested, 'White spirit to keep your feet hard,' as we chatted in the street, and a friend I had travelled to India with and who sounds like a retired colonel said, 'Two words. Double. Socking.'

'What?'

'That's how they got to the Arctic. Double socking. Stops the rubbing.'

People wanted to be helpful and encouraging but usually had little, if any, practical knowledge of the West Bank, and so in the absence of that would give me hiking tips. That was until I met a complete stranger at the theatre one evening who, amazingly, turned out to know the head of the UN Human Rights team in Jerusalem. She had his phone number to hand and duly passed it on.

She also recommended blister plasters.

Some offered views on my personal motives for doing the walk, as it transpires that any forty-seven-year-old male whose behaviour deviates from the approved script is struggling with mortality and existentialism, apparently.

A friend called Nicky said, 'I thought a midlife crisis normally involved sports cars or motorbikes?'

'I can't drive,' I replied.

'So it is a midlife crisis, then.'

Confused, I asked, 'How can rambling be a midlife crisis?'

'You're at that age.'

'I'm forty-seven years old.'

'Exactly!' she said in triumph.

Shortly before setting off, I bumped into fellow London comic Mark Steel, in the BBC canteen. Although the location sounds unpromising, I knew that if anyone could offer a political perspective it was he.

'What have you got coming up then?' said Mark, asking the perennial question comics ask of each other.

'I'm going to write a book.'

'Oh, yeah, on what?'

I told him and he laughed, spluttering in disbelief.

'Why can't you just write a joke?' he blurted out, in his London twang. I grinned, powerless before his coming tirade. 'Oh, no, you couldn't write a joke ...' he started, red-faced with incredulity '... because *anyone* could do that. *You* have to have a mission. You have to make it difficult. You have to do something that no one else would do. I'm going to walk to Afghanistan ...' he starts impersonating me, 'I'm going to walk to Afghanistan but to make it interesting I'm going to do it with no shoes AND find Osama bin Laden. But not just that, 'cos anybody could do that, that is not enough of a mission, no, I'm going to find him, take him prisoner, build a cabaret club in the caves, get an entertainment licence from the Taliban, open a venue, then strap him to a chair and make him laugh. I will force Osama bin Laden to laugh, but not just laugh, I will make him laugh so hard his cock drops off and I will have defeated Al-Qaeda and only then will I be happy because I will have done something no one else has.' He paused and looked at me, shaking his head. 'Fucking hell!' he finished. 'Just write a joke, go on stage and do it!'

Others were even more brusque in their questioning.

'Are you walking on both sides of the Barrier?' asked a woman who worked for Amnesty International in the West Bank cataloguing human rights abuse, which in these globalised times is the nearest you can get to 'a job for life'.

'Yes, that's the plan: to walk on both the Israeli and the Palestinian side.' The idea was to walk the entire length of the Barrier, crossing back and forth between the two sides at checkpoints along the way. In this manner I hoped to experience as much of the Barrier's effects and talk to as many of those involved as possible.

'Good. You should see both sides. How long are you giving yourself to complete it?'

'Six to eight weeks should be enough.'

With a brief, non-committal shrug she said, 'It should be.' She didn't need to add the words: '… but you are utterly ignorant of the situation so this "six to eight weeks" is an arbitrary amount of time plucked at random: you could have used exactly the same amount of factually based analysis and arrived at the answer "Blancmange" and it would be just as valid …' She didn't need to and didn't. Instead, she asked flatly, 'Why are you doing it?'

Put that bluntly, I stammered jollily, 'Well, well … for all sorts of reasons really … but I suppose I shall really find out when I get there.'

'Huh,' she had replied, in a manner suggesting that I could not be more stupid if I had replied, 'Trifle.'

Why *did* I want to do it? Well, I love rambling, I am fascinated by Palestine and Israel, and I like doing normal things in abnormal situations. In my mind, nothing made more sense than Walking the Wall. Palestine compels the attention of everyone from Barack Obama and Desmond Tutu to bin Laden and back again. For me, though, it asks seemingly contradictory questions: how and when will a people be free; and yet what must a country do to protect itself from suicide bombers? I have sympathy with the Palestinian cause but despised the methods of the Second *Intifada*'s and, for a while, like many, I simply switched off about the whole issue. The war on Gaza in December 2008 changed that and with a re-acquired curiosity I found myself wanting to find out more about the West Bank and, in particular, the 'Wall'. Why was it put up in the first place? What does it do? How do people cope with it? And what is going to bring it down? The only real certainty I have is that, at some point, this wall will come down.

Although I refer to 'Walking the Wall', strictly speaking my walk would be a 'ramble'. It's a fantastically English word, full of playfulness. A ramble can be an aimless stroll or an organised route or both, as the word manages to both embrace and undermine seriousness at the same time. I could be talking or walking or both. And what could be more English than rambling, with the possible exception of an irrational hatred of the French, and a lust for the death penalty? Indeed, what could be more subversively English *than* rambling? In 1932, over 400 ramblers took part in a mass trespass in Derbyshire at Kinder Scout: in defiance of the police, they walked onto the moorland to, 'take action to open up the fine country at present denied us'. According to the *Guardian*, the walkers – mainly from Manchester – sang 'The Red Flag' and the '*Internationale*' on the way, trespassed on the land, fought the gamekeepers, had tea, and strictly observed a self-imposed no littering policy. Later that evening, five of them were arrested and the event went down as a milestone on the road to the 'right to roam', which was introduced legally in 2000. The story conjures images of the everyday and the extraordinary, of the dubbining of boots, Thermoses of hot tea and hundreds of people breaking the law to 'open the fine country'. It is, for me at least, a perfect example of an event that defines Englishness, where hundreds of working people risked arrest in order to enjoy the view.

If one of the attractions was walking and the second was Palestine, the Wall was the third. I was in Berlin just after that wall came down, and was struck by how suddenly it fell: a structure that had seemed so impenetrable, so permanent, seemingly crumbled in a moment. Then there is Morocco's 'Berm' (which, as everyone knows, is one of Inspector Clouseau's best gags). But it is also a 2,700-kilometre-long military structure erected across Western Sahara by the Moroccan occupying army, in order to keep the 250,000 refugees living in the desert from reclaiming their homeland. I have stayed with Western Sahara's native Sahrawi refugees in the Algerian desert and was gripped by their belief that one day they would get their homeland back.

Walls like these are an admission of the failure of politics: when the solution to a problem is to throw a wall around it, discourse has come to end and graffiti artists might as well scrawl upon the damned thing: 'WORDS FAILED US'.

*

The Israeli authorities operate tight control of the Wall: after all, having gone to all the trouble to put it up, they are hardly going to piss off, leave the key in the door and an honesty box for any drinks out of the fridge, that would be tantamount to handing operational control over to English Heritage.

Along the Barrier there are a series of checkpoints to control movement in and out of the West Bank. The Israelis compel Palestinians to apply for permits, many of which are refused, if they want to leave the West Bank (Israelis, however, do not require permits to enter or leave the West Bank); and they must also show their ID card, which is green for West Bank Palestinians. Even car number plates are colour-coded: Israeli cars have yellow number plates and West Bank cars white and green. Nor are West Bank vehicles allowed past checkpoints: Palestinians predominantly cross on foot, getting transport to, and then from, the checkpoint.

Things happen by separation walls, for all this control, which do not happen elsewhere: people behave differently in these places. What seems impenetrable is nearly always more porous than imagined. The very structures built to keep people out become the havens of those most adept at getting in. These places become the frontline for different struggles, for better lives, for more money, a way out and more overtly political struggles, too. The area around these structures is often just plain fucking weird. Which of course is an added attraction.

All of this created in me a compulsion to Walk the Wall, although I would learn to explain this venture to friends more succinctly by asking, 'What better way of understanding a conflict about land and identity could there be, than walking it [the Wall] and talking to people?' But I also had a small confession that I would only mention in a whisper and only after checking the coast was clear. It was this: I want to find a really good walk.

I know, I know, I could have gone to Cumbria or got a train to Brighton and bounced along the wonderful chalk of the South Downs, but these places are well hiked and everyone expects the Lake District to be beautiful. Which is why it is so fucking *dull*.

Anyone with any taste knows that predictability is the woodworm of joy. And joy was what I was after. The joy unlike any other in finding a good walk, is genuine bliss. It comes from a combination of the landscape, the route, the company and exposure to the elements that stays on the right side of exposure. Most of all, what makes a 'perfect walk' is losing yourself in a sense of freedom. The West Bank might be the last place a London comic might look for joy, but I was sure I would find it there. And I wondered if it was possible to have a 'perfect walk' along the Barrier? I also wondered if I was turning into a knob.

To organise the logistics of the trip, I assembled a team of people to work with me. First and foremost there would be a schedule. Inevitably a walk like this involves a huge amount of improvising, but I needed to know where I would need to be at the end of each day. If I didn't have a schedule and keep to it, I would run out of time and money and if I didn't reach the end of the Wall, nothing of the walk would count. 'Walking the Wall' means just that.

My long-term researcher, Susan McNicholas, would co-ordinate the entire ramble. 'First you need to go to Jerusalem for a few days and talk to people, and see if they think the walk is possible,' she had said.

Which is what I did. I talked to people at the UN, lawyers, Israeli and Palestinian campaigning groups opposed to the Wall, and Israeli and Palestinian fixers – journalists with good local knowledge and contacts who could help arrange interviews and meetings. Together we worked out the shopping list of things I would need. Firstly, translators – I speak very little Arabic and the nearest I have to any Hebrew is a smattering of north London Yiddish slang: enough to know the difference between a *schmeckel* and a *schmairel* but no more. Then there were the questions of where to stay, what places to avoid and who to try and interview.

Jamal Juma is the coordinator of a grassroots group called Stop the Wall, and he offered to help find translators and places to stay for the first part of the walk on the Palestinian side. Some of the time we would be staying in villages along the route, and some of the time staying 'off the Wall', in guest houses. This would sometimes mean getting a taxi in the morning and driving to the place I had finished walking the night before, picking up the route and starting again from there.

My Israeli fixer was a woman called Nava Mizrahi, an award-winning ex-journalist who now works with foreign film crews, sorting out interviews and logistical problems. She was brilliantly blunt: 'I have never worked on a book before,' she said. 'But I am willing to try and make this work because I think you need someone to help you here. [And] If you only walk with the Palestinian activists then you will do the walk, yes, but you will miss a lot of what is going on.'

The final person was Phil Stebbing, a cameraman who came to film the walk. He had just finished covering the election campaign in Afghanistan, and was another award winner, although you wouldn't have thought it to look at him. He looked like a retired drug dealer with a penchant for not shaving, and the remnants of a Mohican. Half the reason I took him with me was so that if we got stopped and strip-searched, they'd go to him first. I could tell you the things I like about him but we have a whole book ahead of us and that can wait.

Pooling our knowledge, we concluded that the best way to do the ramble and the interviews, *and* keep our families and bank accounts happy, was to split the walk into three rambles, each lasting eighteen days, returning to England in between them. The first ramble would start in the north-east, the second would finish in Jerusalem and the third would hopefully take me south of Hebron to the finish point at Beit Yatir.

With these rudimentary preparations done, the ramble was ready to commence. Any journey of this type is a quest for knowledge, which by its very nature is predicated upon a certain degree of ignorance. And so, fully equipped, I set off for the West Bank.

PART ONE
THE FIRST RAMBLE

ONE OF MANY REASONS FOR THE FENCE

Sdei Trumot, an Israeli village just north of the West Bank. It has an air of suburban calm, or at least it would have but for the highway that runs through it. The homes have red-tiled roofs, high spreading palm trees in their gardens and hedgerows you could balance a spirit level on, but there is also an intermittent background din of someone driving somewhere else.

One of the buildings by the highway is the grocer's: a long, single-storey affair with a front and side porch giving it the appearance of a homely warehouse. The words 'car park' would be too formal a description for the arrangement here; nonetheless, drivers can pull over, get coffee and pastries, and take a seat on the porch under flapping plastic bunting.

The porch has room enough for a serving hatch, a couple of tables and a public toilet. Between the porch and the highway lies a tiny flower bed, sprouting shrubs, cactus and a couple of small, long-leafed cordylines. The plants share the space with some fading hoardings advertising eggs, cheese and milk, amidst the more recognisable symbols of Nestlé and Coca-Cola. Throw in some telegraph poles and a spiky palm, and it's just another piece of roadside clutter you'd drive past in an instant, a second's worth of blurred view out of a side window.

In the middle of this clutter is a white stone about a metre and a half tall; it sits by a young pine. Few people would select this spot, opposite the toilet door, for a memorial stone but this is the spot that marks where Avner Mordechai was killed by a suicide bomber seven years ago. He was fifty-eight.

Dror is Avner's son, and he runs the grocery shop on his own now. This morning he was up early, making the pastries that sit on the porch table, collecting flies as we chat.

'It is the time of year for flies; most of the year it is fine, but not now,' he says, as he shoos a small cloud off the pain au chocolat. Dror passes a photo I had seen earlier hanging inside the shop; a picture of his father taken at a family occasion.

'My father was murdered in 2003.'

'He looks the epitome of a hard-working man,' I say, looking at the tired eyes of a man dressed in a suit that looks like it didn't get worn that often.

'He lived and worked here in this area since 1954. Where we are sitting is where he was blown out ...'

The police believed the suicide bomber might have been waiting for more people to congregate at the bus stop opposite. It is understandable conjecture as, eight days earlier, a suicide bomber had killed seventeen people and wounded one hundred in an attack on the number 14A bus in Jaffa Road, in the centre of Jerusalem. However, regardless of what the bomber may have intended to do, what he had done was to detonate himself inside the store at 6.15 a.m. on 19 June 2003, killing Avner and destroying the shop completely.

Dror describes what greeted him as he came into work that morning: 'I saw the crowd of people and the smoke. I was not allowed past the police line in case there was a second bomb. I felt scared. I didn't know if my father was alive or dead.' Dror was following the ambulance carrying his father to hospital when he heard on the radio that he had died.

When most Israelis are asked about the Barrier they give one answer – it is for security. For them the Barrier is a necessary evil, put up precisely because of what was happening to people like Avner. His death happened at the height of the Palestinian uprising, the Second Intifada, and 2003 saw twenty-five bomb attacks in Israel, which killed 142 people (figures that showed a decline from the previous year, when 220 died). The suicide bombs were detonated in hotels, shops, restaurants, ice cream parlours and a bar mitzvah but the most likely targets for these attacks were buses, bus stops and stations.

This is why Israelis call the Barrier the, 'Security Fence'. And most Israelis think it has worked; since the Barrier went up, suicide bombings have stopped.

But Dror expresses a curious lack of certainty when I ask if the Barrier makes Israel more secure. 'The Fence is a border. Two countries, two people, and the Fence divides the two people.'

Before the shop, Dror's father was a farmer, eating, drinking and working with Palestinians, 'but the good relations we had with them before is over now. This attack made me frightened, scared for the future of the country.'

'Would the Fence have made it safer for your father?'

'If the Fence existed, then 50–50 ... If they want to come to make an explosion they come; the Fence will make it harder but they will find a way.'

As we continue to speak, Dror gets up and shows me around the outside of the store. After the bombing, he set to, rebuilding the shop straight away. 'I am the only son in the family and it took time for the state to help, and so I needed to get back to work to support everyone: wife, family, mother ...'

'When did you put the marker stone here?'

'After we finished building, we put the stone there. It reads: "In memory of Avner Mordechai, killed by terrorists 19/6/2003".'

'Would you mind if I took a photo of you standing next to your father's stone?' I ask.

'OK.' He shrugs and places a hand on the stone. I realise that what I like about Dror is that he doesn't have any profound words to offer the world. His experience has not led him to make great announcements on dignity or reconciliation or revenge; nor does he have to – he has a family to support. There is a hint of sadness to him but, in truth, it is outweighed by tiredness.

chapter 1
AS I WALKED OUT

Walking to the edge of the flat roof, I stand, legs apart, hands on hips, looking through the hazy winter sunlight and to the distant hills. Two men, Palestinians, are standing behind me and together we survey the route we are to take. Slowly, I raise my arm and point to a spot on the horizon.

'There,' I declare with all the gravitas of an Old Testament prophet. 'That is where we start our walk.'

'Where?' enquires a man called Fadhi, with a voice that sounds as if he is squinting.

'There, where my finger points. That is where we will start.'

The wind blows lightly, and high, high above a black bird circles. Then a voice from behind says, 'But that is Jordan.'

Fadhi pauses with the natural timing of man who has spoken at many meetings before he diplomatically suggests, 'You can start in Jordan if you want, but it will take some time to arrange ...'

The bird circles closer and I remain still, facing the hills, looking out to the valley and say one word. 'Ish ...'

'I am sorry?' says Fadhi.

I wobble my pointing finger, as if I'd always intended to be vague. 'There ... *ish* is where we will start.'

Fadhi is the Jordan Valley coordinator for the umbrella organisation Stop the Wall, who have agreed to help with translators and guides. He joins me in pointing and declaiming. 'That is the no-man's land, the border, we shall walk up to there ... and see,' he says, leaving the final words hanging in the air, surrounded by possibilities.

Jacob, the second Palestinian on the roof and our translator for the day, smokes and smiles.

'Jacob farms this land,' says Fadhi, 'so he will be able to take you westward, right up to the Wall. What can the soldiers do? Tell him not to farm? We will see.'

The two of them debate where to start the walk, but I am distracted. From up here, the Barrier is some 400 metres in front of us, and it appears as a rather dull-looking, long fence, stretching across a plain before disappearing into the wonderfully crumpled geography of the Jordan river valley and the hills beyond.

The mundanity of this first impression of the Barrier is confounding. A line of wire mesh doesn't fit into the image of 'The Wall'; from my visual lexicon of walls that carve through countries, I expected romantic martyrdom, a dash of Expressionism, a nod at George Orwell and the odd soundtrack of David Bowie songs recorded in Berlin. I expected the Barrier itself to be more dramatic, more epic, perhaps. The last thing I expected was a long mesh fence in a flat muddy field. I am about to spend eight weeks walking alongside this Barrier and will come to see it dominate the land in the most dramatic ways but for now this could be Runcorn on the outskirts of an industrial estate, guarded by a sixty-year-old bloke with a dog and a Portakabin that smells of rolling tobacco and messy divorce.

This first day of any journey is full of emotions, but I wasn't expecting disappointment to be one of them. I just don't think I envisaged myself saying, 'Well, it doesn't *look* very oppressive.' But one thing is sure: if the view from the roof is anything to go by, the walking should be easy. A nice flat plain, with no major rivers, mountains or fjords that we can see; just flat farming land, a slight incline and a main road to cross about halfway through. There are a few clouds in the sky but these are wispy specks that quickly get blown across to Jordan. The going appears to get a little hilly towards the end, but it doesn't look hard. This is what you need on the first day: no big climbs, no real prospect of rain; no surprises.

*

Twenty minutes later I get a familiar feeling of worry and excitement as we cross the fields towards no-man's land. Phil the cameraman, Jacob, Fadhi and I are trudging directly towards a mass of barbed wire covered in red signs. The writing on them is indecipherable at this distance, but red signs on barbed wire rarely say, 'St Luke's Church Fête this Saturday'; they're generally more likely to read: '*Blah blah* Do not *blah blah* own risk *blah blah* death.' (Later it transpires I am virtually fluent in red signs.)

Phil the cameraman is a good judge of the mood and his eyebrows signal his emotional well-being. They are currently half-raised, set to 'Caution' .

'Is it OK to be here?' I ask Fadhi.

'No,' Fadhi says calmly. 'We are not allowed.'

'Not allowed,' I repeat dully, as we keep walking.

'Not allowed to be even here.'

But still we keep on towards the wire, doing the very thing we are not allowed to do.

'Is it safe, though?'

Fadhi shrugs.

'What will the authorities do if they find us here?' I ask.

Fadhi mimes bringing a gun to his shoulder.

'We might get shot?'

'Perhaps,' he says, cheerfully. 'Who knows? … We shall see.'

It is hard to tell how serious he is because it sounds as if he is making a political point rather than expressing a genuine possibility. Phil's eyebrows are now at DEFCON 1.

Fadhi continues: 'If the soldiers ask you what you are doing, you must tell them you are writing a book about birds and flowers.'

'Well, there might be a mention of birds and flowers, I suppose …'

'Do not mention anything else. Birds and flowers, that is all. Do not tell them the truth.'

'OK.'

'If you want to walk the Wall, you have to be a very good liar.' And with that Fadhi departs, leaving Phil, Jacob and me next to the barbed wire and the Barrier.

Standing in the corner of the field, we are exactly where we want to be. We about-turn and start walking.

We have begun. The walk to Jacob's farm is a relatively short and simple one, but we're distracted ten minutes in by the whining hum of an armoured vehicle on the Israeli side of the Barrier. It stops, sitting squatly behind the wire. Then it sounds a siren, an electronic honking sound, a warning squawk. It is an odd noise this whoop: a mixture of draconian disco and electro camp, but it saves the soldiers from having to get out of the vehicle and shout, 'Fuck off' in Hebrew, Arabic and English. It works, too, as we all are startled by it and possibly a little embarrassed by that.

'We should move further from the Wall,' says Jacob.

'Is that what the noise meant?'

'They do not want us so near.'

Jacob smiles, but I am slightly nervous. The path twists away from the wire, onto the farm's dust tracks for a while, and the military departs. Ditches run by these tracks as we leave the Barrier behind us, crowded with the burnt stalks of reeds, their short, charred stems leaving black lines of soot on our trouser legs as we brush past. We circle around an Israeli settler farm[3] planted with tall, date palm trees; cut through a grove of short trees where grapefruit-like pomelo fruit hang unripe and low; turn up a stony track and in front of us, once again, is the Barrier.

'When do we get to your farm?' I ask Jacob, as we stop for some water.

'You are on it.' Jacob grins, spreading his arms open then laughing his throaty laugh. His looks are rakish, his chin chiselled, his hair swept back; his natty roll-neck jumper, however, is tattered and frayed, but you can't have everything: if Edward Fox was a Palestinian farmer, Jacob would give him a run for his money.

Right alongside the Barrier's barbed wire is an old blue tractor, parked sideways on an incline.

'Is this yours?'

'Yes,' he says, cocking his head playfully.

Hell, I think, *even his parking is rakish.*

Jacob's rented farm stretches out over forty-five *dunam* (just over eleven acres) and slopes right up to the Barrier. His fields are covered in thin straight lines of plastic wrapping, under which plant life vies for space: leaves push out from under the edges and the tears in the material which reveal squashes, their stems twisting to fruition. He leads us across his land, past his greenhouses, calling out the names of vegetables and pointing: 'Aubergine … cucumber … beans …' until we reach the very edge of the Barrier, where he tells us, 'Here we can walk right by the Wall.'

The Israeli use of the term 'fence' (eschewing the term 'wall' as an inaccurate and pro-Palestinian term) is somewhat disingenuous. True, actual concrete wall accounts for only about four per cent of the Barrier, but that does not make the rest a fence. In reality, and for the most part, it is a standardised configuration of fences, razor wire, ditches, roads and military patrols. It starts on the Palestinian side with six rolls of razor wire stacked three at the bottom, two in the middle and one topping it all off in a pyramid formation; this is normally about two metres high and uncoils along the 'fence'. Next to the wire is a trench one to two metres deep: sometimes it is a ditch dug in the dirt, sometimes it is a concrete contraption. After the wire and the trench comes the sand path, enabling soldiers to see if anyone has come near the 'fence'. Next to the sand path comes the actual bit of fencing; this is an electric fence with motion detectors and is about three to four metres high. There is then another sand track, making two in total, one on either side of the electric fence. Alongside the second sand track is an asphalt road, along which military vehicles drive. After this is another trench and finally the 'fence' is finished off with another pyramid of razor wire. The whole thing is constantly patrolled by soldiers and/or the border police in Humvees and armoured Land Rovers, and a series of communication watch-towers monitor just about the entire length with cameras and state-of-the-art spy equipment. From start to finish red signs adorn the 'fence' saying: 'MORTAL DANGER: MILITARY ZONE. ANY PERSON WHO PASSES OR DAMAGES THE FENCE ENDANGERS HIS LIFE' in English, Hebrew and Arabic.

A simple rule of thumb is if you can't buy it in B&Q then it's not a fence and if you can buy all of the above in a B&Q then you are probably in the Phnom Penh branch. To be accurate, it is a military barrier that has some fencing involved in the construction. But the word 'fence' suits a certain way of seeing the conflict here, because it reduces it to the idea of a neighbourhood dispute, a local tussle of equals; few neighbourhood disputes involve, however, one neighbour putting another under military occupation. (It is certainly not a neighbourhood dispute where I live and if it was, I'd imagine Lambeth Council would take extremely stern action on planning application grounds alone.)

As we walk next to the barbed-wire coils, occasionally peering through to the fence beyond, I catch sight of something that is quintessentially English – what appears to be a small trig point, about a metre high: a rectangular stone with a flat pyramid point protruding from the earth next to the Barrier. Moving closer, it starts to look as if the tip of Cleopatra's Needle is growing out of the ground and that if we were to dig deep enough, we would find the remaining twenty metres, a plinth and some benches.

Pointing at it, I ask Jacob what it is.

'What is that? I don't know. I have never seen it before,' says a genuinely bemused Jacob, whose expression also says, 'Where the fuck did that come from?'

It seems odd that something so prominent to my eye has been missed entirely by Jacob; I wonder how anyone can have failed to spot this on their own land. Perhaps he doesn't come this close to the Barrier normally; perhaps he is busy with other things.

'Is it a milestone? It could be, couldn't it?' I say, opting for familiarity, milestones being a frequent feature of British rambles.

'I don't know.'

'I wonder if it has anything written on it?' I say as much to myself as to Jacob and Phil, as we arrive at it. With one hand resting on its top, I lean in to look at its four sides. There is writing.

'It's in Arabic, I think. Jacob, is this Arabic?'

'Yes.'

Jacob and I are now both peering at the writing carved into the stone. The words have been worn slightly smooth by time and weather, but the stone is certainly not so ancient as to make it undecipherable: at maybe thirty or forty years old, for a milestone this would be a whippersnapper. Jacob peers to translate.

'"Palestine. We are coming."'

'What?'

'That is what is says: "Palestine. We are coming."' Jacob straightens up.

We are right next to the Barrier, which here follows the 1949 Armistice 'Green Line',[4] the de facto border of the West Bank. Across the wire is Israel, and someone has stuck a plinth here reading, 'Palestine. We are coming.'

'Does it mean, "We are coming" as in the state of Palestine will soon exist: in effect, "Our state is becoming"? Or does it mean, "We are coming! Beware!" or "Charge!"?'

If it is the latter, you have to admit, it is a classy bit of gang graffiti.

'"We are coming, Palestine is coming."' Jacob shrugs, indicating the former.

In my world, a stone like this would state a fact: the height above sea level, or the distance from a city. This one, with the formality and certainty of something literally set in stone, announces an event that has yet to happen; it is a declaration of intent. It is such an ordinary object, a fixture of the landscape that ceases to be seen: despite sitting right next to the Barrier, it seems to have drawn no attention from the Israeli military. It stands looking at them each day as they drive along in their armoured cars – staring them in the face, mocking them almost, if only they would look at it properly – and saying, 'One day this will be ours.'

Perhaps we have stumbled upon a stonemason's gag. If so, it would be the first time I have knowingly seen anything witty by a Mason.

We ramble on, past the translucent sheeting that covers the tubular greenhouses full of cucumbers and beans, stopping for tea made in a blackened kettle balanced over the flames between breeze blocks, then past demolished workers' huts of flattened concrete sheets, lying like folded cardboard. We pass families in the fields, pass barns with no walls – just roofs stuck on stilts – until we emerge from the track onto the main artery road of the Jordan valley, the A90, by the Bisan checkpoint.

The Bisan checkpoint is primarily for vehicles, and is laid out like a series of toll booths, manned by heavily armed attendants. I should point out this is not a toll road, and no one asks for money (if they did you would be well advised to be sure you had the right change in advance).

The differently coloured car number plates indicate where the driver is from and we watch yellow plates pouring through the checkpoint from the Israeli side and roaring off down the A90, which heads south past Israeli settler farms and down to the Dead Sea.

Walking along the side of the road, a short distance from the checkpoint, Jacob lightly holds his hand up to my chest.

'Wait,' he says.

We have managed to stop right at the point where cars change gear and accelerate away, so we have to talk loudly, amid the roar of revving engines.

'Is it always this busy?' I ask.

Jacob shrugs and smiles. 'Sometimes.'

Phil is lifting his camera to the checkpoint when Jacob says, 'Try and keep the camera out of sight. They do not like people taking pictures of the checkpoint.'

'OK, no problem,' says Phil over the noise of the cars.

We cross the road and, one minute later, I find myself in front of a soldier, saying the words, 'I am writing a book about birds and flowers.'

'What is your name?' asks the soldier.

I want to reply, 'Is your teacher around? Or any other grown-up?' Israel has military service so its army is predominantly conscripts and this one is fresh-faced and hairless.

After I give my name, he asks, 'Where are you from?'

I reply, 'England,' but I'm actually thinking, *If this conversation goes on for much longer, it's going to look like I am grooming him.*

And when he asks, 'Why are you here? What are you doing?' I think, *Just tell the truth, you have nothing to conceal.*

Fortunately, the soldier knows as much about birds and flowers as I do. He hands us over to a private security company, who are also twelve-year-olds in wraparound shades.

'Have you taken any pictures of the checkpoint? Because this is not allowed,' asks one of them, who seems a pleasant enough chap.

'Why is it not allowed?' I ask.

'Security,' he says, on autopilot.

'Well, I don't think we did ...'

'We need to check, and look at your bags and passports.'

In a small cabin just to the side of the checkpoint, they run our bags through an X-ray machine and rummage through them by hand. Security drops my notebook in a plastic tray, along with my handkerchief, some keys, a pen, suncream, and then he stops, turning something over in his hand.

'What is this?'

'Kendal Mint Cake.'

'What is that, exactly?'

'It is the personification of Englishness enshrined in a mint and sugar-based confectionary item.'

'Excuse me?'

'An energy bar.'

'OK.' He slowly puts it onto the tray. I feel a bit sorry for him and I want to offer him some Kendal Mint Cake, but I don't want to spoil his tea.

Outside is a shaded waiting area with seats, so I grab my notebook while Phil is being searched, and start scribbling ideas. Just as I was writing, the lad who searched my bag asks incredulously, 'What are you doing?'

'Writing.'

'What are you writing?'

'Thoughts about being here,' I explain, though not in an overly friendly manner.

'Writing about here? This place? It is not allowed!' he replies quickly.

'Why not?'

'Security,' he answers firmly and, again, automatically.

'What security, exactly?'

'Er ...' His answer is not so quick now. 'You could be writing a report?'

'I am. I am writing a book.'

'A report for terrorists!' he splutters.

'And what would I be writing?'

'You could tell them we have guns and ... shoes.'

'Shoes?'

'You could give them information, yes,' he says, exasperated.

'Do you think your enemies don't know you have shoes? What threat do you face from a terrorist who doesn't know you have shoes?' I knew I should stop but my frustration at being delayed by a group of kids on a whim was starting to get to me.'Do you think Hezbollah are unaware that Israeli security has shoes?'

'It is not allowed.' But his eyes are wide behind his shades, and he knows he has said something foolish.

'Is the fact that you have shoes a state secret? If Hezbollah find out about your shoes, how will it affect security?' I liked the thought of a cloaked cleric reading a report: 'Shoes! I thought so! The time has come,' and, sweeping his cloak around him, he would cry: 'To the Bunionator!'

The young soldier backs away to his cabin, and I feel I have bullied him.

An hour later, we walk away from the checkpoint. On our first morning, we have been detained and questioned, and we are only a third of the way to our evening's destination. I have no idea if this ramble will work. As we traipse away, heading further into the West Bank, an army jeep passes us, heading the other way. It is the soldiers who stopped us earlier and, as it drives past, one of them shouts out of the open door, 'Welcome to Israel!'

It is intended to be a sarcastic greeting but he seems oblivious to the fact that he is technically in the West Bank, the Israeli Occupied Territories of the West Bank. I shout one word at the roaring truck – 'Israel-*ish*!'

But it is too late; I am not quick enough, and the jeep is through the checkpoint, heading to the military road and driving east along the fence, past a stone that looks like a trig point.

chapter 2

THE AL AQABA VILLAGE GREEN PRESERVATION SOCIETY

We are less than halfway to our destination of the village of Al Mutilla, and already it is well into the afternoon: our first day and we are behind schedule. Unfortunately, the next section of the map is covered in irregular, small, black dots: great swathes of them, like an infestation. They are the symbol for a 'closed military area'. At this stage I'm not sure what 'closed military area' actually means, but I make an educated guess by the words that are *not* employed: the area is not 'open' nor is it 'civic' and it has none of the usual redeeming suffixes like, 'World of Adventure' or 'Admission Free'. What lies ahead is probably more red signs and a line of questioning that will test my knowledge of birds further than, 'I like the blue ones.'

Our proposed route from the Bisan checkpoint to Al Mutilla takes us over six kilometres of 'closed military area', and Phil is worried: 'We need to discuss this.'

Phil has just finished working in Afghanistan (as a cameraman, rather than as a mercenary or drug dealer, for anyone who has picked up this book thinking it is written by Andy McNab) and sports the rough tan and goatee beard of a jazz-loving hobo. He is slightly shorter than I and substantially skinnier and, as a counterpoint to my big, fat Middle Eastern nose, he sports a broken, Roman model. Despite living quite close to each other in south

London, we have only known each other for a couple of weeks and are still discovering each other's habits.

One of Phil's habits is to use the word 'we' when he means 'you'. So: 'What do we know about the area? Do we know how heavily patrolled it is?'

'We don't know,' I reply, realising that my habit is to use the word 'we' when I mean 'I'.

Phil presses on. 'Did we know this was a closed area before we set out this morning?'

'Yes, we did.'

'So what contingency plans did we make?'

'We thought it would be sensible to see how it went this morning before we made a decision.'

Whichever way you look at that, one thing is for sure: 'we' have slightly fucked up. So I defer to Jacob, saying, 'You know the area; what do you think? Is it safe to walk this route?'

Jacob shrugs unsmilingly, in a deliberate manner. They are both staring at me expectantly and I feel I must give in to common sense.

'I think we can get to Al Mutilla another way,' I say, 'and, if we are lucky, it won't involve any scrapes with the military.'

Jacob nods, all smiles once more.

I make a few phone calls and a plan is made: we will drive to Al Aqaba, a village on the edge of the closed military area, and from there get help to guide us round the zone and get us back onto our route. Fadhi agrees to drive us, the mayor of Al Aqaba agrees to meet us and so we set off on the only open road through the black dots. The 'closed military area' runs across virtually all of the Jordan Valley;[5] covering most of the map page in black dots, it's like navigating through a rash. The drive towards Al Aqaba is up through the mountains, past steep ravines and Bedouin tents perched on green slopes.

Just short of the village we are stopped at one of the many internal checkpoints the Israelis have set up to control movement inside the West Bank – this one is eight kilometres south of the Barrier and has nothing to do with getting in or out of Israel. After ninety minutes the military still refuses to let us pass on the grounds that, 'It is just not allowed for you to use this checkpoint.' We are forced to go further south, and by the time we find another checkpoint, the daylight has gone.

'Al Mutilla's not happening tonight,' says Phil.

'No, it is not,' I answer, quietly.

It would be foolish even to attempt to walk the mountains at night, so all we can do is sit in silence as the car potters onwards, pondering the fact that we have failed on our very first day.

With the mood still sombre, Fadhi delivers us safely to Al Aqaba. We thank him, wave goodbye and are left momentarily alone, huddling in the street under the minaret of the mosque.

After the warmth of the car, the cold mountain wind is sharp and sudden, matching my profanities. Then, out of the night air suddenly comes an Arabic voice, speaking in impeccable English: 'Mark?'

'Yes?'

'Come with me, please.' A man in a raincoat comes out of the dark, holding out his hand. He waits for us to pick up our rucksacks before leading us across a small compound, half-lit by the moon. 'Haj Sami is waiting for you,' he says, and we turn at the sound of a humming motor as a figure in an electric wheelchair drones out of the shadows towards us.

In the bright light of the whitewashed meeting room, I see the mayor properly for the first time. Mayor Haj Sami Sadeq is sitting upright in his wheelchair. With as much greying hair on his chin as his head, he is dressed in smart institutional wear: a grey, zip-up fleece in care-home casual style; padded old-man shoes (black, comfy, flat and clumpy); and a pair of beige trousers.

The mayor's assistant, the man who had come out to meet us, is Ala'a Subaih and he is fastidiously well groomed. His crisp and clean raincoat is carefully folded and he sits attentively behind a desk in the communal hall.

'First, we will show a short presentation, then we can talk, then some food,' says Haj Sami when we are all settled, and he signals with a flick of his hand for the lights to be turned down. A film bursts onto a screen hung in the corner of the room.

My heart sinks. I have seen an inordinate amount of short campaign films in my time, and the only good thing about them is their length. They usually run with an opening shot of the village/factory/military base, with a commentary running over the top to explain the issue; then there's a shot of a banner with a campaign slogan; shots of local resistance and demonstration; and then there will be the key incident (usually violent) in grainy footage (which if it is not shot on a mobile phone will look like it is) that has sparked the film; then a school photo of a victim; grieving relatives; and poignant statistics finishing with a plea for justice. I may sound cynical, but even if Che Guevara had been there, he'd have been thinking, 'Please God, let it be *Rambo* by mistake ...'

The reality is worse. It's a three-minute video comprising a series of photo-montages set to a group of local schoolchildren singing what appears to be their own composition, 'We sing a song of peace'. Pictures start flashing up of kids dressed in matching white baseball hats and T-shirts marching in a line around the village and then waving peace signs, all the while singing their song of peace. When they get to the lyrics: 'hand in hand across the land', guess what? Yes, shots of kids walking across the land and, by golly, if they are not hand in hand, too. Look carefully and you can spot Mayor Haj Sami in the background: while the kids dance wearing black and white *keffiyeh* headscarves, he is in the corner smiling, like an Alfred Hitchcock cameo.

All of this is carefully stitched together with the starter kit of video tricks: screen wipes, starburst fades and page-turn edits. It leads to a climax featuring a child's plaintive plea for, 'No more hate, no more fears, no more pain and no more tears', before rising to a crescendo of unaccompanied chanting and hand-clapping: 'We see ...' *CLAP* '... a peaceful world ...' *CLAP* '... in harmony ...' *CLAP* and so on, until drums break in with a classic Phil Collins series of sloppy thuds, and everyone is back to singing the song of peace set over photos of a school trip to some local caves. and trotting about the village again.

The lights come on abruptly, Ala'a is smiling expectantly and Haj Sami is staring majestically into the middle distance, as if he's posing for a portrait. I feel under enormous pressure to applaud but the juddering silence of the room is broken only by the sound of me pushing my jaw shut. At this point I would not bat an eyelid if Pudsey Bear were to walk into the room shaking a collecting tin.

And as we sit basking in the saccharine after-taste of the film, I realise that I'm going to have to interview Haj Sami on the plight of his village – which appears to be an infestation of singing kids – and that I'm to start my interview now.

Gathering my wits about me, with Ala'a and Haj Sami looking on, the first question that splutters from my lips is: 'So, Haj Sami … how did you end up in the wheelchair?'

He tells me how it happened. After the Six Day War in June 1967, when Israeli forces moved in and occupied the West Bank, the Israeli military decided to use the area around Al Aqaba to prepare soldiers for future combat and so, one day, the village woke up to find itself in the middle of a military training zone.

The Israeli military, it would seem, have a distinctly literal definition of putting people in the firing line. In this instance, an entire village. The sixteen-year-old Haj Sami was in the fields tending the family sheep, when he was shot three times in the back by stray bullets fired by Israeli soldiers who were practising shooting people. He was left a paraplegic. The Israeli army apologised, paid a little compensation and promised to get better at practising shooting people*. They didn't, however, stop the training practice around the village.

Most countries have places, usually in remote rural areas, where squaddies can rehearse hostage situations, or run in and out of empty buildings firing live rounds and shouting. The key difference here is that where other countries use deserted villages for this practice, in Al Aqaba, Israel has happily opted to use an undeserted village (although they are working on that last part). Incredibly, the

---

* *I might be making that last bit up.*

village has had eight inhabitants killed by stray bullets and ordnance, and over fifty people injured. No soldiers have been punished.

It continues to this day. Large concrete blocks placed to resemble a village lie on the hillside opposite Al Aqaba, and Israeli troops train there often. Added to this, it is only very recently that the soldiers ceased the habit known as 'shooting between the houses': the practice that saw live ammunition flying through the streets of Al Aqaba.

Haj Sami holds his hands up, 'All the time training: morning, evening, night.' He looks at me, incredulous: 'Why training in between the houses of Al Aqaba? Everyone ask me, "Why Israeli army train in Al Aqaba?" The Israeli army tell me Al Aqaba like southern Lebanon, and therefore good to practise in.'

Perched high on a hill where the green ravines and steep valleys are cursed to resemble Lebanon, Al Aqaba is, in the eyes of the army, the perfect terrain for its troops to practise. However, as Haj Sami goes on to explain, it's not merely lead and shrapnel the villagers have to fear: Al Aqaba is also under threat from an even blunter instrument – planning laws.

The West Bank is divided into three types of area: Area A is under Palestinian control, Area B is under joint Israeli and Palestinian control and Area C is under full Israeli control for security and 'planning'.[6] Nearly two-thirds of the West Bank is under Area C and, as a result, Palestinians need a permit to build everything from a greenhouse to a hospital. Given that almost all applications are turned down, building anything 'legally' is almost impossible.[7] There is a reason IKEA doesn't have a branch in the West Bank and it is not just that their meatballs are shit.

Al Aqaba is not a big village yet still the Israeli authorities have declared thirty-five of the forty-five structures illegal, and have issued demolition orders against the mosque, the kindergarten, the health clinic and a tarmac road called Peace Street.

The orders have turned Al Aqaba upside down. 'A man in the village,' says Haj Sami, 'has to live, with his sheep, in a barn because the army refuse to give him permission to build a house. The school, they have my house.'

'Pardon?'

'Because the Israeli army refused permission to build a school, it is in my house.' Nothing is where it should be. 'My office,' says Haj Sami, 'is under a tree because the army refuses permission to build.'

To verify this, the next morning I go to his office. It is indeed under a big tree, that has a circular concrete bench running round the trunk. Next to it is a large sign with the words: 'Palestinian National Authority'.

'When the army came here, they said this bench is not allowed. "You have no permission for this."' Haj Sami's square face smiles broadly, 'I said to the soldier, "Please therefore serve a demolition order on the bench."'

Back in the communal hall the hour is late and I am tired, but Haj Sami and Ala'a are still describing the tale of this village and insist on telling the story of the crashed jeep. A few years ago, villagers saw that 'a soldier had accident in a jeep. It tumbled down the hill. The people from Al Aqaba help him. When we saw the soldier dying we help him, take him from the jeep.'

The villagers saved his life but, according to Haj Sami, 'the Israeli army did not say thank you. After the army came and the ambulance came they not say thanks, they say go from here.' So the villagers do just that.

The following day the Israeli army *did* return to Al Aqaba, but only to serve a demolition order on the village clinic.

'He gave it to you the day after?'

Haj Sami nods emphatically. 'We help the soldier and one day after, the Israeli army come and give me the order for the clinic, to destroy the clinic.'

Amazed I repeat the facts, as if to make sure I have heard correctly: 'To serve the demolition order the day after ...'

'After one day,' says Haj Sami solemnly.

And I laugh at the outrage. 'You have to admit,' I stammer out, 'the Israelis have a great sense of timing.'

Their silent stares are a mixture of politeness and incomprehension. I am beginning to recognise that this as a Palestinian thing, their way of saying, ' Anyway ...' With his own sense of timing, Haj

Sami lets tumbleweed drift over the gap in the conversation, and then continues his story.

The British Consulate had helped fund the original clinic, 'So when the demolition order arrived for the clinic I phoned him very quickly and he sent a letter for Jack Straw [Foreign Secretary at the time] and Jack Straw, he called the Israelis and said don't touch this clinic.'

Haj Sami affords a smile. The clinic is still open but he does not know for how much longer.

Slowly it dawns on me, the incredible game Haj Sami is playing. Al Aqaba is physically cut off, isolated in the mountains, and almost the entire village is under demolition orders threatening its very existence. The population has dwindled from 400 to a mere 100 and the soldiers still train here. So Haj Sami has turned, successfully, to the international community for help. The UN, as well as the British, US, Japanese, Belgian, Dutch, Danish and Norwegian governments and also non-government organisations (NGOs) have all invested heavily in the village, by building or donating money for the school, the clinic, roads, water wells and other essential infrastructure. This is not just aid, it is the best insurance policy Haj Sami can find; he is protecting his village with powerful investors.

It is a fiendishly clever game of survival played by a man in a wheelchair, whose best weapon is a DVD of schoolchildren singing about peace.

Haj Sami kindly lets us stay the night in his guest room. Entirely in keeping with a man who has classrooms in his house and an office under a tree, the guest room is in the garage. Ala'a leads Phil and me out into the courtyard and through the wooden double doors of the garage.

'Are you sure you have enough pillows?' he says, pointing at a small pile of them.

'Yes, that will be fine, thank you.'

'I can never sleep unless I have exactly the right number of pillows,' he says.

'You are an exact man, Ala'a,' I say, and he is. As Al Aqaba's clerk, he keeps the files, the documents, the orders, the legal challenges, email lists, DVDs and pamphlets in order. He has to, because in a village where nothing is where it should be, someone needs to know exactly where everything is.

Having said goodnight to Ala'a, I reflect on my earlier words of, '*If we are lucky, it won't involve any scrapes with the military.*' I conclude that it really does take a special kind of luck to end the day sleeping on an Israeli military training range. Not a charmed luck exactly, but special, nonetheless. Military training areas are not generally considered suitable rest stops for travellers, being, as they are, places for red flags, warning signs and occasional headlines in West Country local newspapers that combine the words 'student', 'prank' and 'tragedy'.

So, on the first night of our walk we are to sleep on the floor of a disused garage. I am thrilled. What would be the point of travelling all this way to spend the night in a Travelodge? This is the West Bank, for God's sake, this is Palestine, and the last thing I want is to be curling up with a free shortbread and a complimentary copy of the *Independent*. I have everything I need in the garage, or at least within walking distance if you include the washbasin. The smell of oil and petrol is cheery as it reminds me of workshops and my dad; the combination of the winter chill and the altitude keeps the mosquitoes at bay; and what do I care for a trouser press and a sachet of hot chocolate powder? A cold draught sneaks into the bare room through a broken window, nudging the large wooden double doors into an occasional rattle. Strip lights on the low ceiling bleach the space of colour, with the exception of the nylon blankets, which explode in LSD yellows, reds and browns. Wrapped in this synthetic shroud, the exhaustion and elation and confusion of the day merge into contentment. I take one last look round to make sure all is ready for tomorrow: the green lights of batteries charging, walking boots kicked clean of mud, torch next to pillow. The lights are turned off and moonlight pours into the garage. I hunch further into the blankets, feeling the warm lure of sleep amidst the build-up of static electricity.

chapter 3
DIY

If his living room is to be believed, Fadhi, the debonair, corduroy-wearing activist, has a good pedigree. One framed photo has a young Fadhi shaking hands with Yasser Arafat, while another shows a slightly older version guiding Tony Blair round the Jordan Valley. His bookshelf has a line of reports on the area, authored by him. Outside his home, wherever I go, everyone seems to know him, and he is the perfect person to find guides and translators for us. However, the job is proving far more complex than anyone imagined, even for Fadhi's exceptional skills.

We have had three different Palestinians walking with us in as many days, and it is beginning to feel more like a course in management than rambling. Part of the problem is that rambling is not a popular Palestinian pastime: a stranger approached me in the street to ask, 'What is that?'

'It is a walking stick,' I said, showing him my lightweight, retractable hiking pole. With a mixture of confusion and irritation he replied, 'Do you not have a car?' before he turned and walked off.

It seems that in the food chain of transport, walking puts us well beneath 'Boy on donkey', and probably 'Shopmobility scooter', too. So maybe it is not surprising that my Palestinian guide for the next leg, Matt, simply doesn't understand what a ramble entails.

As we set out from Al Mutilla, I am equipped with everything needed for a ramble, from boots to bobble hat, for the walk over the hilly farmland. Matt turns up in a sky-blue shirt with thin white stripes, a dark blue, two-button blazer, grey slacks, and slip-on black shoes; I'm dressed to hike, Matt is dressed to open the bar on a Sunday lunchtime at the British Legion.

'Are those shoes going to be OK?'

'They are fine. I have walked before, you know,' he says defensively.

Slightly worried, I ask, 'Have you got any water?'

'I don't need any, I am tough,' he laughs. 'As long as I have cigarettes, I am fine.'

If the start with Matt was not promising, walking with him quickly goes from bad to worse, then from worse to really shit. He is completely unprepared for the steep climbs and rocky terraces, and does not want to walk near the Barrier at all. So when a shepherd advises us to be careful, Matt translates it as, 'He says if we go near the Wall we will be shot.'

I have no way of knowing how dangerous it is. But I have just spent an evening with Haj Sami (who was shot) and we have to rely on the guide, so when Matt says, 'I know another way, we can walk on the roads,' Phil and I follow him.

Some time later, and ten kilometres in completely the opposite direction from the Barrier, we arrive at Jalqamus. It is a place with one mosque, half a dozen homes and some greenhouses, so the three of us walking down the road is practically a parade (if someone were to tell me *now* that Jalqamus is a one-horse town, I'd say it had had the developers in since I was last there). But the folk are friendly and point us on our way.

I have given Matt the nickname of Columbus as he, too, is much in the habit of heading off in the wrong direction. He also smokes like he has just discovered tobacco. As he lights up another cigarette, I say, 'You have spent half the walk telling me how Israel is trying to destroy Palestine and the other half trying to give yourself a terminal illness. Why is it so many Palestinian men smoke?'

'Things are changing Mark, honestly, things are changing,' he replies and in all seriousness. 'Nowadays, more and more women are smoking, too.'

*

The following morning, I am hugely relieved when Fadhi tells us he is to walk with us himself, as Matt's fifteen-kilometre detour has put us yet further behind schedule.

The morning is a winter idyll: the sky is blue and the air crisp. Fadhi is a countryman at heart, and while he tramps the hills explaining how the Barrier isolates farmers from land and water, he happily forages.

'Ah,' he says, midflow, 'this you will like.' Bending into a cactus bush he carefully plucks stems from between the prickly pads. 'This is hellion; that is what we call it. You call it asparagus. You can eat it raw.'

He passes me a handful and then is off again, explaining the Barrier while I munch away.

'Once you have a wall,' he says, 'you have to have security to protect it. So people are not allowed to walk near the Wall; they must remain 150 metres away from it at all times.'

As we are standing right next to the barbed wire, I think: *If that is true, the army is being unduly lax in its patrolling duties.* With impeccable timing the military arrives.

We're called to a yellow gate surrounded by barbed wire, over which we hand our passports and Fadhi's green Palestinian ID. Two soldiers guard us while their commander checks our documents; one of them smiles.

'How old are you?' I ask, in dad-like fashion.

'Twenty,' he replies. His helmet is slightly too big and wobbles when he speaks.

'What are you going to do when you finish in the army?'

'University.'

'Do you know what you will study?'

'No. Not yet.'

'I went to college,' I volunteer.

'What you study?'

'Drama.' In an instant, before I really know what I am doing, I proceed to offer him the worst career advice in the world: 'That's what you should do, study drama. When you leave, do a Theatre Arts degree.'

The soldier blushes as Fadhi and Phil laugh.

'But he is a soldier …' giggles Fadhi.

'What's he going to do?' chimes in Phil. 'Express the Occupation through mime?'

The soldier blushes again, and so do I.

An hour passes sitting by the wire. Fadhi lies down to sleep and I discover a Hawaiian rockabilly MP3 track on my mobile phone, so I sit back and let the steel guitar glide over the hula sounds. When it finishes, I return to the barbed wire to where the young soldier is.

'Hey, is it all right to chat?'

'It is good. It helps my English.'

'If I am going to help your English, you must teach me some Hebrew.'

'OK,' he says, his helmet nodding with him. 'Er … what Hebrew you know? You know "*Shalom*", right?'

'Yes.'

The radio cackles from the Humvee as he stands with his gun shouldered, thinking for a moment.

'*Slicha*.'

'What?'

'Say "*Slicha*".' And he coaches me: '*Slicha*.'

'Slick hair.'

Slowly he repeats it, '*Slicha*.'

'*Slicha*?' I say, getting it right.

'That is good.'

'What does it mean?'

'In Israel the word means, "Excuse me" or "Sorry".' And then, with a performer's timing he says, 'We don't use it very often.'

Maybe he will do that drama degree after all.

Finally an officer appears, returns the passports and tells me, 'You must walk away from the fence along here, sometimes 150 metres, sometimes 300 metres away. OK?'

'OK, but where do I walk 150 metres from the fence, and where 300?'

'What?'

'How will I know? When I can walk 150 metres from the fence and where I can walk 300 metres …'

'Never mind,' he says, moving away abruptly, then turns back to add, 'Let us say it is … 150 metres. Along here, 150 metres.'

I have an urge to shout, 'You're making this up as you go along!' as the officer stomps off with his 'My ball, my game!' attitude, while Fadhi smiles with an expression that says, 'I told you so.'

The next morning Fadhi sounds surprised when I call to enquire as to his whereabouts. He greets me with: 'You are walking today?'

'Yes,' I reply.

'In this rain?'

'I am English.'

'Really?' he says, questioning my intentions rather than my place of birth.

'I'm English, Fadhi, it is what we do. If it rains we walk; if it snows we climb Snowdon and wait to be rescued; in heatwaves we become immobile on garden furniture and burn our faces red. It is just what we do.'

In truth, the delay with the army yesterday took up even more time and yet again we didn't complete the planned route. I simply cannot afford to waste another day.

'I have a fever today,' says Fadhi, 'but I will arrange for someone to walk with you.'

Two hours later, standing by a plastic greenhouse crackling noisily from the rain, we meet guide number three, Hakim, a tall, wiry farmer in green wellington boots, old khaki jacket and headscarf. His stubble is white and his English is basic, but he knows the area.

'You want to go Faqqu'a to Al Jalama?'

'Yes, please.'

'I have tractor. I drive you.'

Remembering that rambling is an unknown phenomenon here, I start slowly from the beginning, in a tone more patronising than I had intended. 'We need to walk near the Barrier.' For some reason I am moving my hand in a snake-like gesture with the instinctive belief that it signifies off-road travel.

Apparently it does, as Hakim replies, 'It is tractor; it can drive anywhere.'

'We need to walk,' I stress.

'But the mud. It will put five kilos, ten kilos on your foot.'

He is right, the mud not only sticks to my boots, it grows into large floppy clods. While Hakim lifts his red and white *keffiyeh* over his head, clasps his hands behind his back and walks steadily into the squall, I flail behind in the brown furrows like someone given a pair of clown shoes from the Battle of the Somme.

The surrounding hills are empty, deserted but for the sound of the odd F-16 military plane that interrupts the white noise of perpetual downpour. We traipse under dripping trees, up pathways with rivulets flowing down them, and plough across flooded farm-land. We are soaked. Water runs off our clothes and over our faces, forcing us to blink. My jeans are brown from the knee down and the waterproof coat that clings to my back is a liar.

Phil's goatee-infested face peeks from under his hood, wrapped up tight like a wet monk. He has long-ago packed the camera equipment in his bag, and now he shouts, 'How are you feeling?'

'Like I'm on holiday in Wales, but without my family.'

Hakim, hands still fixed behind and head down, walks steadily on, leading us along the Barrier, or at least 150 metres from it. After two hours, we take shelter under an olive tree for a few minutes, and our voices sound suddenly loud under the relative peace of its branches. Hakim reaches for a cigarette – it should be scientifically impossible to smoke in this weather, but this doesn't stop Hakim, a Palestinian male and therefore able to smoke anywhere (with the exception of a British pub). We drink out of the water bottle in turns, Hakim holding it away from his lips and pouring it directly into his mouth, while I unwrap some bashed Kendal Mint Cake, which turns to mush in my wet hands.

'Would you like some?'

Hakim holds up his cigarette by way of saying, 'No thanks,' so I sit contentedly sucking sugar from my fingers.

'I used to come as … a boy. Here,' says Hakim, speaking in his broken English and erratic inflection. 'With friends we come. Here. No walls. We walk to Bisan, Beit She'an …' He waves his hand in their general direction. 'We. Come here and catch … rabbits.' He joins his hands as he remembers, 'With fires we cook rabbits.' Hakim searches for his words before he continues. 'Then you can go anywhere. Walk anywhere. No problems here.' He nods his head as he makes a list, 'Problems: occupation. Money. Things at home. You can leave it all behind. Here you feel free. You are free. I not come here for many years. I forget.' He takes a final drag on the cigarette and bends down to put the butt under his boot, saying with a grunt, 'I am glad I come today.'

We have another three hours of walking, rain and mud ahead of us. Yes, it will be tiring, yes, we are going to get soaked and yes, I will scramble down the terraces with all the grace and agility of a mattress being thrown onto a skip. But today has been a day of rare joy because today I have found my first Palestinian rambler.

Before the walk, some Palestinian friends of mine had given me some advice. 'You will not,' they said, 'have trouble getting Palestinians to talk. The trouble you will have is getting them to shut up.' And they are right. So far on the walk, four days in, we have probably spent at least half a day listening to farmers talk about their lost land. Frankly, it would save us a lot of time if they could all just pin the number of *dunam*s on their chest like a marathon number and we could all just crack on.

The Barrier is the biggest infrastructure project in Israeli history, and is planned to run for 723 kilometres; something this big and this long simply can't happen without someone being pissed off. The 'someone' in this case is village after village of Palestinian farmers, which is hardly surprising considering over ten per cent of the West Bank's most fertile farming land has been adversely affected by the Barrier. Each village we go through has a story to tell. In Al Mutilla, I see farmers cut off from their land and trees. In Jalbun, the mayor details how his village had lost 2,500 *dunams* (600 acres) of land to the Barrier. In the Arabuna council chambers, a map is spread over the table showing precisely where the Barrier crosses the Green Line and takes twenty per cent of the village farmland.

The northern section, where we started from, was the first part of the Barrier to be erected. It had an immediate and dramatic effect on the Palestinian economy, as many Palestinians reliant on better paid jobs in Israel were simply stopped from entering. Trade between the two communities all but ceased; the fruit and vegetable markets dependent on Israeli custom died and, of course, there were the farmers who now found their land on the other side of the Barrier. So it is no small irony that one of the men responsible for getting the Barrier put up is also leading the attempts to now resuscitate the Palestinian economy.

Danny Atar is the head of the Gilboa Regional Council, a council in the farming area in northern Israel, just on the other side of the Barrier. Phil and I cross the checkpoint to see him.

The council building is like any other regional council building: the stairwells echo, the lifts are small and members of staff have the usual clutter and occasional soft toy next to their work station.

Danny cuts a big figure behind the tasteful wooden desk of his office. He sports a fashionably flimsy black jumper, his hair is two trims away from a mop top and he slouches a little. If a young John Prescott had a TV fashion makeover, he would look like this.

After being offered coffee, we get down to business. 'There are only two solutions when you have suicide bombers: either an all-out war with all that entails *or* a fence. A fence is the lesser of two evils,' says Danny, indicating he has finished his point by waving his hand in the air, as though turning away an offer of dessert.

The suicide bombings that characterised the Second *Intifada* galvanised the public mood for some kind of barrier, but the Israeli prime minister at the time, Ariel Sharon, was ideologically opposed to anything that might resemble a border for a future Palestine state, so he prevaricated. It was at this point that Danny Atar entered the fray.

'How do we create the reality that forces a government to act? We asked ourselves, "Why don't *we* start fundraising for it?" So we went abroad with this idea to raise money, and started building our own fence.'

While his local fence was being built, Danny used every opportunity he could to embarrass Sharon into action: 'Every time there was a suicide bombing, I used to get on the television, on the radio, and attack the indecisiveness of the government.'

'So was building your fence part of the campaign to get your government to build the whole thing, or an effort to stop attacks?' I ask.

'It was both. The campaign put pressure on the Israeli government to actually build a [national] fence but, of course, the fence I built did provide security, too.'

Danny's local fence was to be twenty-five kilometres long, but it was only eight kilometres into its construction when Danny was invited by the Prime Minister's Office to meet him.

'I entered Sharon's office and all the government was there, all the heads of the security forces were there, and Sharon comes and shakes my hand and says, "We have decided to build a fence;

will you now please get off my back and stop attacking me?" And I said, "Yes."'

'Those were his exact words?' I ask.

'That's Sharon,' Danny says, his hand gesture dismissing another portion of imaginary dessert. 'The next day they came and started to build the fence. They dismantled our fence and built one that was much more sophisticated ... Before the fence, there was an average of 365 terror incidents a year, since the fence there is an average of zero.'

'Palestinians we have spoken to have said the *Intifada* had burnt out, that it was defeated. Did the Barrier stop the terror attacks, or had the momentum to commit them burnt out, do you think?'

Danny smiles, 'You can check the army records. As more of the fence was built, so the attacks moved south to where it was not yet built. So it's a myth what you are saying. It's not right. It's because of the fence, one hundred per cent.'

And so the Barrier went up, as did Palestinian unemployment, while the only thing to go down were the wages for those still in work.

Acutely aware of this, Danny is working with his Palestinian counterpart, the mayor of Jenin, to create an industrial zone alongside the Barrier. Aside from being one of the West Bank's largest towns, Jenin was the site of some of the worst violence in the Second *Intifada* and Atar is at pains to point out how he and the mayor are trying to tackle causes of discontent. Now that there is security, he says, they have 'to see how we can improve the lives of Palestinians who are poor and suffering. We have to move very quickly, to get employers to create more jobs. Unemployment is more than fifty per cent in Jenin.'

Coming from England, the concept of an industrial zone fills me with an equal measure of incomprehension and loathing; I instinctively mistrust any address that features the word 'unit'. The companies are usually induced to take space via incentives like tax-free operating periods, and the jobs created are normally badly paid, although I am aware that the one thing worse than having a shit job is not having a shit job.

'So how will this zone work?' I ask, holding back my opinionated twaddle that's so middle class I get points on my John Lewis store card every time I spout it.

'Well, there are two separate industrial zones,' continues Danny. 'The Israeli side is a logistical back-up for the Palestinian side. We have a specific target of 15,000 Palestinians employed, to 700 on the Israeli side.'

'Why are you doing this?'

'First of all, it's basic values: you don't want to see people suffering. But more long-term, you have to understand there are Palestinians with academic degrees who are unemployed, and in that situation it is very easy for them to become terrorists.'

'But,' I stammer, thinking, *Perhaps you would not need to build a zone if you had not built the wall,* 'Palestinian income has been hugely affected by the Barrier, so is this not just a case of causing an injury and providing only a sticking plaster?'

Danny Atar bluntly replies: 'Definitely the fence makes life harder for the Palestinians, but the Second *Intifada* made life very hard for both sides.'

Reviving the economy is no easy job when Palestinian freedom of movement is so curtailed. Danny Atar had to lobby Tony Blair (the Middle East Peace Envoy, and dealer in fine irony) to talk to the military about opening up the local checkpoint at Al Jalama.

'We opened the crossing. It takes three minutes to get through,' says Danny, adding in a flat and deadpan manner: 'And there are many people trying to take the credit for it.'

'This is Al Jalama checkpoint?' I query, gesturing back at the one Phil and I have just come through.

Nodding, Danny says, 'Working from our side, we convinced the Minister of Defence to open this crossing.'

There's an awkward silence. 'We crossed it by foot and it took an hour and forty minutes to get through,' I volunteer.

'By car, you can go by car. You can show a certificate and it will only take a couple of minutes,' says Danny a little impatiently, adding, 'The crossing is mainly for Israelis coming to revive the Palestinian economy, and then it takes them a very short time, a matter of minutes.'

I realise that his three minutes is for Israelis crossing into the West Bank, and not the other way around. The Palestinians can still have the hour and forty minute wait.

Danny has been generous with his time so when he nods and holds his hands apart – brushing aside one final air-dessert – I recognise it is time to finish. After shaking his hand, I leave him to the phone calls and memos that have been building up around him, and the office bustles as folk clamour to see him with the next piece of business.

Outside, the air is warm and fresh and, in the car park, I chat idly with some of the office staff leaving for the day. The other side of the Barrier could be a million miles away.

Departing, I get a taxi to make a diversion via Har Megiddo, the literal translation of which is 'hill of Megiddo', although it is more commonly known as 'Armageddon'. My reason for this has no significance, relevance or purpose, other than that it is nearby. Although there *is* the thought that if ever everything on the planet goes pear-shaped and we wake to the dawning of Armageddon, I'd like to be able to turn to the kids and say, 'Oh, I've been there.'

Back on the Palestinian side of the Barrier, the first thing the mayor of Al Jalama does is to offer tea and then take me to the flat roof of the council building.

A talk on a council roof is a poor man's PowerPoint presentation. From up here you can see everything laid out so clearly: the Barrier, the villages and the farmland stuck on the wrong side; you can see all the individual quandaries. Looking across the plain, a large section of the Barrier appears to run in a straight line and from this distance the Israeli armoured cars whizzing along the military road have the appearance of mechanised hares at a dog track.

By the checkpoint is an empty concrete wasteland, desolate and broken, where the market once stood.

'Here there was a market,' says the mayor. 'All things, fruits, vegetables, goods, everything; there were one thousand stalls. Israelis come from all around to buy. Now they are gone. The market is gone. The Wall has destroyed it.'

'So what are you doing to revive industry?' I ask.

'I try to get Israelis to open their clothes factories here. I give them free electricity if they open.'

'An industrial zone ...'

'Yes,' he nods excitedly.

chapter 4
FARMING TODAY

After a week on the West Bank I have decided that I need a T-shirt with the words: 'Yes, I am British. Yes, I know about the Balfour Declaration.' Every single day someone, finding out that I am British, will say in a manner intended for all to hear, 'Ah, British ... are you aware that in 1917 Lord Balfour of Britain signed away our land to the Jewish?'

They are referring to Lord Balfour's letter expressing the British government's 'sympathy with Jewish Zionist aspirations' for 'the establishment in Palestine of a national home for the Jewish people'. As the British ruled Palestine from 1917 until Israel declared independence in 1948, Lord Balfour pretty much laid out British intentions.

The Palestinian questioner will then, with varying degrees, blame Britain and, by default, me, for the Palestinian situation. Facing this question three or four times a day leads me to the conclusion that this is more of an accusation than a question, and I wonder how I should answer. If I say 'Yes' I am damned; if I say 'No' I am damned, so I decide I might as well reply, 'Actually, I'm his great-grandson and I've just popped over to see how it's working out.'

What I eventually do might be even worse. One evening, I'm introduced to a shopkeeper who starts the familiar phrase, 'You know Lord Balfour ...' Before he can continue, I jump in quickly saying, 'Yes, I do know about Lord Balfour, but it was the *English* who did this, the *English*. I'm *Scottish*! And I can tell you the Scots have suffered far longer at the hands of the English oppressor than anyone else in history! Now, have you heard about the Highland Clearances?' It seemed to work. He looked baffled, offered me some tea and then changed the subject, none the wiser.

Afterwards Phil turned to me and said, 'You're not actually Scottish, are you?'

'No' I reply. 'I am not "actually" but I am "tactically" Scottish.'*

Our identities are often as much defined by how others see us as by how we see ourselves, so when talking to the Israeli military I am very British; thrusting my hand out, and shouting, 'Mark Thomas, how do you do?' When I am with Palestinian officials I turn English, and to everyone else I am from south London. In truth, my identity is less defined by a notion of country and flag than by the fact that my nan was an air raid warden at the end of our street.

Our new guide is Mustafa, an ex-schoolteacher, and he looks it in a grey sleeveless V-neck jumper and white shirt. He grumbles and moans, gets blisters, occasionally shares out bread with *za'atar* (a sort of herb mix) baked inside, can be chatty one minute and sullen the next, chain-smokes relentlessly, is as quick to judge as he is to pontificate, and never tires of blaming others. We like him a lot.

His first walk with us is from Al Jalama to Zububa, across the plains by the straight line of the Barrier, picking, as we go, either light brown mushrooms or live ammunition out of the soil. The mushrooms are a good size, as are the bullets, too.

'The mushrooms come up after rain on this type of earth,' says Mustafa. The ammunition appears in furrows particularly after ploughing; in that respect at least, both are seasonal. Mustafa, his pressed trousers fastidiously tucked into his white socks in an attempt to keep the cuffs clean, plods gently through the mud,

---

* *I would like to apologise to all Scots for any insult caused by temporarily adopting their heritage, with the exception of one Scot, that one being Lord Balfour.*

giving an occasional commentary that doesn't wander past the certitude of his knowledge as he points out, 'These shoots are carrots' or, 'Over there is a hazelnut orchard.'

When darkness finally descends, we are lead off the field by both the imam's call to prayer and the green fluorescent lights shining on the local minaret. Getting into the village, Mustafa lets out a great sigh with the last of his energy, 'I am sooo tired.' He has quickly grown used to our company.

In every village, the streets are lined with memorials to dead fighters: pictures of young men in green or black headbands stare out, weighed down with ammo belts and machine guns, or posed with arms crossed over their chests holding a pistol in each hand. The posters are Photoshop-ed using old snaps and pictures, and the process makes the colours slightly garish. They are also printed onto illuminated signs, the type used by fast-food shops. In Jenin, there are so many of these posters hanging from lampposts and buildings that, illuminated at night, it looks as if the city is full of armed chip-shop owners.

On one hand it is easy to arrive at an intellectual and logical conclusion: that a people under military occupation, denied the right to a state in their own land, have a right to defend themselves and to use the armed struggle to achieve freedom. Indeed Article 51 of the UN Charter goes some way to affording people that right in law. But some of these pictures will invariably be of suicide bombers, and the thought of celebrating them is alien and disturbing. It raises all sorts of questions about moral legitimacy but, stupidly, I don't ask them: the certainty of the posters seems to intimidate me.

A short distance from Mustafa's home village of At Tayba, we walk into Rummana where, attached to a telegraph pole, is a poster that dominates the street. It is a picture of two men, one holding a machine gun with a banana-shaped clip.

'Who are they?' I ask Mustafa.

'*Shahid*. These are *shahid*; they are the martyrs of the village.'

'People involved in the *Intifada*?'

'Er' – he fidgets slightly as if looking for the right definition for me – 'people killed by the Israelis. We believe we should keep the memory of the martyrs alive.'

'A memorial ...'

'These two are Mohammad's brothers,' says Mustafa, pointing at the boys in the picture.

Mohammad is Mustafa's close friend, and the man who turns up at night in the middle of nowhere to drive us to wherever we are sleeping.

'He lost two brothers?' I ask.

'Yes, his father two sons,' he says, then adds, 'His father used to teach me at school. A very great man, very great.'

Ahead of us, just past a bakery, is another shaded sign that sticks out from a building, and beyond that hangs another from a pole; another picture of a young man clutching a machine gun, in happier times. Everyone seems to know someone with a gun.

Almost as prominent and noticeable are the hoardings for government or NGO aid projects. Every single village I have seen has at least one project supported by foreign aid: in Zububa, the Japanese have funded a sub-pumping station; in At Tayba, the UN's World Food Programme has funded efforts to rebuild the terraces for olive trees; the council building in Al Jalama is built with EU and Irish government funds; Oxfam helps provide water for Bedouins; and so on. The buildings and schemes they sponsor proudly bear their names and logos on plaques. Boards on stilts spring up by the roadside proclaiming NGO mission statements, UN slogans and the words, 'A gift from USAID', or some such.

Every village has a banner thanking someone for their money and a poster thanking someone for their life; and so we walk the roads in the sunlight by the pictures of the dead and the giving.

Our days merge into climbing terraces full of olive trees, clambering over low fences and taking off layers of jumpers as the sun quickly heats the morning's chill. By midday, the shade in the groves is as refreshing as the oranges and tangerines local kids gather for us, when they appear at our elbows happily passing around their illicit bounty. Lunch is a shared affair, Mustafa bringing *lebeneh* (a thick yoghurt) and home-made bread smelling of thyme and olive oil, while Phil and I provide the Pringles. Then it is back to the Barrier, and rocky paths, hills and roads till dark. There is no real need for a watch as the Imam's call to prayer is never far away, and nor is Mustafa's, 'Oh, I am sooo tired,' around about three thirty, just to remind us it is time for a cup of coffee.

Mustafa's English is good, and he continually asks me for the meaning of words, carrying a piece of paper and a pen in his top pocket to make occasional notes. Sometimes his vocabulary runs dry: sitting down for a break he takes his boot off, saying, 'I have a painful water bubble.'

'Blister.'

'Blister,' he repeats thoughtfully then, getting out his piece of paper, says, 'Spell this for me.'

Between admiring the country, Mustafa's explanations of all that surrounds us, general banter and long discussions on linguistics, we continue. The big problem is time. I am rambling like an alcoholic. I look at the map, I look at the schedule and for the life of me cannot work out how we have lost two days. The finishing point of this walk is forever changing, too, as it becomes more and more obvious that our itinerary is not a timescale of obtainable objectives, and has actually been reduced more to a prayer.

Originally the walk was to stop at Deir Ballut, then Mas-ha and now I will settle on getting to a city called Qalqilya. The most important thing is to get to our appointed destination each day, but it is impossible to miss the trail of consequences created by the Barrier as it chases itself across the mountains and along steep ridges. Initially it is the small oddities, the daily absurdities, that catch my eye. In At Tayba, the Barrier cuts right across the football pitch of the boys' school, which seems a wonderfully Israeli way to play football: if you want to stop the other side from scoring, stick an electric fence in front of the goal. In Anin, farmers have to queue at the crack of dawn to pass through an agricultural crossing gate to get to their own land, now on the other side of the Barrier. A large yellow sign is attached to the gate reads:

'*Gate no:* [Blank]

The passage through this gate will be permitted between the hours of [Blank]

In case of emergency or a closed gate during the opening hours, please adress [sic] *at the local DCL at the following phone number:* [Blank]

Different cultures have different ways of saying things: in France a bottle of wine might say, 'I love you'. In Italy flowers might mean, 'I am sorry'. But no one says 'Fuck off' with a blank form quite like the Israelis.

Having been intrigued by relatively minor oddities along the Barrier, the sheer scale of the one at Tura ash Sharqiya is both devastating and captivating. In this area, two towns sit next to each other – Tura al Gharbiya on the Israeli side and Tura ash Sharqiya on the Palestinian. Pre-Barrier, a huge market ran along the street from the Palestinian Tura to the Israeli Tura, and sold everything from fruit and meat to furniture and clothes. Arab Israelis came here in their droves but, like many border towns, it was a place where Jews came, too; it was a place where Jews and Arabs met.

The market closed down the day the concrete went up. Raheed, a municipal councillor, stands in his brown tracksuit and slip-on sandals on the broad walk by the shut shops in the Palestinian Tura.

'These shops here are closed now because of the Wall,' he says, before reeling off statistics. 'There were about 400 shops here alone. Each shop supported 15 people.'

'Where have they all gone?'

'All the shopkeepers? Left to try to find another job … this area lost about half a million shekels a day because all the income was generated here in the market.'

Producing some keys from his tracksuit pocket, he starts to unlock a shop door.

'I own this shop and used to rent it out to another person who ran it; I earned $2,000 a year from it. Let me show you what I use this shop for now …' and he steps into the cool shade of the store. The smell inside is distinctive, though I don't quite recognise it before I see the rabbits hopping across the concrete floor; the smell is pet piss.

'This is all I use the store for now, to keep rabbits,' he says, his voice echoing in the emptiness as the rabbits lollop away from the centre of the room, cordoned off with some old plywood panels to stop them escaping when the door is opened.

'How many do you have?'

'Fifteen.'

'And how much income do they generate?'

'Oh,' he says smiling, embarrassed. 'These are for eating, just for the family.'

The economic impact of the Barrier is writ large here, in decay. Back in Al Jalama, where the mayor pointed from the rooftop to a concrete area by the checkpoint and told me that a thousand market stalls had gone, I could only attempt to equate that fact with the reality for those stallholders. Here, rust and rubble tell the story clearly in a fifteen-minute walk along the old market road from the Palestinian to the Israeli Tura. The street is inhabited only by empty shops, derelict warehouses and deserted workshops; and all that is left of these is some oil stains, and spaces in the roof where the corrugated iron sheets have fallen in. Where once there was hundreds if not thousands of traders and workers there is now an empty road with a wall at one end, and a closed shop housing fifteen rabbits.

Dusk settles as we arrive in the West Bank town of Tulkarm, home to an industrial zone far more established than Danny Atar's plans for Al Jalama and Jenin. Somewhere between getting to the giant meat factory by the Barrier and using the toilets at the petrol station, the sun drops out of sight, or maybe it just dipped low enough for the pollution to reach up, drag it down and beat it unconscious.

The Nitzanei Shalom or 'Buds of Peace' industrial zone is a proper industrial zone, with eight chemical factories, respiratory illness clusters and a thriving sector selling doomed canaries in cages. Its name suggests its purpose: it was set up after the Oslo Accords in 1993 to stimulate the local economy and promote better relations between the two sides, although its appearance suggests it may not have worked. The area is dominated by this heavily guarded complex, which sits right on the Green Line. There is a single door on the Palestinian side for workers, which is opened only in the morning and at night. Once you are in, there is no getting out. It is cold, unwelcoming and intimidating.

Strangely, Tulkarm has a *nouveau riche* area where gated gardens, colonnades and balconies befuddle the boundaries between grandeur and ostentation; essentially this is a working factory town, with a small yuppie enclave and a university in the middle of it.

The town doesn't look like an ideal place to be an organic farmer – with the factories, students, traffic jams and crowded, late-night streets, you would have to be in a peculiar type of predictive-text hell to describe Tulkarm as 'rural' – but that is what Fayez Al-Taneeb is, and it is him I have come to see.

A West Bank farmer whose land happens to sit between the Barrier and a chemical factory, Fayez sits in his living room or, at least, he occasionally sits; mostly he jumps up and paces, gesticulates, draws maps, enacts the story of his farm and, in stiller moments, leans over his son who sits at the family computer, playing film footage of their lives. Fayez is lean and fit, with grey cropped hair in the Palestinian style (by which I mean he has a moustache). He has the appearance of a boxer's second, a ring man with a towel and a fast line of advice, and the demeanour of a trial lawyer putting the Israeli authorities on trial in his own living room. The jury, for tonight at least, is me.

I'm a city boy but even I know that one of the last things a farmer wants is a chemical factory as a neighbour. But that is what Fayez got in 1984, when the Geshuri chemical factory set up on the Palestinian side of the Green Line – it had intended to operate in Israel but failed to get a licence so moved to the West Bank. The factory is actually an award-winning building designed by Lord Rogers and constructed in reflective glass and Italian marble … like fuck. It's a chemical factory. It has lots of pipes and chimneys popping out of the top: a concrete fortress that can't decide if it wants to be a factory or a prison.

Down the side of this ugly building and in its shadow, lies a narrow, muddy path. It leads to Fayez's farm, which is sandwiched between the factory and the concrete slabs of the Barrier: when *that* was built in 2003 the military took nearly two-thirds of Fayez's land, leaving him only 12 *dunams* (just under three acres).

The consequences of putting a chemical factory next to a farm are as predictable as they are ruinous: as Fayez says, 'So you are a farmer and you grow beautiful organic things and they dump a chemical factory next to you.' He pauses, then continues, 'I took a sample [of plants] to the Palestinian Agriculture Authority; they told me the plants were poisoned.'

'When the factory was first built in an Israeli village, a Jewish farmer took Geshuri to court and said they were causing problems for land and health, and it was shut down. So they moved here. We took the factory to court in 1989 and they said we can't do anything because it is in West Bank, on Palestinian territory.'

But the factory is not the only worry for Fayez, who leads me again to the family computer, explaining how the Israeli army destroyed his farm for the first time. It was 2000, and the Second *Intifada* had started. Fayez had already had the legal tussle with

Geshuri and was now the leader of the Farmers' Union, so when the factory was attacked, the army decided to destroy his farm in retaliation.

'Did they serve any sort of notice?' I ask, and with that I unleash the full torrent of the story.

'They don't send to me letter, they don't speak with me, nothing. Me and my wife we were working between the greenhouses and we heard there is a bulldozer in our farm. I go out to look [and] I cannot believe that the bulldozer has lowered the bucket down and starts to demolish the farm. I said, "What are you doing? Stop!" He says, "Don't challenge me," and carries on.'

Instinctively, Fayez jumped in front of the bulldozer bucket and grabbed it with his hands, but the machine moved forward picking up more earth, pushing Fayez with it. The soil relentlessly surged around his legs, threatening to push him over, so Fayez turned to put his back against it, but the bulldozer just kept moving. The earth came up his back and then to his shoulders and, just as he was in danger of being buried alive, his wife started hurling stones at the driver with all her might, hitting him full in the face. That stopped him.

'He said, "OK, you pelt me with stones; I'll show you tomorrow what I can do." Next morning they came with a hundred soldiers and two bulldozers. They destroyed all the farm, all the 32 *dunams.*'

A neighbour filmed what happened from a safe hiding place as the army declared the area to be a military zone and that no one was allowed there. Fayez's son presses play on the computer, and this film starts. The camerawork is shaky and slips in and out of focus, moving in amateur haste from one thing to another, trying to catch everything that is happening. The camera rushes from newly broken metal tubes and bulldozer-ruptured irrigation pipes to earth massing in the bulldozer bucket and there, in the middle, is Fayez. His hair is longer and darker, but without question it is he on the screen, twisted in torment, wanting to step forward to stop the destruction of his farm but unable to do so, caught between impulse and self-preservation. In despair, he lifts his hands to his head and shouts, knowing there is nothing he can do, surrounded as he is by so many soldiers. The bulldozers start to rip up his greenhouses, ploughing up the soil as peppers and cucumbers disappear under great mounds of earth. He steps forward and stops, but then is unable to stand back and his friends have to grab him and lead him away.

Sitting at the family computer, his son watches the pictures, and tears silently start to fall down his face. He remains motionless, one hand on the computer mouse, ready to stop the film with a click.

'And why?' continues Fayez. 'Just to destroy me and my wife? Three times they did it – 2000, 2001 and 2002. The second time was one week after I had put in new irrigation pipes and planted, and two tanks came from the Israeli army. Just smashed everything up.'

It seems a trivial question but I ask it anyway: 'Does the army ever give a reason?'

'Sometimes they say industrial area, sometimes military zone and I should not be here.'

Witnessing the family watch their sufferings played back to them is intensely uncomfortable, and I am amazed they are all still here.

'Do you ever think, "I've had enough, I should move"?' I ask.

'To where?' Fayez snaps. 'To where? To where can I go? Have you been to Lebanon? I was there in 2005, and I visit all the Palestinian refugee camps there. I have been to Jordan, I visit all the Palestinian camps there. You cannot believe our situation. Where would I go? There?'

The next morning, Fayez is much happier. He practically skips around the farm explaining how to hang tomato vines to get the biggest crop, smelling thyme for *za'atar*, showing me his bees and telling stories. He guides me through a greenhouse door, ushering me into the damp heat and quiet, where I wander down a row of cucumber plants. They grow fast and tall, forming a leafy corridor decorated with delicate tendrils and small yellow flowers until, surrounded by foliage, I can no longer see the entrance I came in through. And, just for a moment, I can forget that above the plastic sheeting is the looming presence of a watchtower.

Heading back to the door I emerge to find Fayez looking at his watch: 'I have to meet some journalists from Japan and Denmark today.'

'OK,' I say, thinking I have half an hour to ask a few questions, but just then Fayez waves something at me.

'You try?' he says, smiling, as he hands me a large, bright red chilli, warning: 'Very hot. You try it.' Halfway down the pepper, I think, *Whenever I want someone to leave my home I will say I have an appointment and give them a chilli.*

There is a lot to ask about a place like this, but I want to know how you manage to run an 'organic' farm next to a chemical plant. At the risk of sounding middle class, exactly who is running the Soil Association Certification programme around here?

'Aren't you worried that chemicals will get onto your organic farm?' I ask carefully.

'Now you want to know about the weather here in Palestine,' Fayez says with a smile. 'The wind all the time blows from Israel to Tulkarm city. It doesn't blow onto the Israeli side.' Ah ha, so the pollutants get blown into Palestine but, as Fayez's farm is on the other side of the factory, they do not blow onto his farm. Which sounds a definitive if dubious argument.

'Except for forty days when the wind changes. The Egyptian wind comes directly from the east to west.'

Which means the pollutants from the chemical factory blow onto his farm for forty days? Well, no, it doesn't, apparently. When the wind blows from the factory into Israel the factory shuts down, or at least the offending production line does, according to Fayez.

'Our Jewish neighbour, a Jewish farmer, found a white chemical powder on his plants which damages them … and the Israeli farmers came to the owner of the factory and he promised them every year the production line [that produces the problem] will stop.'

So Fayez is telling me that an Israeli-owned factory based in the West Bank is happy for its pollutants to blow into Palestine, but turns off the offending production line when the wind blows into Israel. He's the only Palestinian beneficiary of the plant's actions, which means his crops are now safe from the chemical detritus. I tried speaking to the factory owner but after initially agreeing to an interview he proves impossible to get hold of. It's an incredible tale but everyone I speak to on this side of the wall, at least, supports the story.

In the search for more information, I go to the market in Tulkarm. Above a dress shop, the Palestinian Medical Relief Society has been running a general practice and women's advisory service for over twenty years. Dr Mohammad Shaban has been studying Tulkarm's problems with chronic diseases for all that time from a surgery equipped with orange kids' chairs, and an eye chart that uses pictures instead of letters. He beckons me in, shoots a passing glance at the 'No smoking' poster and starts our interview about the rise in respiratory illnesses in the traditional Palestinian way, by fishing out an ashtray and sparking up a fag. Accompanied by his colleague, Mohammad Abusi, Director of Public Health in Tulkarm and Qalqilya, Dr Shaban begins: 'Here in Tulkarm we have a serious problem in our area. It began when these factories were built here, since the Geshuri factory and others are making paint and gases and fertilisers.'

His colleague steps in, 'We follow a protocol devised by the World Health Organisation and what we found was clusters of cancers and respiratory illness from the gas fumes from the factories.'

'The rise in cancer, was it lung cancer?'

'Yes.'

'And this is linked to the arrival of the factories?'

'There is no other reason, only the factory.'

'Did you talk to the factories about your findings?' I ask.

'We did,' says Dr Shaban dryly. 'The municipality took the factory to the Israeli court but they said no one in Israel is affected so no offence in Israel, so no crime has occurred.'

Whatever its original intentions, the reality is that the industrial zone allows Israeli companies to operate outside Israeli environmental, industrial and employment laws by using the peculiar status of the West Bank to get away with things they would not be allowed to do in Israel. It would appear that Israelis can be protected from pollution but Palestinians cannot. And it would also appear that the economic benefit is not quite so enticing, either. Although there has been legislation passed making it mandatory for Palestinians working in Israel or on the Israeli settlements to be paid the minimum wage, several factories in the Nitzanei Shalom industrial zone argue they don't fit into either category, and therefore do not have to comply. One, Solar Gas Industries, pays its workers according to the Jordanian legal system[8] in place in the West Bank before 1967 and the Occupation which, needless to say, doesn't offer quite the same minimum wage requirements or benefits enjoyed by anyone working for an Israeli firm elsewhere.

I ask a welder at Yamit factory making agricultural filters – someone whom Danny Atar would argue had benefited from the factories being here – what his reaction would be if they were to close.

'If they shut the factory here it would be a good step. I am a worker but I will find other work. This factory affects us so much that for the public good it should be shut down … if they shut this factory down it would be a better life here.'

Breakfast the following day is at Fayez's house – home-made bread baked with fresh *za'atar* and cups of tea served on the porch – and there is a gang of folk around the table. The Japanese journalist Fayez met yesterday stayed the night in the family home; he is discussing his travel plans and is uncertain if he will stay here another day. Fayez interrupts with a steady stream of hot fresh bread and instructions on how to grow thyme; our guide Mustafa smokes and has a small morning grumble about his lack of blister plasters; and passing neighbours shout greetings and are invited to eat as they walk by on the street. Nursing a small hot cup of tea, I quietly realise that sharing bread and tea and swapping stories is one part of Palestinian culture I feel very comfortable with. And so we sit for longer than we might before we shake hands, offer thanks and set off into the flickering shade of a street full of trees. The Japanese journalist might not have a firm itinerary but we have seventy-two hours left in which to finish the first part of the walk.

Fayez, of course, has a farm to run, in between talking to more reporters today; telling his story to anyone and everyone is his way of fighting back. As we leave the front porch behind us I hear him say to the Japanese journalist, 'You should try a pepper, very hot.'

chapter 5
AFTER-SCHOOL DETENTIONS

No one starts a ramble thinking, 'I hope this is shit.' True, my children have walked out from holiday cottages muttering, 'I *bet* this is shit,' but that is altogether different. We might hope it doesn't rain or that a nice café *en route* is open, but the desire to escape the humdrum, to experience the elements or enjoy a bit of nature usually means a ramble starts with optimism.

I am beginning to wonder if this usual expectation is at odds with walking here, where simple things can go awry and frequently do. This time, the day after International Human Rights Day, the Israeli army has detained me in the middle of a field of greenhouses.

There is no connection between the two events – the Israeli army are not confined to barracks during Human Rights Day to then leap into their jeeps at the stroke of midnight shouting, 'Right, back to work!' It's just my irony radar is set to 'high'.

'What religion are you?' shouts one of four heavily armed young men as I am beckoned over to the Humvee.

I have been here long enough to know the answer should be straight and honest. 'Atheist, though technically that is not a religion,' would be appropriate, at a push, and with a twinkle in my eye I might have got away with, 'Buddhist Presbyterian – I'm coming back, but as something more uncomfortable.' Instead I blurt out, 'What religion am I? That is the most stupid fucking question I have been asked outside of Northern Ireland.'

Two and a half hours later we are released.

Every day something goes wrong: our tardiness outrages a farmer at Tura al Gharbiya as we don't have time to talk to him; water and patience run out at Kafr Sur, where we collapse on a street corner in a heap; we even manage to get lost. How could I lose the Barrier, for God's sake? One minute there is a blocked road and a diversion, and the next we're standing on a rubbish dump in the middle of nowhere wondering why seagulls are eating our sandwiches.

Later, when I tell Fadhi I lost the Barrier, he replies, 'Do you think you would be able to do it again, on a more permanent basis?'

Yet every day I start out with optimism. Not through strength of character on my part; no, it is the sight of the hills. I keep finding myself proclaiming to Phil or Mustafa or anyone who happens to be nearby: 'Look at that! It calls out to be walked!' The West Bank gives good geography: the hills roll in curves under a sky that fills your eyes. Each day I am amazed at their beauty – sometimes I nearly cry in awe – and there is always a moment when I just want to be still and enjoy being part of the landscape.

Despite this, the perfect walk still eludes me. Perhaps it is because the feelings of joy and exhilaration that make a specific walk 'perfect' come with a feeling of freedom, and it might be that this is too much to ask for in a place surrounded by wire and concrete and a cold absence of liberty. Coupled with this, my fears of failing to complete the route play out at night, and the days are dogged with doubt. It is a relief, therefore, on this the ninth day of our walk, to be spending the afternoon with someone who has walked some of this very route.

Taysir Arabasi has the swept-back hair of a romantic lead, and the white jumper and black padded gilet of a market-stall holder. He is also the Palestinian director of Zaytoun, the Fairtrade olive oil cooperative, while in 2005 he was one of the organisers of a protest walk along part of the Barrier.

In 2004, the International Court of Justice ruled Israel to be in violation of international law in its chosen route for the Barrier. It demanded Israel stop construction, dismantle what was already built (some 200 kilometres at the time) and pay compensation to those who had lost land and homes.[9] This moment of victory for the Barrier's opponents was short-lived, however, when it became apparent that Israel had no intention of complying with the legal ruling.

'People felt forgotten: the Wall has been constructed, end of the story.' Taysir explains the reason of the 2005 walk. 'We wanted to say even if this construction is completed we want it to be demolished; the International Court of Justice decided that the Wall is illegal and it has to be removed.'

It is a truism that the rich have no need to protest, that those in power do not march. Instead they memo to themselves little Post-It notes left next to the kettle: 'Go to bank. Kids' piano lessons. Vet. Blockade Gaza.' Thus marching is the preserve of the poor and the downtrodden: Ghandi marched 240 miles to pick salt from the beach at Dandi and defy British colonialism; in Alabama, the black civil rights movement marched from Selma to Montgomery to fight for voter registration; and England witnessed the epic, 300-mile march against poverty and unemployment that was the Jarrow Crusade.

The West Bank villagers march follows a great global heritage. Men, women and children marched over twenty-two days from village to village along the Barrier, sometimes travelling ten to twelve kilometres a day, holding meetings, protests and non-violent actions.

'It started in Zububa and went through At Tayba and Anin; the same villages you walked through,' Taysir tells me.

'And where did you finish?'

'The whole thing finished in Jerusalem, at Qalandiya checkpoint.'

Following in the footsteps of such grassroots dissent, sharing the roads they took, feels auspicious and exciting, but I would be lying if I did not admit to a sense of relief on hearing the villagers had not walked the entire length of the Barrier. Strangely, I suspect I might be a tad miffed if the villagers had walked the whole way, thereby robbing me of making the claim to be the first to walk the entire thing, and I am not altogether happy with these feelings. They cast me in conflicting roles: on one hand I'm following the spirit of solidarity shown by the International Brigades, while on the other I'm just one more public-school explorer in a foreign land. It leaves me unsure as to whether to sing, 'Viva La Quinta Brigada', or scream, 'Bagsey first up Everest!'

We have two days left to finish the first walk, and we have become 'rude tired' – a mental state arrived at when exhaustion erodes social skills. When discussing the local police, Mustafa says, 'I don't know this area so I don't know who is the headmaster of the police.'

Normally this would be the starting point for a discussion on the word 'headmaster', but instead I tersely reply, 'Commander.'

'Commander?'

'Yes.'

'I don't know the commander, then,' he says. But he doesn't get his piece of paper out to make a note of the word.

Being 'rude tired' affects everything from conversation through to dress sense, and I am reduced to wearing things that smell least. I enter the hilltop village of Jayyus looking like I've just robbed a Barnardos shop, with a dignifying tickle of sweat rolling down my neck from behind my ear.

I reach for the Ventolin and Mustafa reaches for his cigarettes.

'What do you think?' says Phil.

'I think I need to get my blood pressure checked,' I reply, breathing deeply.

'About this place.' Phil is the first one to pick up on the odd feeling there.

Out here, on the edge of the village, there is no buffer from the cold wind, and puffs of dust and litter scud around in the air. Every other house looks half-built; just shells of concrete waiting for windows and paint.

'Looks like folk ran out of money,' says Phil, nodding at the empty homes. 'Or cleared off.'

'Something is weird about this place,' I agree.

The main street is full of hubbub and old men milling around with cups of coffee. Anyone who has visited a northern seaside resort out of season will recognise the looks we receive, looks that ask, 'Why are you *here*?' Phil is right, something is weird here.

At the local school, we have arranged to meet staff. In the headmaster's office, chairs line the room and pictures of Yasser Arafat and Mahmoud Abbas decorate the walls.

The headmaster looks like a headmaster: perched on the edge of his desk as he is, he could pass for a detective in a homicide department.

Three students and some teachers join us, and start by telling us how the Barrier has taken the village land. Its placement put 900 acres of village land on the other side of the Barrier, land which included 50,000 fruit and olive trees and all six of the village irrigation wells. This has, of course, been catastrophic for the village. True, there are two crossing gates, run by the military for farmers to access their land. These are supposed to be open at regular times but it doesn't always happen, and even if they are opened it can be for a mere fifteen minutes, dependent on the army's mood. But the biggest problem the farmers face is permits – less than twenty-five per cent of the farmers have permits to cross, and unemployment now runs at seventy per cent in Jayyus. Meanwhile the land the farmers have been forced to abandon is regularly vandalised by settlers.

'The children worry about their families, about the land, about their future,' says the English teacher.

It is an all too similar story to many others I have heard, and I scribble out a list of follow-up questions about irregular gate-opening times and settler damage to crops. But as I am writing, they start a new story, a different story, one I am not expecting at all: 'Our students are suffering from this Wall because their lives are always in a state of fear, and worry and upset,' explains the English teacher.

The students in the room look at the floor, in the way teenagers do when being talked about by adults. The teachers look at me, waiting for my reaction, so in response, I nod my head. If nods could speak this one would say, 'I have no idea what you are talking about, but I don't want to look stupid.' The headmaster isn't a headmaster for nothing and 'hears' my nod loud and clear.

'Let me explain,' he says. 'Some of the students were arrested last night and this really affects the students here. They are always thinking and worrying about their friends who have been arrested.' His tie is loose and he looks tired. 'Every day there are students not attending school because they can't sleep at night … The army come at night, knocking at the doors, shooting guns in the air. Every night.'

I look round the room, but no one even bothers to nod in agreement. 'I think seven students were arrested by the Israeli soldiers last night,' says the English teacher.

'What was this for?'

'They said they were throwing stones at the soldiers near the Wall.'

The headmaster holds his hands up imploringly. 'Education,' he says, 'needs stability. We need to be able to give our students a calm environment to study in. They need peace and quiet to think, and we are losing these things in Jayyus.'

Outside, the playground is empty and looks much like any other playground, until you take a second look at its murals. If the Workers' Revolutionary Party had a design-a-playground competition, this is what the winning entry would look like. At one end of a whitewashed wall is a large portrait of a young boy behind prison bars. Next to this image is a child wrapped in barbed wire, holding a candle aloft. The one concession to childhood is a picture of a camel, though that might be a post-modern nod at bourgeois sentimentality. The most striking picture is of a chained fist smashing the Star of David. The sight of this in London would have me calling the police and the Department of Education, under the belief that Iranian President Ahmadinejad had opened up a 'free school'.

'I see you are looking at the pictures.' The geography teacher's side-parted grey hair is ruffled by the wind, and he has zipped up his red tracksuit top against the chill. 'One month ago, soldiers came to this town, gathered all the women and children into this yard and turned it into a police station. They broke into the sports hall and used it for interrogations.'

At the side of the playground he opens the door of a small hall to show me, then gestures back to the empty playground.

'This isn't the first time they have used the yard like this. In the past they ordered the students, young men, to put their hands up against the wall and then they beat them in front of the crowd.'

'They publicly beat kids?'

'Yes, in this place. So this is why the paintings; we wanted to transform the playground.'

The geography teacher is friends with the PE teacher, who tells me: 'When the army came and arrested the children last night, most of them, except one of nineteen years old, are twelve years old.'

'*Twelve?*'

'Yes.'

'Twelve years old?'

'Yes.'

'And the army came in the middle of the night and took them?'

'Yes.'

The PE teacher knows a family who had one of their children taken by the army a few nights ago. 'I can take you to him.'

Ali, a teacher in another village and a member of the local council, welcomes me into his living room and offers tea. He cuts a figure of mannered propriety with his sports jacket and wire-rimmed glasses. He sits down on an ornate sofa, a single pat of the empty space next to him brings his son, Yaya, alongside him, and they tell their story.

At 2 a.m. a few nights before, banging and shouting woke Ali. Opening his door, he found Israeli soldiers pointing their guns at him. He was told, 'Wake your family! Get them out on the street!'

One son, Achmed, was already up but the two youngest, Yaya and Zachariah, were still in bed. Ali took a glass of water up to the boys so they could have a quick drink when he woke them. His son Yaya is twelve years old, and it was him the soldiers wanted.

'We have a picture of him, wearing a blue and red shirt, throwing stones at the army,' said the soldier in charge.

'He doesn't throw stones,' Ali replied.

'We have a picture.'

'A football shirt?' asked Ali.

'A Real Madrid shirt,' came the reply.

'But he doesn't have one like that.'

The soldiers searched the wardrobes for the T-shirt in vain, but remained intent on taking Yaya. By now his mother was crying and his younger brother, Zachariah, tried to hit the soldiers when they moved to arrest Yaya. Fearful of his family's safety, Ali said: 'I will come with him. Let me come with him, OK?'

'OK,' replied the soldiers and, handcuffing Yaya, led him to a jeep. Ali quickly calmed Zachariah, and left with the soldiers.

The army vehicle drove a short distance into the village square and parked. There were some eighteen other army jeeps and two armoured personnel carriers in the square, all of which had picked up other children from the village. The soldier told Ali they needed to transfer vehicles. The door was opened and Ali got out of the jeep, but then the door was shut behind him, and Yaya was left alone in the jeep.

'But what will I tell his brother? I told Zachariah I would look after him. What will I tell him?' Ali implored.

'Go home,' said the soldier, 'and when you get there, catch Zachariah by the ear and tell him, "Don't throw stones like Yaya, don't throw stones at the army."'

As Ali sits on the sofa telling me this story, the family cat jumps lightly onto his lap. It is ginger, with a white belly, not yet an adult. It takes a few cautious steps around Ali's legs to find a comfortable spot, then curls up. Sitting next to his father, still visibly shaken but attempting defiance, Yaya can't resist the purring and reaches out to stroke the cat.

After being taken to a military base – handcuffed and blind-folded – Yaya was questioned about the village, school and throwing stones at the soldiers.

'They showed me a photo and said it was me, but it wasn't,' he says, arms folded and his lips tight. 'Then they asked me to sign a paper saying they had not hit me. Then they let me go.'

'How long were you detained?'

'About twenty-four hours,' says his father, as the ginger cat searches for a more comfortable position.

'Did you get any food?'

'They gave me some cold rice and beans and some water, but I didn't eat it. And when I went to the toilet they would not take the handcuffs off.'

'Did you get access to a lawyer or an adult like a social worker?'

'No,' he says.

The Israeli authorities released Yaya and another boy from Jayyus on the roadside five kilometres from his home. His parents were not informed of his release, the boys had no money and it was dark.

'Fortunately,' says Ali, 'a doctor was driving past and stopped and gave them a lift home, or they would have had to walk.'

Yaya is lucky. In the West Bank, children of twelve and over can be held without charge for up to eight days, with no access to family or lawyers.[10]

Before leaving Jayyus, I talked to the town's mayor about the arrest. He said, 'The problem here is that in Palestine the children are soldiers, and in Israel the soldiers are children.'

On the day of Yaya's detention his brother Zachariah, by all accounts, did not have a good day at school.

QALQILYA / ALFEI MENASHE

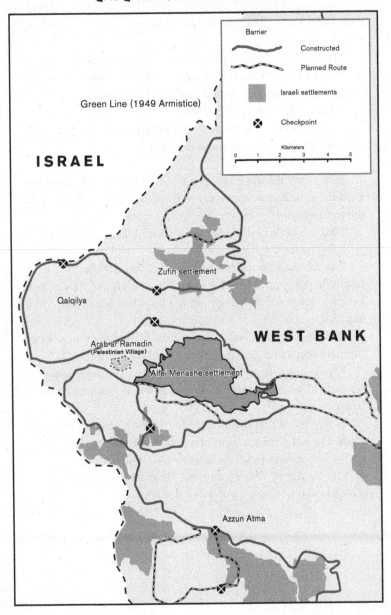

Green Line (1949 Armistice)

ISRAEL

Barrier

Constructed

Planned Route

Israeli settlements

Checkpoint

Kilometers
0   1   2   3   4   5

Zufin settlement

Qalqilya

WEST BANK

Arab ar Ramadin
(Palestinian Village)

Alfei Menashe settlement

Azzun Atma

chapter 6
ALBERT AND
THE ~~LION~~ GIRAFFE

Today is the final day of the first part of our walk and we are even more 'rude tired'.

Phil is up first and has gone to the window.

'Fuck,' he says, from across the room.

'Weather?'

'Fucked.'

'How fucked?'

'Semi-fucked.'

'Rain fucked?'

'Cloud bollocks.'

'Is that fucked or bollocksed?'

'Bollocksed.'

'Not fucked then.'

'Right.'

'Coffee; shower; fuck off. Yeah?'

'Fuck yeah.'

Phil hasn't bothered to shave in a while, and his goatee beard is losing its shape. It is now a thatch of unmaintained face topiary swamped by uncut stubble. I intend to suggest that he might like to remedy this but the words come out as, 'You look shit.'

'You look shitter,' he says, meaning, 'Thanks for your concern.'

Like I said, we are rude tired.

The final destination is Qalqilya Zoo, it adds a sense of fun for the last day and Mustafa has never been before. It is some twenty-five kilometres short of the planned end point, but frankly I couldn't care less. Waving goodbye to people this morning, I shouted, 'Have a happy Christmas.' It is the first time I have uttered those words this year and at once I felt horribly homesick. I want to go home, have a bath, cuddle the family and get some sleep. Everything else can wait.

We restart our walk from where we left off at the school the night before. The village seems on edge once again after another raid last night. Officially, no one should be on the streets this morning as the army put out a military order to that effect, but life goes on.

Mustafa is as grumpy as we are, and is having a sulky smoke when, suddenly, a group of young kids runs, shouting, at us. The oldest can only be around nine years old, and there is playful confidence to the group; but a couple have their hoods up and one has a face mask on. A pebble flies and bounces off my rucksack, a couple of lads shout and make the victory sign, and one comes at me screaming, 'Rooooaaar,' but his voice hasn't broken yet so it sounds rather squeaky.

Mustafa snaps, '*Halas!*' Enough.

But the kids have seen Phil's camera and swarm, though it is more *Lord of the Midges* than *Flies*. A couple more pebbles ping off our bags and I make out one word in the shouting children's melee: '*Yahod!*' Jew.

'*Halas!*' says Mustafa again, reaching for his phone.

'Just tell them we are internationals,' I say.

But Mustafa is on his mobile.

'Just tell them we are not Jews,' I insist. And then, 'What are you doing?'

'I am calling the mayor.'

'What for?'

'To get an apology for these children's behaviour,' comes the testy reply.

'Let's not waste time,' I groan. 'Let's just go.'

'I must talk to the mayor,' says Mustafa, and starts mumbling into the phone.

'Bollocks to this.'

In truth, I am furious with myself: 'Tell them we're not Jews,' I had said. Despite being factually correct, it feels cowardly and wrong. A few years ago, I was included on a far-right website listed under, 'Influential Jews Controlling the British Media'. I was delighted, thrilled to appear next to my comic hero Alexei Sayle, who was also included. It didn't matter that I am not influential, nor in the British media nor indeed Jewish: it still felt like a badge of honour. In a world that is increasingly complex on issues of identity, it felt nice to know I could 'pass', that I could cross the line from Gentile to Jew and back, even if it was only with anti-Semites. But just then, I had gone from being proud of being mistaken for a Jew to being quick to proclaim I am not one. Nor is this the first time this trip.

Talking to a group of teenage Palestinians in an orchard near Tulkarm, one lad had said, '*Yahod?*'

'No, I am not a Jew,' I had replied quickly.

'Oh, where are you from?'

'I am from Eng– ... Scotland ... Yes, I am a Scot and have you heard about what the English did to us in Culloden?'

Declaring myself a strategic Scot (once again) nullified the discomfort I felt about declaring my Gentile origins so clearly. But why *should* it matter if I was Jewish? There are lots of Jews who are opposed to the Occupation, and surely this is the issue: this conflict can't merely revolve around religion, can it? And should a nine-year-old boy who, along with the rest of his village, was woken by Israeli soldiers at two o'clock this morning, be conscious of these arguments?

Jayyus comes to an end abruptly, the way that villages do here: the last house in the village is the start of the countryside. The hills run immediately in front of us, dropping down into a valley and shooting out into the horizon demarcated by a grey sky. To our left is a road that winds along the ridge from where we stand, dipping in and out of hills, disappearing behind mounds and gullies only to re-emerge later in the distance.

'Let's follow this road,' I say. 'It has to be easier than scrambling down the hills with no paths.'

The road is new, with a long white line stretching perfectly along the middle of the tarmac, and yellow lines that run along the edge at each side: a proper road. This is no charity-project either: there is no proclamation of the donor's name with a grandiose project title like, 'The Jayyus Rejuvenation Bypass – a gift from Oxfam'; no signs announcing that it was paid for by the EU or *Top Gear*. This makes for a peculiar sort of road, made more so by the site of a huge, stripped olive tree, charred black from burning, standing by one side of it in some newly worked ground with replanted olive trees that look as if they have narrowly escaped a similar fate. Then the familiarity of it dawns. At the edge of the tarmac is a sandy track, next to which is a continuous line of concrete footings buried into the ground and just past *that* is a ditch running along the side of the road. This is the Barrier. The concrete footings have evenly spaced circular holes in them, into which will slot the poles for the electric fence. The sandy path is to identify activity near the fence and the ditch is part of the whole standardised structure. This is simply an old bit of the Barrier that has been taken down.

'We're on the Wall!' I shout to Phil, who has walked off to set up his camera for some shots.

'Yes,' says Mustafa, slightly bemused at my sudden joy. 'This is where the village won a court case and forced the Israelis to move the Wall back towards the Green Line. The Israelis had to come and take this down by the order of the court.'

'And is it just left for anyone to use?' asks Phil.

'We're on the Wall!' I yell, jumping on it. 'The Wall!' Ramblers often walk on old walls and ruins, ancient paths and traders routes, but not like this. This is an old bit of a new wall.

This is special. This is a vision of what the Barrier should look like, the mere path that it might become. That the Barrier will eventually come down cannot be in question; the question is, what will be left here when it goes? Will it be the border between two states? Will it be left to crumble and decay? Or will the Wall be ours to walk? Sure, we'll need some signposts; those upright wooden ones with a symbol for the trail and an arrow carved into them. And, yes, we'll need some rest stops at viewpoints with good panoramas, wooden benches and circular concrete tables. There will have to be guidebooks and maps and perhaps a badge on completion of the route. Plus flapjack with far too many bits of cereal and oats in it. But this is what it *might* be like. Are we walking on the future? Are we walking on possibilities? We are walking the Palestine Way.

The joy of following the 'old' Barrier as it cuts across the hilltops has eased my tiredness and lifted me out of my gloom just as surely as Mustafa seems to sink lower into his. To prevent a soaking from the rain, he has rolled a plastic bag onto his head that comes to a pointy peak and he wanders, head down, looking like a chain-smoking Smurf.

Taking a path from the 'old' Barrier leads to a main road that branches in two directions: one to a checkpoint leading to Israel and the other into Qalqilya, our final destination for this part of the walk, and a city that is almost completely encircled by the Barrier, which here consists of eight-metre high concrete slabs.

The narrow road into Qalqilya is referred to by most Palestinians and observers as 'the bottleneck'. A map of the Barrier does give the encompassing route a bottle shape: an odd bottle admittedly; a sample bottle perhaps, or an old seventies bottle of rosé. The road also has an army checkpoint in the middle of it: a small booth, the bottom half of which is metal slates, while the top is Perspex window. As we pass by it, I wonder if a driver being pulled over by the army has ever been tempted to lean out their window and shout into the booth, 'Er, I'd like two chicken nuggets, large fries, a shake and a Coke.' Tempted perhaps, but only tempted.

We walk into town, Mustafa and I both in childish moods: him sulking and me overexcited at the prospect of going home. On the outskirts of the city we move past nurseries full of seedlings, palms and ceramic pots; walk past a petrol station with a pizza concession and bright neon fizzing against the grey sky; we step around the second-hand sofas and chairs laid out under awnings on the pavements, and run a slalom of Formica desks and cupboards.

As we walk further into town, the furniture shops turn into electrical shops that are full of reconditioned TVs and lines of washing machines; there are even a couple of exercise bikes sitting forlornly in the drizzle.

In the centre, city life picks up: shops sell goods that come with a receipt and yellow taxis go about their business of braking sharply and hooting. There are clothes shops, sweet shops, music shops, street stalls and in *shawarma* cafés there are pans of oil bubbling with falafels.

We are trying to find our last objective and suddenly, to our left, there is a side street where the walls are painted in faded colours and an elongated Palestinian flag hangs across the road, supported on either side by pillars covered in drawings of rhinos, horses and koala bears. Under this arch are the metal gates of the zoo. With one hand I reach out to touch the gates and the first part of our walk is done.

'This is brilliant,' I say to Phil, so relieved to be here. 'Good work mate.' I reach out and quickly hug him.

'Well done.'

'Well done all of us – a team effort and all that,' I reply, grinning broadly.

'I have a question,' Mustafa suddenly pipes up, ominously.

'What's that then?' asks Phil.

'It is for Mark.'

'OK.'

He pauses, staring at me, then says, 'Is there a difference between the animals in this zoo and the life Palestinian people are living with the Wall around them?'

'Well, yes, I think there is,' I begin. 'The animals are looked after by their keepers, they are fed regularly and they are not dependent on pass cards to get to work to get that food and ...'

'No,' Mustafa's voice is curt with emotion. 'There. Is. No. Difference. Between the lives we lead and the animals' lives.' His eyes look hurt and his face tightens, and with sudden passion he shouts, 'We are trapped in one great prison. Stuck in a cabbage!'

'Cage,' I correct automatically.

'What?'

'You're not stuck in a cabbage; you're stuck in a cage.'

'A cage,' he says, his anger spent as quickly as it had arisen. He quietly finishes, 'We are stuck in a cage.'

'I have a question for you,' I say to Mustafa.

'Yes?'

'If this is a zoo, does that mean I am just a tourist here?'

He shrugs, then says, 'Maybe ... maybe.'

'What do you think, Mark?' asks Phil.

'I think, maybe, too,' I say slowly and, with a crushing sadness, I enter the zoo.

I realise then that the reason Mustafa has been in a bad mood for the past couple of days is because Phil and I are going home. We are about to do the one thing he cannot: leave.

In the zoo, the first sight to greet us is of a young monkey, with an erect penis, gripping the bars of its cage and screeching as a boy pokes at its genitals with a stick. The boy's father looks on, laughing, throwing chunks of pitta into the cage, while the monkey howls in rage and all-too-apparent excitement.

All three of us move away from the spectacle and wander our separate ways round the zoo, bumping into each other twenty minutes later by the hippo enclosure. The metal railings around it are painted a murky blue, the water in the pool is brown, and rain-drops dimple the surface. On seeing us, the enormous creature lumbers with surprising speed towards us, opening its large but oddly delicate-looking mouth of mottled brown and red.

'If this thing makes a break for it, we're doomed.' I attempt to raise the mood.

'I know,' smiles Mustafa.

At this, the creature turns away from us, forces its backside against one of the blue poles and starts to defecate loudly, using its stubby tail like a fan to disperse the excrement, which flies through the air like a Catherine wheel of kak.

'It is like a machine,' cries Mustafa, stepping back to avoid getting hit.

'It is!' I laugh, in part that we are talking again: the sight of the spraying shit turning the air a blurry brown has eased the tension between us.

'Here,' says Mustafa, calling me over to a glass display case behind us. Inside is a snake, and it doesn't look well.

'That is the skinniest snake I have ever seen,' I say, mesmerised by the emaciated stick of a reptile. 'It is the weediest snake ever.'

'The words,' says Mustafa, pointing at the information plaque, 'say it is the Palestinian snake. That is our national snake.'

'You have a national snake? Well, it looks exhausted,' I blurt out before I can stop myself.

'Just like the people,' says Mustafa, suddenly cackling at his own audacity.

'Your snake is knackered,' I return, warming to the theme.

'I know,' he says, 'and the sign says it is not even poisonous.' He gasps, his face full of mock outrage: 'Our snake is not even dangerous!' He is laughing hard now, to my relief.

As our giggling judders to an end, I wonder aloud, 'Do you think it is possible to see something with a little less symbolism?'

It is not. In one corner of the zoo stands a stuffed giraffe, Brownie, which died in 2000 when the Israeli army opened fire near the zoo. The sound of gunfire induced a panic in Brownie who stampeded, banged his head, collapsed and died.

Coincidently the director of the zoo happened to be an amateur taxidermist and despite the scale of the project decided to work on the giraffe himself. What he appeared to lack in precision equipment he made up for in love.

A giraffe has many noted physical aspects, one being its eyes: huge and lovely, great black shiny orbs of beauty. Unfortunately, it would appear that black glass eyes were not easy to come by at that time and the director had to make do with the nearest suitable replacements, which were Day-Glo green in colour. Not only this, but the lower part of the jaw is out of line with the upper jaw, and protrudes to one side. Perhaps it has not weathered well in the open; the neck looks over-stretched and the head over-stuffed. The legs are set at an angle that means it leans back, as if the animal is about to collapse.

The overall effect of the eyes, jaw and frame was to give the look of the animal still in the midst of the gunfire that did for it, In that respect the representational skills of the taxidermist are exemplary.

But the true wonder of this place is to be found in its very existence. Founded in 1986, the zoo has survived *intifadas* and clampdowns in a city that is now virtually encircled in concrete and wire. According to Zayed, the zoo's manager, it was, 'set up to draw people to the city for tourism, to bring people in to the markets'. In this it was successful, with many of the visitors coming from the Arab Israeli community as the entry price is much cheaper than Israeli zoos. But the Barrier has been problematical for the zoo, due largely to the restrictions and vagaries of the checkpoints, which have meant a decline in Arab Israeli visitors.

Qalqilya's markets have suffered the same fate as those in Tura ash Sharqiya and Al Jalama. Yet the zoo stays open. 'It is important for kids to find places like this, like the zoo, because they are closed in. All around them is the Wall. Without places like this they will be crushed,' says Zayed. In the summer the place is packed, the zoo has a pool for kids, and parkland, too. On this bleak winter afternoon, a group of women in long black *abayas* and white *hijabs* giggle as they come out of the cafeteria, young children wrapped up in anoraks and woollen hats spilling around them. By the swings and the slides, on a bench, a dad sits huddled in a driving jacket, sharing some tea with his two sons. It doesn't seem to matter that the dead giraffe is a little out of shape or that the hippo runs a muck-spreading service; people want normality, and for some this is as close as it gets. It may be a symbol for Mustafa and for other Palestinians, too, of the captivity of their lives, but above and beyond all of that, it is a day out at the zoo. It's very existence a minor miracle. A moment when kids can forget the Barrier, the Occupation, the lost land, the night raids, the destroyed homes, the pass cards and the army patrols. A moment when they can enjoy saying the magic words: 'Can I have an ice cream?'

PART TWO
THE SECOND RAMBLE

THE COMMUTE TO WORK

It is 3 a.m. and the road is on fire. Both lanes are alight; a line of flames burning in the darkness as if the rest of the street was already scorched and the blaze was now heading towards us. I expect the cab driver to turn around or at least stop, but he doesn't – instead, he lets out a low growl and continues driving straight at the inferno. Shadows flicker over the inside of the cab as we approach the wall of fire and still the cabbie just keeps driving towards the line.

Great. Of all the cabbies in the West Bank I get the one who thinks he is in the Royal Tournament. I haven't had enough coffee for this.

As he heads into the blaze my hand grabs the door handle, ready to bail out the moment we stall, start to burn or the cabbie bellows 'Muwhahahaa!' But in the wall of fire there is a gap. Not a big one but a gap nonetheless, and the cab moves slowly through it, while I stare mesmerised by the flames.

The driver chuckles and says, 'Welcome to the Holy Land.'

'Are all your welcomes this biblical?'

'The army are in the town tonight, so the youth put tyres in the road and light them.'

'Is that normal?'

'For here, yes.' He shrugs and pulls a cigarette from his top pocket.

The flames fade behind us as we roll on into the darkness ahead. The centre of the city slips past the side window: shops huddle, wrapped and locked in roll-down shutters indistinguishable from one another, row upon row of night-black storefronts, each turning into a blurred memory before it is barely realised. On the side roads and narrow lanes, the taxi's headlights reflect back at us from approaching junction walls. Dogs haunting the rubbish bins are caught in a brief glare before slinking off as we rattle through the alleyways. A little further on lies the Barrier and a checkpoint and, as we turn onto a main road to approach it, other headlights start emerging in the rear mirror, while red tail-lights sparkle in front of us.

'Here, this is the workers' checkpoint,' says the cabbie. 'It's for Palestinians working in Israel; they have to go through the checkpoint to get to work.'

'What's that?' I ask, peering at an odd structure:, a cross between a large barn and a bus shelter.

'This was put up by the municipality. It is a shelter for the workers. To keep them dry when it rains. Just behind it is the checkpoint.'

The cabbie stops the car and Phil and I wander over to the shelter. Straight down the middle of the concrete floor run two rows of benches, back to back, but no one sits here. Instead, small groups of early arrivals sit by the stalls that have sprung up around the shelter. Carts and trestle tables selling breads are set up under the tall, corrugated-iron roof: flat loaves, long loaves, buns, twists, sweet pastries and parcels of dough, with the ubiquitous za'atar *or meat, all laid out in their respective piles. The battered metal doors of the small coffee carts are flung back, revealing water boilers and gas rings that burn with a roaring hiss while men frantically stir bubbling pots of coffee and juggle plastic cups. From the edge of the shelter the stalls spread out – they resemble shipping containers with a front that lifts up to form a metal awning. Anything the workers will want and buy is here. Kettles boil tea, pans fry falafel and* kibbeh, *there are crates of pitta, pots of hummus, olives and pickles, and shelves lined with cigarettes, lighters, tins of meat and beans, oranges, avocados and tomatoes. Plastic chairs squat around braziers fuelled by broken-up delivery pallets. Here the men sit, as the grey haze of the wood smoke spills across the shelter, picked out by stark striplights hanging above. I get coffee in a plastic cup that yields under the heat of the drink and sit to watch the steady increase of the throng.*

'Why is everyone here so early?' I ask a man by the fire.

'So they can get to work on time.'

'What time does the checkpoint open?'

'Five, maybe.'

It is barely past three in the morning and already workers have come for a place in the queue outside the checkpoint – not to cross it, but to queue for when it opens and, with luck, get to work on time by seven or eight. Beyond the shelter lies the checkpoint; an industrial-looking building surrounded by metal barriers, with a turnstile that allows just one person through at a time. Above it are two lights, one presently glowing red, beneath which the workers have begun to queue, waiting for the green one.

At the market under the shelter, trade is steady when we arrive, men drink and smoke, stamping at the cold, clutching at warmth by the braziers before disappearing into the darkness by the Barrier. These are the early ones and more soon descend. Headlights begin to swarm on the road, tyres crunch in the dirt and engines are left running while the vans unload their human cargo into this graceless hour. Shuffling, running, rushing and pushing, workers start to flow across the concrete floor, a torrent of featureless men, their faces stripped of detail in the pallor of the blunt low light. Pouring over the concourse, hunched shapes in the grey mist; builders in layers of jumpers, clutching lunch bags and canvas holdalls. Their clothes dull with dust and splashes of plaster and paint; a group of women in long coats and headscarves cutting through the throng in a group. More taxis pull up and mini-buses too, decanting people for the crossing.

At the stalls, traders frantically wrap bread, take cash, shout and listen to orders while handing out change from the last. And still the workers flow through, heading to the closed checkpoint to wait in line for the green light to glow. Patches of light leak from the checkpoint: the glare of a CCTV screen lights the upper window of a watchtower, and light from the tunnel beyond the turnstile throws a weak, yellow colour onto the waiting figures nearest the gate, turning them into silhouettes that fade into a mass as they queue along the wire. Here they wait, in the cold under the bars, the lucky ones with permits and security clearances. But it is only half-past three in the morning; there are hours to go before they are through to the other side.

This line of workers is but a smear of black shapes in the dark night. It strikes me that for an occupation so obsessed with identity, it does so much to obliterate it.

chapter 7
IF IT LOOKS
LIKE A DUCK

Since the moment we left Israel at Christmas, I had been worrying about our return.

We had spent some time on our first trip with people from Stop the Wall (STW), a campaigning group that advocates non-violent protest. They had helped us coordinate guides and accommodation but, while we were on our walk, their principal organiser, Jamal, had been arrested and detained on the basis of secret evidence that he was not allowed to see or challenge in court. Jamal was the second of STW's organisers to be arrested and held in this way in the space of three months. Just before the arrest, their offices and that of another NGO in Ramallah were raided in the middle of the night and trashed.

Coupled with this, an Israeli group, Breaking the Silence, which publishes testimony of soldiers' experiences in the Occupied Territories, had agreed to walk some of our walk with us, but they too were facing pressure from the Israeli authorities. Publishing the soldiers own words strikes at the heart of Israel's perception that it has a 'moral army' and has unsettled the authorities enough for legislation to be proposed that would ban NGOs critical of Israel from receiving funding from abroad, an act many believed to be directly aimed at the group. NGOs I had spoken to or worked with in the past were getting worried about new Israeli restrictions on them and, just weeks later, the Israeli Interior Ministry announced it would stop issuing work visas to foreign nationals, an announcement that targeted most of the aid agencies that work in East Jerusalem, Gaza and the West Bank, which include Save the Children, Oxfam and Doctors Without Borders. A serious clampdown was taking place.

In this atmosphere, I started the New Year of 2010 concerned about the people I had left behind and for the future of the walk. We had planned to do the remaining walk in two trips, but friends involved in various NGOs began to warn me about trying to get back into Israel: if they were facing entry difficulties, the chances were I might face them, too. Getting in even once without any scrapes or attracting unwanted attention was, in their opinion, going to be difficult enough.

'I don't mind doing it all in one go,' Phil had said cheerily when we met after Christmas. 'In fact, it makes sense to do the whole thing in one last push.'

'That would mean five … six weeks away from home,' I had replied, rather faintly.

'I reckon we have to treat this as our one shot at getting it done,' Phil, the Afghanistan-hardened cameraman, continued. 'Imagine if we got in for the second time, got two-thirds of the walk done and then get stopped going in on the third trip. No, we have to make a serious attempt to finish this walk.' He tugged at his newly emerging goatee and smiled cheerfully.

'Yeah?'

'Yeah.'

So, decision made, we set out to finish the entire walk in one trip.

Beginning to assemble my gear again, I stock up on blister plasters and make a hopeful guess that my walking boots will last long enough to make the final walk. Phil and I also work on synchronising our stories and working out a procedure for when we get to Tel Aviv airport. We will split up at Customs, avoid any mention of the West Bank and, if the worst comes to the worst, Phil will defer all questions about the itinerary to me.

So it is a little disconcerting, when we arrive there, to find Phil standing next to me in the Customs and Immigration hall.

'You should join the other queue,' I whisper awkwardly as security guards look on. I am beckoned forward, stepping from behind the white line to the Customs booth, where a young woman with more hair than human warmth reaches to collect my passport. I slip it under the glass and try not to chew gum in an anxious manner. Just then, however, another passport is slapped perkily onto the shelf next to mine. The officer looks up, and I look round to come face to face with Phil, who is peeking over my shoulder, wide-eyed and grinning. He has blond highlights in the coxcomb of his Mohican, and he flicks his hair mischievously.

'What is the purpose of your visit?' the officer says blankly, while flicking through my passport.

'I am writing a book on walking.'

'Walking?'

'Yes.'

'And what is his relationship to you?' she says, looking up and gesturing at Phil with one of the passports.

'Er ... he's a friend.'

'I'm his friend,' says Phil, coyly.

'Friends ...' she says slowly, lifting her eyes to examine us.

'Yes,' says Phil, from over my shoulder. 'Good friends.'

'And where are you staying?'

I take a composing breath to list our Israeli destinations rather than our West Bank ones, but before I can answer Phil leans over my shoulder again and says, 'Together. We're staying together.'

With that the official stamps our passports, smiles knowingly and says, 'Have a good time.' We are in.

Despite all the warnings, we have got back into Israel with ease. I feel foolish at pandering to paranoia. But in fairness if you are going to be paranoid, this is the place to be. Mordechai Vanunu blew the whistle on Israel's nuclear weapon programme, kidnapped from Rome in a honey trap operation run by Israeli secret services and served eighteen years in jail, the majority of which was spent in solitary confinement.

I had seen him last year when I visited East Jerusalem on the recce trip. I had been having coffee with an Israeli activist called Jeff Halper when he had suddenly looked up and in his broad American accent had said: 'Hey, there's Mordechai Vanunu.' And there indeed was the legendary figure of the peace movement.

'Wow,' was all I could think to say, 'I did a benefit gig for his release years ago.'

In a booming voice Jeff had called across the café: 'Hey, Mordechai! I want you to meet Mark Thomas. He did a benefit to get you released!' in such a manner as to imply that I and I alone was responsible for his release, and that this would be the perfect opportunity for Mordechai to come over and personally thank me. With that one shout, seemingly, Jeff had managed to wipe away the international campaign for Mordechai's release, the protestors and supporters, the letters of protest, demonstrations and diplomatic pressure – all gone, and the only thing that had sprung him from his prison cell was the benefit gig I took part in at the Quaker Friends Meeting House in Red Lion Square in London, sometime in the last century.

'But Mordechai is not free,' said Mordechai Vanunu, when he had seated himself at our table, and looking at me as if I had, after all, failed him. 'I am not allowed to leave this country.'

Jeff shot me a look as if to say, 'Maybe you should have done two gigs and finished the job properly.'

Of course, I did what British people do best in these situations, which is turn bright red and stammer: 'Well, nice to meet you, anyway, and er … chin up.'

He was arrested for breaching his parole conditions just after our first walk. One of the conditions is that he cannot leave Israel; another that he cannot have any contact with foreigners. As his girlfriend is Norwegian this is problematic. He was arrested for speaking to her.

*

Back in Israel we begin our first day's route on the Israeli side, yet we remain in the West Bank. The walk is around Alfei Menashe, an illegal Israeli settlement on the Palestinian side of the Green Line but which the Barrier encircles. The 'fence' cuts into the West Bank, lassos the settlement and returns to Israel; this will not be the last time on our walk that we see the Barrier twisting into the West Bank for the sake of including a settlement on the Israeli side. If Britain's colonial map-makers were guilty of overusing the ruler, then Israel can likewise be accused of cartography with spaghetti.

With a military barrier surrounding Alfei Menashe, the place is inaccessible from the West Bank and so to get there I have to leave Palestine, enter Israel and then re-enter Palestine, or at least a part of it with settlers on. In a car you can tell which side of the Barrier you are on blindfolded, as the lack of swerving and sudden braking indicate and absence of potholes which immediately place you on the Israeli side. I recommend you don't try this experiment, as being blindfolded in a car on the West Bank has an altogether different connotation.

Driving through Israel, we start to notice the absence of certain familiarities with the West Bank.

'Do you know what we haven't seen in a while?'

'What?' says Phil.

'A boy hitting a donkey with a stick.'

'You're right!'

Neither had we seen a man standing at the roadside selling coffee from a Thermos flask, nor a single poster of the *shahid* martyrs.

In fact, at some points the Barrier itself seems to disappear: driving right next to Tulkarm and Qalqilya in Israel, you would need a keen eye to spot the Barrier in places. Instead of concrete slabs and barbed wire, this side of the Barrier features embankments of municipal shrubbery, like those seen on any British motorway, where saplings and brambles scramble for life as traffic roars past them. The Barrier has been landscaped out of the view. All that remains of it is a thin and continual strip of grey concrete running above the grass, like dull icing on a green cake.

The walk in Alfei Menashe will be our first in an Israeli settlement. I have been to Israeli communities, *kibbutzim* and the like, but all of those have been on the Israeli side of the Green Line. Alfei Menashe is not. It is a controversial settlement even for a settlement, and the charge sheet against it makes for quite interesting reading: as the Barrier expands around Alfei Menasche, it squeezes the room left for Qalqilya and turns a once vibrant market city into an enclave, with only one narrow road in and out of the place. Then there are plans to use Alfei Menashe as the starting point to extend the Barrier along a corridor of settlements even further into the West Bank, by some twenty-five kilometres. This is referred to as a 'finger' and, rather aptly, two 'fingers' are planned, one from Alfei Menashe, called Qedumim, and another to the south, called the Ariel Finger.

These two 'fingers' will effectively take a hundred square kilometres of Palestinian land – almost half of the region's area – onto the Israeli side of the Barrier,[11] while between these 'fingers' to the west and the closed military area of the Jordan Valley to the east, Palestinians will be sandwiched into a twenty-kilometre strip of land which, it is hoped, will form part of a 'viable state'.

There are two schools of thought on the legality of the Israeli settlements built over the Green Line: Israel believes them to be legal, and the rest of the world does not.

The Fourth Geneva Convention (to which Israel is a signatory) protects civilians under military occupation. Article 49 states that, 'The Occupying Power shall not deport or transfer parts of its own civilian population into the territory it occupies.'

The United Nations and the International Court of Justice argue that as Israel is the 'Occupying Power', the settlers are Israel's 'civilian population' and the 'territory it occupies' is the West Bank, therefore they deem Israeli settlements to be illegal under international law, a view held by the entire international community except Israel.

There are four legal points that Israel develops against this global view.

Israel argues that the West Bank cannot be 'occupied' as they say it wasn't anybody's to begin with. It is, therefore, 'disputed territory' and hence not covered by the Fourth Geneva Convention. Ergo their behaviour is legal.[12]

Israel goes on to argue that even if that isn't the case, the treaty means *forcible* transfers of the civilian population and as nobody *forced* the settlers to move to the West Bank, Israel isn't in contravention.[13]

Even if *that* isn't the case, the treaty was only created because of the Second World War, and was only meant to deal with similar circumstances.[14] So, unless there is again a global conflict involving a small man with a moustache, then the Convention doesn't apply.

And finally, even if *that* in turn isn't the case, they advance the legal invocation of 'bollocks to you'.*

Whether you are of the official Israeli view or that of the rest of the world, it is hard to see the Israeli settlers as anything but a significant part of the problem. There are 121 illegal settlements on the West Bank[15] housing some 304,569 settlers (one in nine people on the West Bank is an Israeli living in illegal settlements). When it's finished, the Barrier will encircle sixty-nine illegal settlements, bringing eighty-three per cent of the settlers on the West Bank into Israel – a process that is causing enormous hardship for Palestinians. And it's true the illegality of the situation makes the settlers somewhat ... well, er ... lawless, an image only reinforced by the media coverage of their forced evacuation from Gaza a couple of years ago. (There, settlers were portrayed as religious zealots defying the rule of law, not dissimilar to American 'survivalists', and thus equating them with religious gun-nuts who can't wait for the Apocalypse and the chance to live off their own urine.) But the closer we get to the settlement of Alfei Menashe, the more aware I become that many Palestinians regard the settlers simply as *Yahod*

---

* *I think the lawyers use other legal phrases.*

– Jews, the race of the enemy, equating military occupiers with an entire religion and people. This is not something I am comfortable with. So I try and think of positive things that can be ascribed to the settlers, warming to the idea of a pioneering spirit of adventure – tough, hardy folk who live off the land and have a love of it, too. There must be plenty to admire in people who can create buildings and communities in uninviting environments. In no time my mind has wandered off into the hinterlands of my imagination and quickly recast the settlers; they are no longer survivalists they are a Jewish version of the Amish, except armed and not frightened of turning on the electricity – except on Shabbat, of course.

Lost in thought and in the line of hills on the horizon, the settlement arrives sooner than I had expected, and I emerge from these cursory musings in a good frame of mind and more than happy to have my preconceptions demolished.

The first person we see is a security guard in a plain coat, *yarmulke* and a machine gun.

There are some 10,000 folk who live up here. The air is clean and clear and the wind gently plays round the hills. The main road past the council buildings is a street of detached homes, some built onto the hillside in descending levels. There are tall garden walls covered with creeping vines and bright orange flowers, and there are low garden walls offering tempting glimpses of yukka plants on garden lawns, and clematis tendrils twisting in trellises. There are hedges and kumquat bushes, ornaments and wrought-iron chairs.

The only sign of the frontier spirit is a decorative wagon wheel.

We follow the paths around the settlement where olives trees grow. There are rows of thyme and horses in paddocks and, in the distance, cranes standing by the newer builds. Eventually, we re-emerge back into the bosom of tarmac and mini-roundabouts as the sun's light turns a dusky evening hue. It is the hour of children's final shouts, the last noises of play, of clinking cutlery and garden chairs scraped up to the meal table. Along this road of split-level gardens, swings, car ports and al-fresco dining, are garage doors open to the street. They reveal bicycles and skateboards leant against walls; plastic washing baskets in corners and piles of trainers; lines of shoes and boots scuffed and unlaced; roof racks; tool boxes and power drills; shelves with sticks and string; boxes; brooms, rakes and spades; coats; racquets and bats; jump leads; rods and line; and mowers, lots and lots of mowers: the clutter of suburbia. We are as far from the pioneer spirit as it is possible to be, we are halfway between Torquay and Disney. This is the stuff of Spielberg dreams, just with the picket fences uprooted and electric ones erected in their place. This is what the fuss is about? This? Is this what people have died for? For rose bushes and hedges, for wind chimes and off-road parking?

The first thing you notice about the mayor of Alfei Menashe is that he looks tough. His shirt is unbuttoned down to his middle showing a lot of white vest, and he doesn't give a damn. Some might say his tanned face has a lived-in look; I'd say someone probably died in there, too. The second thing you notice is the glass cabinet full of sporting trophies, including a karate black belt with his name on it, which means he is certifiably tough. He has short grey hair, smokes, and is so craggy Ordinance Survey probably do his passport photos. He has been the mayor of Alfei Menashe for twelve years and in that time he has seen the place grow from about 900 homes to 1,900.

'Alfei Menashe was established in 1983,' he explains, 'to help people coming out of the security forces; basically to give them an affordable, good quality of life.'

'Affordable?'

'Yes, it was open to other people, too; however, you can see most people are not here for ideology but for a good, affordable quality of life.'

The ideology to which the mayor refers is the idea of *Eretz Israel*, The Land of Israel, which refers to the land promised in the Bible to the Jews by God, as his Chosen People. Ultra-orthodox Jews seek land as the fulfilment of this promise. It's also a great way of claiming land, religious prospecting if you will, it's a mixture of 'Praise the Lord' and 'Fill your boots!'

The mayor talks fast and while his voice isn't exactly gravelly, there are certainly some loose chippings in there. Sitting behind his office desk, he lights a cigarette, grabs a novelty ashtray of a toy duck lying on its back and explains one of the settlement's main attractions.

'When I speak to the young couples that move here, they say they come here mainly for the schools.'

Schools. Well, that puts things into perspective, then, doesn't it? What motivates settlers? Ideology? Religion? Zionism? No, a good Ofsted report. In fact, I have half a mind to spread the word when I get home, sit back and watch the British middle classes swarm in, trilling, 'It might be illegal, but their SATS results are brilliant.'

The inhabitants might not be ideological but the mayor certainly is, and the Barrier put him a dilemma. Being a Zionist he believes in a 'Greater Israel'; that one day Israel will exist from the Mediterranean through to the River Jordan and possibly beyond, so the very idea of a Barrier through this land strikes at the heart of his belief. As he says: 'The Separation Wall will probably be the border and this could mean giving up the dream of a Greater Israel for ever.'

With framed photographs of Peres and Netanyahu looking down from the wall, the mayor flicks the ash from a Marlboro Light into the ashtray duck's stomach and continues: 'But I had to defend my citizens and make sure this settlement would be on the west side of the fence, on the Israeli side.'

The mayor got his wish. But the Barrier does not just go around the settlement and return to the Israeli side: it captures Palestinian land and villages in its net, thereby trawling them, too, onto the Israeli side. Technically, Palestinian villages caught in this way remain in the West Bank but on the Israeli side of the Barrier, and thus cut off from the rest of the West Bank.

The settlement of Alfei Menashe, by its inclusion into the Israeli side of the Barrier, originally pulled five Palestinian villages along with it. One of them is Arab ar Ramadin and it is to this village that I am now heading, with the Israeli human rights lawyer, Michael Sfard.[16]

Michael has a small law firm that represents Palestinians, activists and NGOs. The villagers in Arab ar Ramadin are his clients and they have agreed to let me sit in on one of their legal meetings.

Michael could not be described as flash. His suit is black and off the peg, and he doesn't so much as wear it as accompany it. Like myself, if he lost a couple of pounds, I doubt he would phone in to report them missing. As he drives through the Tel Aviv traffic, Michael explains the situation in Arab ar Ramadin.

'In every practical sense the villages are cut off from the West Bank, cut off from their communities, their teachers, their doctors, their customers and left in this enclave that was created by the fence. They are not able to keep on the contacts they had before because there is a fence between them and the West Bank. Not able to create new contacts with the state of Israel because they are not allowed to cross into Israeli territory. It is illegal for them to enter Israeli territory. If they do they are outlaws.' He occasionally breaks from his discourse to change lanes or while concentrating at a junction, but neither cones nor contraflows derail him from his line of thought. 'The area between the Green Line and the fence is called the Seam Zone. It is a closed military zone and people have a right to enter there or reside there *only* if they were living there before, and have a permit to keep on living in their homes,' he says, then checking I have understood adds, 'Right?'

'So they don't have to get the permit to cross into the village; they have to get a permit to live there?'

'That is right.'

'Do Israeli settlers have to get a permit? Do they need to get a licence to live in Alfei Menashe?'

Michael smiles, looks out of the driver's window and flicks the indicator, but his smile has answered the question before he tells me: 'The settlers do not have the restrictions of the permit system.'

Once again, there is one rule for settlers and another for Palestinians – quite literally as it turns out, as the settlement of Alfei Menashe is under Israeli law and the village of Arab ar Ramadin is under military law.

Turning off the road, we arrive at the village. The abrupt departure from tarmac and entry onto a dirt track has a juddering intensity that leaves my internal organs realigned and my mind ungraciously wondering if Phil's kidneys would be a match.

'Blimey, this is like NASA training,' says Phil, holding onto the dashboard. 'It feels like G-force!'

'There are two types of everything here, including road surface!' I mutter under my breath.

Michael does not miss a beat and calmly continues his discourse: 'Whenever they put down asphalt here, the Israeli civil administration comes and takes it off because the village doesn't have a building permit for a road.'

The visual landscape of Arab ar Ramadin lacks the familiar sights of a village; like houses, for example. There are no houses to be seen. There is no road, pavement or kerb either, nor street lights or pylons, and no roundabouts. Instead, the pitted track navigates a line of tin huts basking in the sun. They are either grey or covered in peeling white paint, the front doors are large, the windows few and of glass there is little to be seen. There are no doorbells or letterboxes. The Israeli military have forbidden the construction of permanent homes and even the mosque is a tin hut, a green tin hut admittedly, but a tin hut nonetheless. As well as the refusal to allow homes and roads, the Israel military also forbids an electricity supply, so the entire village uses generators. There is a water supply, but the pipelines come through Alfei Menashe and recently the settlers turned the water supply off. It took a day of legal activity to get it back on.

I have been here two minutes and learnt one thing: Arab ar Ramadin might be called a village but it is not one – it is a village being bullied into becoming a shanty town.

At the top of the track is what looks like an actual building. The village council building is essentially a two-up two-down, with a desk at the end of the living room. Sitting in a chair with his three-year-old son standing between his knees is the village's representative for the legal action, Kesab. He nods a welcome at me as the rest of the village council gather around.

'We have no electricity, we have no roads, our houses are not permanent brick houses and ninety per cent of the shanty houses have a demolition order issued against them.'

He then moves on to the business in hand and, turning to Michael, says, 'Things have got worse at the checkpoint: the soldiers are insisting that if you drive a car, all the passengers have to get out 300 metres before the checkpoint and walk the 300 metres, while the driver goes through. The passengers are taken to a security room to be checked. Then they have to walk to the car on the other side.'*

I scribble notes but frankly don't understand why this problem has half the significance as the lack of houses, electricity and roads. As if noticing my incomprehension, Kesab adds: 'These are people who go through the checkpoint every day. They might be elderly people, pregnant women or sick people. Still they have to get out and walk. Yesterday, there was a woman ill with diabetes and high blood pressure. She had to get out and walk. Driving my son back from surgery, he had to get out of the car and walk.'

None of which is good, but I can tell there is something of greater significance that I am failing to grasp. Having just arrived, the entire situation appears absolutely awful. Trawling through

---

As the village is on the Israeli side of the Barrier residents are permitted to bring their cars from the village through the checkpoint and back.

the minute details of the checkpoint doesn't lessen the impact, but nor does it offer any greater clarity for this state of affairs.

'I have a small grocery store here,' Kesab says with the air of someone going back to the beginning. 'If I want to bring merchandise into the village from the West Bank I have to give the Israeli civil administration a list of what I want. Sometimes they say, "You ask for twenty sacks of floor. This is too much." You understand? They tell me how much flour I can bring in.' He laughs and in a final attempt to make me see his point he says, 'Eggs.'

'Eggs?'

'Eggs. Sometimes people are not allowed to bring in eggs through the checkpoint.'

'Eggs?'

'Eggs.'

What possible reason could there be for this? What nefarious act can you commit with an egg? The worst thing I can think of doing with an egg is shoving a poached one between two damp bits of bap and calling it a McMuffin. Admittedly, we do throw them at politicians back home but that is normally regarded as filling in time between elections. What possible threat is an egg?

'The soldiers look at an egg and treat it as if it is drugs.'

'Eggs?' I still find myself captured by the inanity of it. 'Treating eggs like drugs?'

Does the Israeli army think eggs are habit forming; that they lead to a dependence on other dairy products? Are eggs a gateway to cheese?

'Eggs?'

'And chicken.'

'What?'

'Sometimes people cannot bring in a chicken through the checkpoint.'

'Well, naturally, there might be an egg in them ...'

'You can choose between waiting for two hours until they make all the enquiries and see if you actually are entitled to bring a chicken in, or throw it into the garbage and cross the checkpoint without it.'

'Is this a policy?'

'It depends on the officer. Every officer in the checkpoint decides whatever he wants.'

Everyone in the room is now looking at me: Kesab; the village councillors on the high-backed chairs; Michael on the sofa; even Kesab's son, still standing between his dad's knees. They are all looking, waiting for me realise that this village is totally controlled by the Israeli military, down to the last egg.

I leave the village council to their business, and wander down to the sheep pens, chatting to villagers and admiring a rose bush growing by the side of one of the huts. Half an hour later, the meeting over, Michael comes to find me, his sleeves rolled up and his jacket slung over his shoulder, and we start to stroll back towards his car. I ask him the most obvious question: why are the Israeli military doing this?

'Is it a case of the famous Sharon quote?' I ask.

'Which one?' he says, laughing.

I try and remember it as best I can, '"You don't simply bundle people onto trucks and drive them away ... I prefer to advocate a positive policy, to create, in effect, a condition that in a positive way will induce people to leave."[17] Is this what is happening here, is this that policy in action?'

Without pause, Michael says, 'In the Seam Zone [the area between the Barrier and the Green Line], no question about it. The civil administration is doing everything it can to create the desire in these people to leave their lands. Then, if they leave, the civil administration can say, "Well, it was their wish." This community has been offered a chance to leave many times.' He throws his jacket in the back of his car. 'Israel wants the Seam Zone to be Palestinian-free. They don't want Palestinians living in the Seam Zone as then it will become an Israeli territory ... So the Wall has nothing to do with security! If the Wall was about security it would be placed on the Green Line and it would separate Israel from the West Bank. The Wall was a genius tool to grab more land for Israel with as few as possible Palestinians in it.'

With that, it is time for Michael to go, leaving Phil and me time to take a final look around. Just then, a young man appears, 'Would you join us for coffee, please?'

He gestures to his shack, which is a one-room hut with two chairs and a small table under the shade of some tin sheeting.

'Thank you,' says Phil.

'*Shokran*,' the young man replies, and he disappears inside. Normally when calculating the schedule for the day, I will add forty-five minutes to an hour for Palestinian hospitality. So frequent and persistent are the offers of tea and coffee that I have started to refer to them as the, 'Palestinian Roadblock': Israel has checkpoints, the Palestinians have hospitality 'blocks', and neither are easy to get past. But this place is different. Sitting on the stoop, we could be on the front cover of every blues album ever made.

Our chap emerges with a tray and on it is a pair of truly splendid coffee cups. They are old and art deco, the saucers white with sculpted curves, the cups fluted with thin, silvered rims and silver wings for handles, like a thirties design for a plane freight delivery company. They are perfect and delicate. Just sitting here holding one feels special.

On this hillside of tin and mud, there is a sense of pride and propriety that is rather calmly defiant. No matter how many times the water is cut off, no matter how many demolition orders are placed on a building, people still bring out the best china for guests.

'You were right,' says Phil.

'About what?'

'You said there was something admirable in the pioneer spirit, about building communities in inhospitable places.'

'Ah, but I was wrong, because I thought we would find it in the settlement.'

'Right sentiment; wrong place.'

'Indeed.'

And we sit back, sipping coffee from the most beautiful cups I have ever seen.

chapter 8
ANTHONY PERKINS'S SHORTER COUSIN

In most circumstances there would be something uniquely undig-
nified about a man on the wrong side of forty-five carrying wet
wipes for personal use. But they form a vital part of the morning
checklist, made up of items to locate by frantically unpacking each
and every pocket of the rucksack.

'Checklist' is probably an over-formal description of a process
that is essentially a freestyle swearing competition thinly disguised
as a last-minute memory test. It is a seventies TV game show for
foul-mouths involving the words: compass, map, suncream, cock,
torch, pacamac, arse, hat, bastard, fuck, first aid, fuckfest, pen,
shades, water bottle, piss breath, Tupperware, wet wipes, notebook,
shit-stick, cock burn, wank and sandwich, although there is a strong
improvisational element as to the order in which they appear.

The daily routine of ransacking the rucksack to check our kit
is one of an increasing number of rituals. Every morning liberal
doses of insect repellent are applied followed by suncream, working on the basis that if I get sunburn the last thing I want is insect
bites. Every evening I clean my boots, stuff them with paper when
wet and slather them in dubbin when dry. Every day I check to
see if the repairs to my boots are holding up as the only thing
keeping them from turning into flip-flops is superglue. I've started
checking my feet, too. They have never warranted much attention
before, but every evening I peel off my socks and peer down at a
pair of crumpled white things, wondering why I have been given
a dead man's feet. Part of this new obsession is due to increasing

paranoia about having to stop the walk because of something embarrassing like corns. So the medical kit carries foot-care products and medicated talcum powder.

I am not sure if I want to know what medicated talc does exactly, but it does conjure up thoughts of live things in damp places, and the phrase, 'Could some of my medical students come in to see this?' Every morning and every night there is always a small cloudburst of medicated talc in the room, accompanied by a coughing yelp of, 'Where did I put the clean socks?' This lurking fear of having to stop the walk because of something stupid also extends beyond worrying about in-grown toenails and the like, to encompass the horror of a groin strain incurred by over-stretching on the hillside terraces, or worse, returning home because of chafing. I have visions of friends querying me on the possible scenarios for my sudden reappearance: 'Deported by the army or death threats from militants?' and being forced to utter the words, 'No, it was insufficient absorbency in my underwear and a sweat-related friction rash.' So, powdered, scrubbed and defoliated I set out each morning.

We quickly leave the settlement of Alfei Menashe behind us. Crossing to the Palestinian side of the Barrier from here will make for a couple of good days' walking. The mornings are hot and I am grateful of any wind that finds us, but we have plenty of shade and, with a few exceptions, the going is light. Two shepherds – in their teens but only just – are guiding Phil and me through this part of the ramble and they leave us puffing on the terraces as they scamper around the hillsides, playing soldiers. Holding sticks against their shoulders, crouching behind boulders and walking through olive groves as if they are on patrol, they shout into their collars as if they have walkie talkies and crouch behind boulders.

'I love action movies,' one lad says over his shoulder to me, and I shoot him a 'dad' smile. His friend waves his arm forward and shouts, 'Company, move out! Search and secure the area!'

They run to some nearby branches, ducking under the lower ones while I look up for signs of the Israeli army near the Barrier, slightly concerned that they might mistake the sticks for real guns.

'Let's move further this way,' I call out, motioning away from the wire and watchtowers.

'Received and understood!' one of them shouts, before they race across the terrace towards a field dotted with poppies. The boys vanish ahead and I take a moment to sit on a clump of rocks to drink some water. The sight of the flowers is captivating. Their stems yield in the soft breeze, while their brief red petals turn and twist. Next to me a single poppy shudders in gentle gusts that ripple the grass around it and I happily while away ten minutes watching the field and its fragile beauty, thinking of nothing, engrossed in the waves of the wind and the spots of red that seem to go on and on. I realise I am happy and that if I could, I would shut my eyes and sleep long here, breathing the air full of the smell of soil and grass.

In the next village, Habla, we stop by a row of shops. 'This area is funded by the European Union,' says one of the shepherds.

'Including the shops?'

'Yes, this shop, too,' he says, pointing at the coffee and falafel shop.

'EU-funded falafel! We have to get some.'

'I'm not hungry,' says Phil politely.

'And miss the chance to piss off UKIP! Are you mad?'

We get a bag each and two for the shepherds.

Arriving at the village of Deir Ballut, the Barrier continues its way south. We take a left. Our route goes east, further into the West Bank, along the proposed route of the second 'finger' – the Ariel Finger – the planned corridor that will jut out from the Green Line almost at right angles to it, and run some twenty kilometres into Palestinian territory to Ariel.

According to Israel's current prime minister, Benjamin Netanyahu, the settlement of Ariel is 'an integral, inseparable part of the state of Israel'[18] – a statement easily contested with the most rudimentary map. Ariel is clearly in the West Bank and clearly some twenty kilometres over the Green Line. However, the Barrier is to surround the settlement of Ariel and rejoin the existing Barrier. A future Palestinian state is being whittled away with wire and brick. A nick here, a settlement there: bit by bit, picked at, gouged at, and eroded by the flow of Israeli expansion, these 'fingers' take more than land. They take with them the possibility of a viable state.

At the very eastern end of the Ariel Finger is the only bit of this planned Barrier yet built. It runs some ten kilometres around the tip and is nicknamed 'the fingernail'. If I am to walk the Barrier then I should walk the 'fingernail', too.

The settlement of Ariel started in 1977 with just two army tents erected on a hill near a Palestinian village. A year later, Ron Nachman, Ariel's future mayor, led a group of forty families with Israeli government backing out to the hillside in order to build a city. The place now has a university with 10,000 students and a population of about 20,000. This is where I will walk and stay, in a city built in the heart of the West Bank: an illegal city about to be surrounded by the condoning military embrace of the Barrier.

We are staying in Ariel in a bed and breakfast for a few nights. It is in a quiet street, decorated with tidy lawns and Toyota trucks parked neatly along the roadside. It feels like a suburban new town but it's getting late. We are only five days into this walk but it is out first proper sighting of hot water on tap and I drag my rucksack from the taxi with high hopes of clean sheets and a shower. Having rung the doorbell, we wait in the front garden next to a plaster seagull and an Israeli flag until the door opens.

A small, cross man with hard, confused eyes leans back in the doorway to examine me. I have stayed at a number of guest houses over the years, but never before has my arrival been greeted by the owner trying to stare me down. In the ensuing silence I fumble for a scrap of notepaper to check the address and find it just as the small, cross man says, 'Mark?!'

'Yes.'

He gives me another long look. The owner of the B&B is obviously a 'character', with all that entails. There is something disconcerting in his lack of height or rather, the way he looks up at me and down on me at the same time. Finally, sounding as if it is against this better judgment, he says, 'You'd better come in.'

We step into the house.

'Welcome,' he lies.

Dragged by his grumpy orbit we follow him into the living room. A huge fish tank burbles away behind the sofa, world championship skating is on the widescreen TV with the sound turned off, and the walls look as though they have had a collision with a trinket gift shop. Flags hang from them, as do rugs, daggers, swords, a ship's steering wheel, clocks, barometers and plates – lots of plates.

With a slight Eastern European accent, the small, cross man introduces himself: 'I am Natan. I run tours, religious tours. We have one tomorrow, four people want a special tour. I know all the places. I take them and show them. You like gardens?' he asks, though it would be a mistake to think it a question. 'Come, I show you my garden. Come, come.'

Conversation with Natan would just about qualify as a dialogue, but only on a technical point. Outside on a wooden porch stands a birdcage and a statue of the pissing boy of Brussels to which someone, probably not a master craftsman, has added a home-made concrete penis. The new penis is much larger and more erect than the original. Patting the boy on the head, Natan says, 'It was too small,' then leads us down some wooden stairs onto a small, sloping garden. He walks to one of the trees lit by a series of garden lights and says, 'These are pomela. We still have a few fruit on the tree. See.' The fruit look like large grapefruits.

'You know why they call them "pomela"?'

'No.'

'Because of "Pomela" Anderson,' he says, cupping his hands over imaginary breasts.

'Pomelas?' I say, not quite believing Natan is telling me tit gags.

'Pomela Anderson!' He asserts, eyebrows arched and cupped hands shaking with emphasis.

'Oh,' I say.

'Ach,' he says, and flips his hand dismissively before returning to his routine. 'What is this?' He holds up his middle and fore-finger, his thumb pressing against them.

'I don't know.'

'A dead Jew, because a live one would be doing this ...' and he starts to rub his thumb on his fingers, in the universal sign of money.

Ever the diplomat, Phil interrupts, 'What is this over here?'

'That?' Natan says, turning to follow Phil's sight, 'Ah, this is Snow White.'

There, standing in the middle of a small pond, is a statue of Snow White holding a basket.

'She is guarded by her dwarves.' As Natan says this, figures become apparent in the night-lights: little men around the pond. Great. So the small, cross man has a garden of gnomes guarding a virgin overlooked by a child with an adult's erect penis. This is where we are staying the night: sleeping in a homoerotic Hitch-cock thriller. We had been told that there was only one B&B in this city; the lack of competition is beginning to tell.

Dinner is served by Natan's wife who smiles silently; my coping mechanism for the situation, too. Natan starts, 'I am originally from Romania and when I split with my first wife I put an advert for a wife in a paper, that she should be a Romanian Jew.' His wife smiles while he points his fork at her and continues, 'She is Romanian but a Christian.'

That dealt with, he starts off on a new tack: 'I was in the army in '67.' He nudges me and says with mock sincerity, 'The Arabs wanted to drive us into the sea but we couldn't swim, so we fought and we won. This is our land. And here we are.' He stops and looks at Phil's plate.

'Are you eating the chicken?'

'No, I'm a vegetarian.'

'Good. More meat for me,' he says, and spears another piece of schnitzel onto his plate.

'Why are you here?' he asks, actually waiting for a reply for once.

In the shock of the silence I say, 'Well ... we're going to talk to a general called Shlomo Gazit ...'

'I know him,' he shrugs, 'in the army. I know him. If you see him tell him Natan says hello. Who else?'

'Well ... er ... if the mayor has time ...'

'I know him, the mayor, I know him. He is a good man. Why else are you here?'

'Well, I'm walking along the length of the Barrier, on both sides of it, and talking to lots of people as I go. Both Israelis and Palestinians.'

Natan stops and holds his fork aloft. 'There is no such thing as a Palestinian.'

'Er ... there is. We have met them.'

'There has never been a state called Palestine,' he says emphatically, 'so how can there be Palestinians?'

'Well, they call themselves Palestinians and it's really up to them to decide what they like to be called,' I say, adding softly: 'It is not up to you.'

'Arabs. They are Arabs.' His voice is raised now.

'Palestinian Arabs.'

'There never was this place! They are Jordanian, in fact.'

'What you call Palestinians is your decision, but they do live here.'

'Ach, this is our land. God gave us this land. It is ours. There are twenty-two Arab states and only one Israel: let the Arabs take them.'

I am tired of this spouting. I have heard Israelis say it all before; it was dull and bigoted then, and it is dull and bigoted now. I have listened to this long enough and can feel myself reddening with anger. Phil calmly jumps in at this point, saying, 'Oh, is that a picture of the Pope?' He points to a knick-knack on the wall.

Before he can stop himself, Natan says, 'I know him.' Phil smiles and Natan continues, 'From the seminary. I know him.'

After supper things take a calmer turn. The plates have been cleared away and Natan leads us into the relative calm of the living room. We sit on the sofa and start to relax with the bubbling hum of the fish tank and silent figure-skaters on TV. Natan, however, is still in full flow: 'I show you something. You will like this. I used to do security.' Opening a photo album he says with a wink, 'Here, this is me as a younger man. I look good then, huh?'

He is wearing a white shirt and has permed hair and a moustache.

'Yes, you look very fit,' I say.

'I look good.'

'You look very handsome,' says Phil.

'You know who this is?'

'No, I don't ... looks familiar, though.'

'Richard Clayderman.'

Prompted by his silence and staring, I say 'Ohhh, Richard *Clayderman*! How did you meet him?'

'I do security. After the army.'

I smile, content to look through the photos of him posing with famous celebrities, making the appropriate noises when needed, leaving arguments to one side for the time being. It might be boring but you can't go wrong with a photo album.

'You recognise this person, don't you?'

It is a photo of Denis and Margaret Thatcher.

*

When I get up the next morning, Natan and his silent wife have already left for their guided tour. Making coffee in the kitchen, I look out of their kitchen's massive glass windows. The West Bank's hills are magnificent from this vantage point as they unfold in all their scuffed glory. In the garden, the daylight shows Snow White and her small companions to be even more hideously saccharine than I'd supposed. And a few metres beyond them is the Barrier. We were sleeping almost next to the Barrier with its electric fence, military road and red warning signs. From here, the fencing appears to be protecting Snow White, as if miles of barbed wire and motion sensors and military patrols have been designed to specifically guard this unfortunate king's daughter and her diminutive plaster protectors, as though the Israeli military machinery is there to keep her safe from woodcutters and evil stepmothers, safe indeed, from any random crone clutching suspiciously delicious fruit.

Here on the ridge, secure from demons, the Barrier protects a fairy story.

ARIEL FINGER

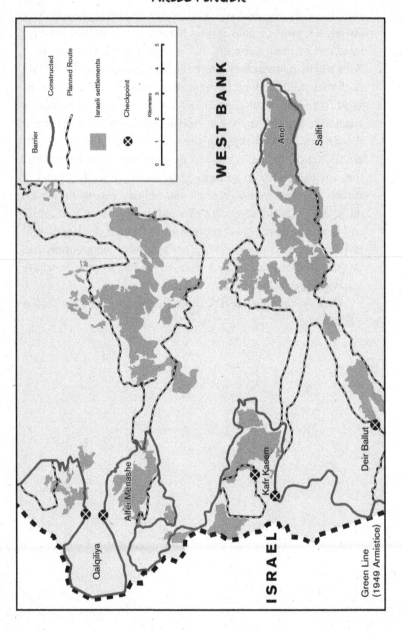

WEST BANK

Ariel

Salfit

Barrier — Constructed
Planned Route
Israeli settlements
Checkpoint ⊗

0 1 2 3 4 5
Kilometers

Qalqiliya

Alfei Menashe

Kafr Kasem

Deir Ballut

ISRAEL

Green Line
(1949 Armistice)

chapter 9
SETTLING IN

With a cloud of profanity and talc the day begins.

The Ariel settlement is essentially a long rock ridge and as the road leaves the settlement, the Barrier runs left and right; we are at the middle point of the fingernail.

Our starting point for the ramble was to have been Ariel university but in an unplanned and almost unconscious fashion we have ended up walking onto the Barrier itself, trespassing onto a closed military area. There is a checkpoint here, but no soldiers in sight.

'They are very relaxed now the terror has gone,' says Itamar. We have two Israelis walking with us today, Fred and Itamar, who are both instantly likeable. Fred is the shorter of the two and originally hails from the USA. With a scruffy, short moustache and wearing a baseball cap, you could be forgiven for thinking he is a car mechanic from a small town in the Deep South. Itamar was in the Israeli army but refused his reservist call-up for the second Lebanon war, earning him time in jail. He is also very active in Combatants for Peace, an Israeli/Palestinian group of ex-fighters working to end the military occupation through non-violent struggle. He sports a classic bald look: letting his unshaven stubble grow long enough to merge with his remaining haircut so you don't notice the join. He wears a checked shirt and carries a rucksack, and looks like the ex-army peacenik he is.

For some reason – rather than coming off the Barrier – we feel compelled to keep walking. With a casual curiosity we simply wander, passing the unmanned checkpoint and turning right through a set of open gates onto the military road, the central core of the Barrier. We know that the army patrols this road, which trails along the ridge flanked by the usual barbed wire and fencing on either side, but we all step onto it in unvoiced agreement and literally Walk the Wall.

On one side of the tarmac lies the settlement; on the other is scrubland and thermal currents, good only for birds. There is nothing above us but sky, and below us, Palestinians. The day's grey hazy cloud is easier to define than the lives unfurling under the shadow of the ridge, down amidst the blurred mass of buildings, toiling invisibly. The view alone makes masters of us.

'Israel thinks it cannot have a minority of Jews and have a democracy,' Itamar says, explaining Israel's eternal obsession as we stroll confidently in the light breeze.

'For Israelis, you have to have a majority of Jews in order to have a democracy ... the Wall means you can have the majority of settlers in the West Bank and bring them on the Israeli side of the line. This is our demographic fight.'

As we chat of politics and walk to the clack of my hiking stick – on the tarmac surface it occasionally skitters, forcing me to hold it out at right angles like a dandy's cane – it occurs to me that being on the Israeli side of the Barrier has made me approach it in a completely different way. Oh, I still hate it and can rail about its effects on Palestinian lives, but, interestingly, being on the same side as those who put it up means the Barrier is no longer aimed at me. The Barrier was built to keep the Arabs out, ergo, on this side, I am no longer in its sights; I have nothing to fear from the Barrier and feel completely at ease walking upon it.

My comfort here is entirely logical: on the Israeli side of the Barrier, the gate is open, there are no soldiers and the signs that say MORTAL DANGER face outwards, none of it is directed at us at all. I have none of the fear of the closed military area that I had in the north. Just by being on this side of the Barrier we seem to have developed a strange sense of entitlement. Onwards. We stroll like we own the place and nothing will dent our confidence. Even when an army jeep appears at the far end of the yellow line heading towards us, I feel completely calm and merely ask, 'Should we be worried about this?'

'Nooo,' says Itamar. 'There was no sign up telling us not to come in. So why should we not be here? Just leave the talking to me,' adding with a shrug, 'What is the worse they can do?'

The jeep pulls up and stops directly in front of us. A soldier climbs out wearing shades but no helmet, no jacket, not even webbing of any kind; he holds his rifle loosely at his side.

'It must be "Dress Down Friday",' I say to no one in particular. The presence of the army is irritating rather than worrying, and in the fashion becoming of a dandy with a walking cane, the encounter bores me.

Itamar and the soldier speak for a few minutes in Hebrew. Itamar points this way and the soldier points that way, then they shake hands and the lad climbs back into the vehicle and starts to drive back the way he came.

'So?'

'So he wanted us to go back to the start. I said there is an agricultural gate maybe a kilometre ahead of us, so if you let us keep walking in this direction we will get off the Wall quicker.'

'And?'

'He said OK.'

We continue walking on the Barrier and when we come to the agricultural gate, we open it and step off it. Itamar promptly sits under an olive tree, gets a gas burner out and starts to make coffee, chatting to Fred who has propped himself up against a stone wall. Phil and I find a discarded red sign that reads: MORTAL DANGER: MILITARY ZONE. ANY PERSON WHO PASSES OR DAMAGES THE FENCE ENDANGERS HIS LIFE and start mucking about, posing with it for photos as the sun comes out and shines upon us.

Our day's illicit wanderings have taken us around the southern side of the Ariel finger, and now on the northern side our best option is to use a pathway that has the Barrier beneath it and suburban gardens rising above: on one side, the path is decorated with garden porches, trees and satellite dishes (we even spot Snow White peaking over the brow), and on the other side, down the hill, is the 'fence'. The pathway is used by few folk at this time of day, mainly dog walkers striding purposefully with a lead in one hand and a plastic bag in the other; even settlers, it seems, must suffer the universal indignity of handling warm canine stool in a Tesco carrier.* A few couples are out too, taking a stroll and soaking up the early evening sun.

The path periodically stops and we are forced onto residential streets for a while before the thin dirt trail reasserts itself. We are wandering the back end of suburbia, and to that extent at least it provides a break from it. In one of these quiet streets, a white truck reverses into a parking bay and out of it gets a thick-set man nearly as wide as he is tall, with a layer of work dust clinging to him. Slinging a grey sweatshirt over his shoulder, he nods a greeting to us. We nod hello back and a minute later we have struck up a conversation in the street. His name is Elias, he's Romanian, and came to Israel in 1961.

'Do you mind if I ask why you came to Ariel?'

'No, you can ask,' says Elias. 'I moved here from Tel Aviv about ten years ago because my daughter wanted to. There is no ideological reason for me moving here; we just wanted a nice place to live.' He gets a chiller box from the truck and kindly passes round bottles of water for us as we chat.

Normally, the English middle classes are struck with near terminal squeamishness when it comes to discussing how much they paid for something, and if you ask, a look creeps over their faces as if they have just defecated through a sieve. The exception

---

* *There is no Tesco in Ariel but you get the point.*

to the rule is house prices. Reverting to type I ask, 'How much did you pay for your house?'

'$250,000,' he says proudly. 'It is big, too, as you can see; three storeys, and a lot of space inside. In Tel Aviv you would pay $700,000 for it. And here we have this too, look,' and Elias points to the hills and land glowing in the evening sunlight. 'Only the snow is missing,' he says, 'If we had snow it would be like living in Switzerland.'

The comparison is not an apt one, for starters the aspect of neutrality might be a sticking point as also, I suspect, would the whole Nazi gold thing, but I take Elias's point: why would anyone want to pay more money to live somewhere that didn't have this view? Only this morning, Fred and Itamar had been inspired by another view; one of new developments and cranes, prompting them to discuss why houses cost less here: 'Purchasing homes here in Ariel is much cheaper than purchasing homes inside Israel and that is the main reason people move here, because of cheap housing. Normally when you buy a house on a new build, you pay for the infrastructure, too, but these places are subsidised. The price doesn't include the cost of bringing in the roads, water, sewage and electricity,' said Fred.

'Or the land,' adds Itamar.

'Here you only pay for the materials, labour and the contractors' profit, nothing else.'

'Remember, the land doesn't belong to anyone.'

But this only goes partway to explaining why life here is cheap. The Israeli government has funded the settler movement to the tune of $100 billion,[19] and every year spends $556 million maintaining it.[20] The settlements are deemed to be 'national priority areas' and, as such, receive benefits and subsidies from six government departments to provide more cheap housing, tax breaks, better social security and key worker provisions than anywhere else in Israel.

Elias's dog comes over wagging its tail as we finish our drinks in the street. My dad was a self-employed builder and I feel comfortable in their company, recognising the way Elias gulps down his water to damp down the dust of the day.

'Thanks for the drink,' I say, 'but we should be going. We have all of Ariel to walk around.'

'Have you been to the country club?' Elias says.

'You have a country club?'

'Yes, we have a country club.'

'Are you a member?'

Elias leans casually against his truck, 'Of course,' he says. 'While you're here, you should go and see it.'

Over that evening and following morning, I meet a number of other settlers. One of them is Palti, who makes green tea in his new kitchen while cradling his daughter in his arm. She has blonde, wispy hair that sticks straight up in the air and wide eyes, like a toddler Stan Laurel.

'Shall I pour?' I volunteer.

'Thanks,' says Palti. He is wearing tracksuit bottoms and a white T-shirt, and is rocking slightly the way parents holding young children do.

'The first time I came here I fell in love with it: clean air, free from traffic; a good place to live and good house prices.'

His daughter sucks her dummy noisily, once, twice, and then returns to staring in bemused interest.

'How do people react when they find out you are from Ariel?'

'When I talk to people who don't know Ariel they think I am religious. That I walk around with an Uzi. That we are all fanatics looking for a fight and carrying weapons.'

I want to tell him that this was exactly how I had imagined the settlers to be, but the words come out as, 'Some people are happier demonising each other, rather than looking for the truth.'

'Exactly,' he says.

We chat and drink tea, and I unconsciously start swaying slightly in an act of parental solidarity.

'And the fence – do you want to see the Wall built all the way along the Ariel finger?'

'Yes, I want to see the whole fence up ... It is the only way I can live in Ariel and Israel.'

The cost of diverting the Barrier from the Green Line to capture Ariel adds approximately fifty kilometres to the Barrier, at a cost of about $75 million. But from Palti's point of view, it makes sense; if you live twenty kilometres into the West Bank in an illegal settlement and want to be part of Israel, then you need to change the border. Looking at it from this angle, you get quite a lot for your $75 million.

On our second day in Ariel, we meet our first religious settler. Though many settle here for economic reasons, there is an undeniable ideological presence, too.

After the morning rituals of swearing, foot care and coffee, we head to a container-home park near the city's university. Container homes are the settlers' tool of choice when starting a new outpost as they can be easily loaded onto a truck, driven to the required site and unloaded, providing a cheap and instant home. There is a swathe of them in the city, providing accommodation for students and new arrivals. One of whom is Elzak, who waves at me from the entrance gates.

'Good to meet you,' I call out. 'Are we going to your home?'

He shakes his head. 'It would not be appropriate.'

'Really?'

'Yes, my wife and children are there.'

'OK,' I say. 'Have you got any suggestions of where should we go for a chat?'

'I don't know the city very well.'

'There is the country club ...' suggests Itamar.

'The country club!'

'The country club,' agrees Phil.

'OK,' says Elzak.

Elzak is a religious man and from his appearance you might indeed guess he is more interested in the spiritual aspects of life than the material. His beard is bushy, his *yarmulke* green, his shirt is button-down and if it got any plainer it would be a sack. But he has a warm smile that is quick to appear and, in all fairness, I shouldn't judge too quickly as I currently look like an ageing David Cassidy impersonator who has just woken from a coma.

At Ariel's country club we pass through the double swing doors into a leisure centre.

'They have a swimming pool here?' I ask, aware of a warm smell of chlorine.

'Yes,' says Elzak. He suddenly looks small and a little bit lost in the entrance hall.

'Have you been here before?'

'No.'

'Really? It's only up the road from your home, so why is that?' I blunder.

'Men and women in the same pool ... I am religious,' says Elzak smilingly. 'It would not be appropriate.'

Walking into the café bar, I whisper to Phil, 'Are you Catholic?'

'I'm atheist,' says Phil. 'Born a Catholic, though.'

'I was brought up Protestant.'

'So?'

'So, a Protestant, a Catholic and a Jew just walked into a bar ...'

The bar is a bar in the sense that it sells alcohol, but basically it is a mix of sofas, throw cushions and waitresses who serve a lot of cappuccinos. A few women sit in the comfy chairs with their legs neatly folded to one side and designer shopping bags by their feet.

'Why don't we sit here,' I say unthinkingly, motioning to a table. It is next to the glass wall that runs floor to ceiling down the entire length of one side of the bar, giving us a perfect poolside view.

'Er ... OK,' says Elzak. As we both catch sight of the bikinis and Speedos, he continues, 'But perhaps we can draw the curtain across?'

We drape the curtain, which is only a thin muslin veil, over our section of the glass wall. Elzak pulls up a chair, motioning to the pool behind the cloth and saying, 'It would be inappropriate ...' He sits with an opaque curtain shielding him from the pool, but is unable to escape the TV mounted on our table that periodically pipes adverts onto the screen.

At his insistence, Elzak will tell his story, then I am to ask him questions. He pulls his chair nearer to the table, takes a sip of coffee, issues a short smile and, as a blurred figure of a swimmer on the other side of the glass passes behind the curtain, starts to speak.

Elzak came to Ariel in 2006 with his wife and eight children as something of a cause celèbre in the settler movement. In 2004, the then prime minister, Ariel Sharon, had initiated his policy of disengagement, by which 9,000 Israeli settlers in the Gaza strip and all the accompanying military presence would vacate Gaza, in a bid to improve security and Israel's international standing. The settlers were asked to accept compensation and leave voluntarily. The army then forcibly evicted those that refused to go, which led to fierce divisions in Israel. Elzak was a community teacher, a spokesman and one of the last Jews to leave the Gaza strip.

The Netzarim settlement in Gaza, 'was a very calm and spiritual place,' Elzak begins. 'There were many debates as we examined the true values of Zionism.'

He looks at me through his wire-framed glasses as next to him, on the TV, appears a flashing image of a plate of sushi. He continues, describing a Zionist idyll – the organic farm, the school for religious study and his first home.

'We stayed, even though the state offered compensation. We were sure of our righteousness; we were sure that at the last moment God would deliver us and intervene.' A televised bottle of Sprite hovers by the side of his head, then a plate of fries.

Elzak gave the final address in the synagogue before the army evicted them.

'Just before I gave it, someone said to me, "Remember, we don't cry."' He looks down, pushing his empty coffee cup further onto the table as he does so, and rubs his bearded cheek with one hand for a moment. 'We are not violent. We are not doing this for ourselves; we are doing it for the whole Jewish nation. They have to understand how important it is to hold every piece of land.'

Another bather walks behind the gauze curtain and I glimpse the outline of her swimming costume through the muslin mesh. The image seems to frame a sense of loss. These half-seen bathers are not part of his world, indeed the club itself is a culture that has little to do with his own. The presence of the adverts on the TV screen are almost mocking in their indifference to his experience, and hint at just how far away he is from an organic farm.

'OK,' I say, 'I have a question now.'

He motions with his hand that now would be the time to ask.

'Did your experience of being forcibly evicted and of feeling betrayed give you any empathy or understanding of how Palestinians might feel when they are moved from their land?'

'No.' The answer is sudden and abrupt. One word bluntly hurled, without menace or threat. Yet the total absence of doubt is almost violent. 'No. Because these things are a reaction to terrorist actions and if people are violent, this is what they deserve. I am sure they have done something.'

'What about during Operation Cast Lead when thousands of people had their homes demolished without any direct connection to terrorism?'

'They started a war and during wars this happens. This is why I have no guilt or compassion for these people.'

'What about in Jerusalem now, where over eighty homes are to be destroyed? There is no war there.'

'I don't know about that, but I am sure the judicial system will have considered all their human rights.'

'But your own experience ...'

'The judicial system didn't help, but with Arabs ... they are always more sensitive of their human rights.'

It is now my turn to push my coffee cup away. As I do, the sushi advert flashes back onto the screen for a repeat.

'Thanks for your time and I appreciate the chance to speak to you,' I say, scraping the chair back to stand.

'I want to say something before you go.' Elzak beckons me to sit back down for a moment. 'The whole cultural world is based on the Bible, and this includes Europe and even Islam. Everyone who is involved in the cultural world has to understand that in the Bible it says that the land belongs to the people of Israel. This is simply the place we should be and we do not have to apologise for that.'

For a man who seems so out of place, he seems remarkably certain of where he should be. He leaves the country club with its glass walls, TV screens at the table, patterned sofas and high-backed bar stools, and doesn't pick up a membership form on the way out.

There's a short silence at the table after Elzak's departure.

'What now, then?' pipes up Phil. 'We've walked the fingernail,' he says, referring to the Barrier around the tip of Ariel. 'Anything else to walk around here?'

'Not a lot,' I reply.

'Right then; leisure time. What do people do around here for kicks?'

'I think we are doing it.'

'This is it?'

'We might get one of those individual chocolates on the saucer with the coffee.'

The waitress arrives and pulls back the muslin drape to reveal the glass wall and the swimming pool on the other side. It shimmers in clear, chlorinated glory. The water looks warm and bright as a swimmer does lengths, and a mum in a swimming hat holds her daughter's hand as they try not to totter too quickly along the side. A shriek of fun goes up as a young boy lying on an inflatable rubber ring, his limbs hanging over the edges, is spun in the water.

'I've got swimming trunks back at the B&B,' I say, turning back to Phil, who is looking slightly wistful.

'I have, too,' he says.

'We could …'

'Yes,' he sighs. 'We could …'

'It would be fun.' I nudge him.

Phil blows out his cheeks. 'It wouldn't really. I mean it would be nice to swim, but not here. Not in a settlement. It wouldn't feel right. It would feel like we have been seduced by the comfort of this place.' Phil twiddles with his goatee, slightly hunched and twisted as he battles with his conscience. He grimaces with resolution.

'I just can't,' he says.

There is a very obvious gap here between the water-rich and the water-poor, and the settlement's pool sits firmly on the side of the water-rich. It is a divide we have seen many times on our ramble, and it takes different forms. The most obvious and startling one is that the grass on the Israeli side of the fence is literally greener, not always, but often enough to notice. In fact, the colour of the land is an obvious manifestation of inequality. You would be hard-pressed not to notice the sight and sound of sprinklers on Israeli farms, the jetting sprays and constant stinging hiss of the water as it arcs across the crops. And you would be hard-pressed not to notice the countless pieces of thin, black irrigation tubing stored between the plastic greenhouses on the Palestinian side of the Barrier. These observations do not represent hard evidence; it would be fair to say they are circumstantial – except for the fact that Israel controls Palestinian access to water supplies in the West Bank and Palestinians get on average just seventy per cent of the World Health Organisation's recommended daily minimum water requirement. That figure drops to a mere twenty per cent in some rural areas – a level usually associated with a humanitarian disaster. Israelis, meanwhile, consume four times the WHO's minimum requirement.[21]

Ron Nachman, the – as it turns out – unavailable mayor of Ariel, knows all to well the importance of the settlement apropos Israel's water situation: 'This is the heart of Samaria and underneath the surface of the land there is the water aquifer. One third of the Israeli water is coming from this area. So if you control the land you control what is above and what is below'[22].

These words could have been in the minds of those who drew the route of the Barrier, as it runs over large parts of the Western Aquifer (the main source of potable water in the West Bank) and in doing so, further denies Palestinians the ability to extract water from it. The Barrier not only takes land, but water, too.

A few days before arriving in Ariel, Phil and I had been driven into the countryside south of the settlement on the Palestinian side. The driver was Ashraf Zuhud, the head of Health and Environment for the town of Salfit. Tall and dressed in black, he had a face devoid of hopeful expectation. The track was rough and we bounced along in the back seat as we were driven through the dappled shade of overhanging trees, then out along the bottom of the ridge that Ariel sits on, high above. We had stopped by the side of a brook, a delightfully noisy one, the water flowing by in background blather. On the opposite bank, the slope rose steeply towards the settlement dotted with olive trees and spread with terraces.

Down by the stream, the shrubs and shoots were green and plentiful, grass and weeds sprouted from the bank side and a donkey contentedly munched on them. The sun was deliciously warm, too. It was almost an idyll, though the look on Ashraf's face should have warned me otherwise.

'We are metres away from the Al Matwi spring and this,' he had said, pointing at the stream, 'is where the waste water comes down from Ariel.'

'Untreated?'

'They remove the solids and then dump the waste water. It has a very high BOD, which shows a level of pollution.'

'BOD?'

'Biochemical oxygen demand. If you have less oxygen in the water, that means there are more micro-organisms, more waste.'

Up close, the water in the babbling stream was a battleship grey colour, and it flowed round rocks and stones, by green stalks and under fallen branches, while the donkey merrily munched to the sound of the flowing waste. A short drive, and Ashraf stopped the car again. At this point, the stream was wider and the trees more abundant but we didn't get out; Ashraf just wound down the windows and waited until my face crumpled at the stench that pervaded the air.

'It stinks of shit.'

Having made his point, he drove on. By then, the light had turned to the amber glow of late afternoon. The road along the valley had seemed smoother but perhaps it was just the hour of the day, when the first signs of tiredness creep in. Stopping the car next to a field where the valley spreads a little before turning to the hills, Ashraf had said, 'The plan was to build a water treatment plant for Salfit here.'

The plan had obviously failed because all that was there were some cattle grazing between greenhouses and a caravan.

'We had done all the paperwork, we had got permission and we had got the money to build the plant from the German government. So I was shocked when the Israeli army came here and just asked us to leave. They stopped the work. They said it would interfere with the settlement.'

Having prevented one waste water treatment plant, the Israeli authorities did later agree Salfit could build another but in a different location, and on the condition that the Palestinians would not just process their own waste water but Ariel's, too. The plant remains unbuilt.

*

Back in the here and now of the Ariel country club, as a couple of well-dressed women beckon the waitress to their comfy sofa to take their order, I turn again to look through the glass wall at the pool beyond, still sparkling and still virtually empty.

Phil gulps his coffee down, eager to leave.

'Are you sure you don't want to go for a swim?' I ask. 'There won't be another chance before … well, actually, I don't know when there will be another chance.'

'No, I'm not swimming,' he says, climbing off the bar stool. 'I feel guilty enough just going for a crap in this place.'

chapter 10
THE POPE OF DEMOGRAPHICS

'Fuckity, fuckity, fuckity, fuckity, fuck, fuck, fuck.'

We are late. We are in an old Renault van belonging to Itamar's mother and driving from Ariel, when Phil decides to point the camera at a checkpoint. The security response only just stops short of a colonoscopy. But, more important is the delay, today of all days. I have a meeting with Professor Arnon Soffer, the intellectual architect of the Barrier, and we are late.

The delay has put me in a mood so foul I could curdle dogshit with a glare. Phil and Itamar are in the front seats and silent.

'How much horse power has this thing got?' I snap.

'I don't know,' says Itamar. 'I am going as fast as I can.'

'Would the car go faster if I whipped it?'

'No, that would not help,' he says evenly.

'I'm sorry, everybody,' says Phil.

'I don't think that helps, either,' adds Itamar, concentrating on the road.

'Why don't you phone him and explain we're a little behind?' says Phil.

The professor is at a settlement called Matan near the Barrier. He answers the phone and I calmly explain our delay. Equally calmly, he replies: 'I only have an hour, I have to be somewhere.'

'Well, I really appreciate your waiting for us. I'll be there in ten minutes.'

'I will be in a silver car. Near the fence. Don't be any later, please.'

As we draw level to the professor's stationary car, he glances at the Renault van as if we are here to collect laundry.

'Professor,' I call out.

'Come,' is his simple instruction as he gets out of his car, reaches for his jacket and sets off towards the Barrier.

Soffer does not walk anywhere: he strides purposefully. In fact, I doubt he could queue for an ice cream without it seeming a matter of top priority. He is in his seventies and his dress is casually immaculate: a small, golden belt buckle hangs on the loops of pressed black trousers; his sunglasses are in the 'off-duty military' mould; his hair is closely cropped. But it is his height and dynamism that define his manner: he is tall and animated, like an expressionist cartoon. He also has an impressive array of academic titles: 'I am Emeritus from the University of Haifa. I am Head Chair of Geostrategy at the University of Haifa and simultaneously I am the head of the Research Centre of the Israeli National Defence College of the Israeli army. I share my life as a professor for almost the last forty-one years and, at the same time in the Israeli army that I am teaching in the National Defence College, I'm teaching in the Staff and Command College. I am often visiting West Point and other military academies all over the world.'

But for all his qualifications, after an hour in his company I can safely say Soffer is essentially a cross between a cab driver and Dr Strangelove. He peers from behind his dark sunglasses and rails in florid description not normally heard in academia, against all and sundry. In his heavy European accent, he rasps that Israel is a 'paradise', that Arabs are 'flooding in' and are good for little but 'tahini and hummus', the settler leaders are 'ego maniacs', their ideas 'idiotic', and don't get him started on Tel Aviv.

'The West Bank, *this* is the cradle of the Jewish people. Not Tel Aviv. I say no bloody Tel Aviv. I hate Tel Aviv ... They [the Palestinians] decided to hate Israel and the Tel Aviv people with their cats and dogs demonstrate for peace ... Bloody Tel Aviv with their small dogs and croissants!'

We are standing by the backyards of the settlement homes on the scrubland next to the Barrier and in the mid-morning sunlight, Professor Soffer is doing what he does best: towering and glowering.

'Ask me and I will tell you why I am so eager to see this bloody fence,' he commands.

I comply. 'Does it cheer you to see this?'

His arms dramatically fly open towards the Barrier. 'I am thrilled by this, to me it is beautiful. I am very happy and I will tell you why. Since we had this fence we reduce the suicide bombers to zero. This is the beginning, this is the end, this is the issue.' Then, turning to face me, he smiles and says, 'But I have much more to tell you.'

Professor Soffer doesn't so much as interview as perform: it is half-lecture, half-cabaret burlesque – I'm worried that if he puts one foot in the wrong direction he'll end up in a bowler hat singing, 'Willkommen, Bienvenue, Welcome'.

'I convinced Sharon,' he says modestly, 'that by creeping into the West Bank, we will very quickly become a bi-national state. Very quickly, the Jewish people will be a minority. Very quickly it will be the end of the Zionist state. It was my philosophy.'

At this point some of you might be hearing a strange creaking or hollow straining noise; don't worry, it is just the definition of the word 'philosophy' buckling under pressure. Essentially this 'philosophy' is that if settlers take over the West Bank, Israel will be left with a country full of Palestinians, who will then outbreed them.

'The Tel Aviv people; every family has two dogs and one cat,' says Soffer. Then, pointing to the Palestinian side, adds, 'And each one of them with twelve children. They will win the battle.'

With the glee of a tabloid contrarian he then asserts that this hypothesis is the Palestinians' objective.

'If I was Arafat* or Abu Mazen** or Fayyad or just this guy or that guy I would postpone any solution with the Jewish people … [I would say] we have just to wait, and the demography and the settlers will bring us all of Palestine.'

In his world, the Jewish settlers are falling into a trap where no sooner have they finished colonising the West Bank, than the Palestinian leaders will scream into a giant tannoy: 'BREEEED! BREED LIKE YOU HAVE NEVER BRED BEFORE!' Or perhaps it will be at the sound of a whistle that thousands of Palestinians rise from their slumbers and start humping with gusto, rutting in nationalist fervour to literally fuck the Jews into oblivion. Faced with this vision of a heaving mass of copulating Arabs at the gates of civilisation, who could help Israel in her hour of need? Fortunately, Professor Soffer was at hand.

'I had the pleasure and the duty to teach Sharon, Bibi and Ehud Barak [the then Israeli prime minister] what it is all about,' he says, clasping his hands together and bowing his head in false humility.'Mr Bibi Netanyahu, our current PM, called me, and he said, "Are you ready to be my private teacher?"'

So what did he teach them?

With his arms flailing and torso contorting, Soffer twists himself into the third person: 'From his ivory tower, Professor Soffer tries to analyse the situation. I am in a trap … If I return to [the concept of] the Green Line, I have to evacuate half a million Jewish settlers. It'll be a civil war; it's the end of Israel. My compromise is the demarcation of this Wall. It is a demographic line. Arabs here; Jewish people there.'

To paraphrase: in order to halt the settler charge to the River Jordan and the prospect of Arab-humping techniques overwhelming the state of Israel, Soffer decided the only thing Israel could do was build a barrier, thereby extracting the settlers from the

*Former chairman of the PLO
**Palestinian president and Fatah leader

West Bank by placing them on the other side of the Barrier. Believing that forced evacuations, like Gaza, will tear Israel in two Soffer's solution is simple: redraw the border. Build a barrier over the Green Line and around the settlements on the West Bank, where anything on the Israeli side is de facto Israeli.

'So how important was it to include the settlements into Israel?'

'My plan, the demarcation, in my opinion, was a great victory because eighty-five per cent of all the settlers in the West Bank are now inside Israel; they are west of the Wall ... Only by taking them back home and leaving the Palestinians can we live together.'

'So is the Wall the new border then?'

'This was my idea. The fence is going to be the border between Palestinian and Israeli. It is going to be for a long period of time.'

And so he struts and frets his hour on a stage of his own making, answering questions of his own asking and railing against enemies of his own choosing: religious settlers sacrificing Israel on the altar of their egos; politicians immersed in ignorance; and the ever-indifferent, non-breeding, dog-owning, pastry-loving elite in Tel Aviv. To Soffer, their biggest crime is in failing to comprehend the greatest threat of all: the breeding Palestinians within the one-state solution, with two nationalities living within one country. For Soffer, the economic consequences of a one-state solution are disastrous: 'The income gap between this village,' – he points to the Palestinian side – 'and this one,' – he gestures to the Israeli homes – 'is one to twenty. There is no other such place on earth.'

He pauses as if considering the magnitude of his own insight, and stares off into the abyss of a bi-national state.

'Six million Jews will have to support six million Arabs, and the burden falls onto my middle-class shoulders. I have to support six million Arabs, very poor, *and* all the ultra-orthodox Jews with thousands of children. It's the end of the middle classes. It's the beginning of a dictatorship. When you don't have any more middle classes, you will find the dictator.'

'But what of the criticism of the Barrier? What if the economic impact of the Wall creates the next *intifada*?'

'I am happy to say this is not the case at the moment. More and more money is pouring in there from the West, including from Israel.' Pointing over the Barrier in the direction of a Palestinian village called Habla, he says, 'I would say ninety per cent of the buildings in Habla are new buildings, and you have to see the greenhouses. Go and look for yourself; there is a wonderful panoramic view of Habla – I will show you how to get there. It's a wonderful picture. It speaks for itself. They are so happy, you cannot even imagine.'

A smile creeps across his face as if he is with them and feeling their joy.

'So people in Habla have felt the economic benefit already?'

'Of course. From the road you can see their plantations and you can buy fruit because they are coming into Israel to sell it. Go and see – it's a wonderful place to take pictures.'

Habla is to the north, the village we walked through with the war-game-loving shepherds and where we bought EU-funded falafel. I couldn't recall anyone mentioning their joy at the prospect of selling fruit at the Israeli roadside. I did, however, remember how the owner of a falafel shop had gestured at my walking stick and spoken in Arabic. The shepherds had burst out laughing but he had stood impassive, waiting, grey stubble on his chin and oil on his apron.

'What did he say?' I'd asked.

'Oh,' said the shepherds, translating, 'he asked if your stick with the numbers on the side was for measuring our sadness.'

I had smiled, embarrassed, and the owner had walked closer to me and spoken again in Arabic.

'He said if it is, you will need a bigger stick.'

To which extent, Professor Soffer is right: I cannot imagine how happy they are.

Professor Soffer is late for his next engagement and so with a flourish, hurries to his car. As he drives off into the distance, he has not only left me with a bad taste in my mouth, but also a strange and overwhelming feeling of desire for croissants and chihuahuas.

chapter 11
MY COMFORTING STAFF

As a rule I avoid shopping in places where posters of Saddam Hussein are prominently displayed. Call me picky, but it just doesn't say 'Fairtrade' to me: moustachioed torturers in general, and Saddam Hussein in particular, just don't inspire a sense of confidence in the customer service department, either.

In the West Bank it is not uncommon to see pictures of Iraq's genocidal ex-ruler pinned up in shops or restaurants, and the village of Rantis is no exception. Here, the grocer has a photo of him – in military uniform holding a pistol in the air – displayed above his trays of cucumbers and avocados. The shop itself is dark, small and has the homely smell familiar to good grocers: the smell of potatoes dusted in mud sitting in cardboard boxes.

The shop owner is altogether less pleasant and started to furrow his brow into a frown of casual hatred from the moment we walked in.

'*Shokran*,' I say cheerfully and he nods a nod that is hard to read but doesn't say welcome. Our translator has not arrived yet so I'm relying on the Englishman-abroad-shopping-method: to point, smile and say 'thank you' loudly.

'Er ... cucumbers and bananas, I think, Phil.'

'Yeah, that'll be fine.'

Pointing and picking up two cucumbers with a grin, I say, '*Shokran*,' again. The owner holds a plastic bag open for me, though I can't help feeling he would rather be putting it over my head and wiring up my nipples to the light socket.

'And four bananas.' I take them from the tray, hold up four fingers and say '*Shokran*,' then put them into the bag.

The owner looks at the contents then shuts the bag and hands it to me silently.

'*Shokran*,' I say again, with a smile.

'Fifty shekels,' he says, without one.

'How much?'

'Fifty shekels.'

'That's a tenner for four bananas and a couple of cucumbers. No, that's not right, surely.'

'Fifty shekels,' he insists blankly, thrusting the bag at me.

'It doesn't cost fifty shekels,' I say in frustration. 'It wouldn't cost that much in … in … in Marks and bloody Spencer.'

'Fifty shekels.'

With that, I hold up my hands and walk away. Outside Phil says, 'I don't speak Arabic but I think he just told you to fuck off.'

'This isn't going to be a good day,' I say, as we leave the village and start back towards the Rantis turn-off. The day had started badly when we lost the guide due to walk with us: he had been behaving slightly erratically and in two days' time he will phone me to say, 'Sorry, I can't make the walk.' But this morning he is merely not returning my calls.

'We need to get someone else,' I had sighed to Phil.

So friends and colleagues were contacted, favours begged, arms twisted and time zones ignored, and by 10 a.m. we had a new guide, Mohammad, from Qalqilya.

'I will get a taxi and meet you at the Rantis turn-off, just by the main road. I will be as quick as I can.'

The Rantis turn-off is not as glamorous as its name might suggest. Its highlights are a dry-stone wall and the traffic. A large container truck thunders past on its way to a quarry and in the wake of its roar, I wait for the birdsong to return. This doesn't happen (unless you are including crows).

Arriving early, we had gone into the village to get fruit and, after meeting Saddam's grocer, we return empty-handed to sit on the Barrier and watch the traffic. After a minute a car drives past. Then another. Then a delivery van. On the stone wall I jiggle my legs with nervous energy and continually flick looks at my watch, aware that we are on the verge of becoming our own Pinter play.

'Are you anxious?' asks Phil.

'Yes.'

'Are you bored?'

'Yes.'

'Are you anxiously bored?'

'Maybe.'

'Or are you bored with anxiety?

Pause. Then to no one in particular I whine, 'Oh, come on ...'

Today's walk will be problematic without the added frustrations of finding a new guide. Firstly, the map shows the red line of the Barrier running through a closed military area again, which means we will have to walk around it thereby adding an extra seven kilometres to the route. Secondly, the Israelis regard this area as troublesome: there have been a number of village campaigns against the Barrier and the army has killed non-violent demonstrators, so we need to be cautious. Thirdly, we have to keep to the schedule. We still have half the Barrier to walk and if we are as delayed as we were in the first walk, we are not going to make it. With everyone still talking about the Israeli crackdown on internationals and protestors, this could be our only chance at this walk. Oh, and I'm also skint, so there is neither the time, the money nor the opportunity to dawdle. We have to keep up the pace, and we have to reach the village of Ni'lin before it gets dark.

Mohammad had said he would get here as soon as he could, so technically it is impossible for him to be late, which infuriates me. As well as being bored and anxious, I am now fretful and cross. Midday has been and gone when he finally arrives, and he barely has time to get out of the taxi before I yell, 'Right then, let's get on!'

I move from a standing start like a fat dad at sports day. I glance up and down the road and cross quickly behind a passing cement truck.

'Other side; cross now! Come on!'

The others follow gingerly, peering nervously down the road.

'On the left, facing on-coming traffic.'

A van hurtles past leaving bits of rubbish dancing in its slipstream.

'Four kilometres down the main road and there should be a turning on the right to Shuqba.'

Another car passes with a roaring whine. As it accelerates onwards into the distance I catch Phil muttering something about 'Colonel Blimp'.

I yell over my shoulder, 'We're late starting. We need to move.'

Such is our pace that it is half an hour into the walk before I look properly at Mohammad. His leather jacket is old-school '70s and his jeans and clunky steel toe-capped boots would render him inconspicuous in Camden Market. His black wavy hair and goatee beard would fit right in, too. In short he looks like a student. Moreover, he is the first Palestinian we have met who looks younger than his thirty-four years. Most Palestinians look older than their age. (When I got home after the first ramble, my wife, Jenny, had said, 'You look old and knackered,' to which I replied, 'The good news is that in Palestinian years I am only twenty-eight.')

There may be no pavement to walk on, but for the West Bank this is a good road: new tarmac and freshly painted yellow lines with just enough room for us between them and the crash barrier. Builders' lorries rumble past less than a foot away, our jackets in their wake. Cars speed on leaving a fading trail of blaring horns and dust. Music bursts momentarily from truckers' cabs. Minivan buses splutter and rev as we tramp on. A Humvee whirs down the winding black line, guarding the illegal settlement of Ofarim sitting above us. Ofarim covers part of the hillside with its sprawl of uniformed blocks of white houses with red tiled roofs and air-conditioning units, and fir trees planted between them in an effort to break up the monotony. An orange and white communications mast stands in its midst and Israeli flags hang from poles. A road sign says 'Ofarim' written in Hebrew, Arabic and English, but the Arabic word has been sprayed over with black paint so it is no longer visible – perhaps the settlers don't want the Arabs to know they are here.

Phil has fallen behind slightly and a settlement security car stops as it comes level with him.

'Where are you from?' shouts a man in shades and baseball hat.

'London.'

He stares at Phil intently, as if by looking long enough he will be able to confirm Phil's answer; as if he can read geography on a face. Seconds tick by and still he stares.

'OK,' he says finally and drives off looking disgruntled and unsure: tonight he'll lie in bed thinking, 'Maybe I'm getting old. I had him down for Kent ...'

'*Yalla*, Phil; come on!'

'I'm coming.'

Phil runs to catch up under the gaze of the settlement, and even Mohammad answers my questions at the trot: 'I am not working in a job at the moment. I am a political activist. In fact, this Saturday I am doing a tree planting.'

'That sounds like gardening,' I pant.

'It is an action. At a village near Qalqilya there are settlers, and there are twenty-seven demolition orders ... So we plant trees as a symbolic act of resistance.'

'What reaction do you hope to get?'

'None. The army will be there. So no reaction is good. But we hope this is just the start and it will grow into something bigger.'

'Is this a popular form of action?'

'Planting olive trees? Yes, you can say it is.'

'Still sounds like gardening to me.'

And so we go on, chatting and shouting over the rumble of lorries, the pace steady as the road curves downwards. Our heavy boots clump time with one another as taxi buses trundle by, packed with passengers. Clouds merge into silver streaks across a greying sky. A pack of curs yelp at us from the roadside, raise half a hackle and then return to sniffing each other while we tramp on, hoping to reach Ni'lin by nightfall.

Having left the main road, walked down one side of a valley on a dirt track and up the other on something resembling a road, we have come to Shuqba. From a distance, the village is a picture of cubes and blocks pinned to the hilltop by a minaret.

A rest stop is forced upon us: in the village centre, a downpour catches us suddenly and we shelter under a tiny corner-shop awning.

'Water?' Phil asks me.

'Coffee.'

'Food?'

'Whatever's there.'

Clutching coffee and chomping chocolate biscuits, we huddle and watch people dash, crouching, in the wet, turning up collars and holding anything that comes to hand to save them from the rain; covering their heads with plastic bags, newspapers and even the odd bit of old sacking. As everyone scatters in the downpour, our moments under the awning are strangely calming. The hot coffee warms us, while puddles swell in the street and oily rainbows swirl in concrete ruts. It is a minute of peace, listening to the gurgling of pipes and gutters and the soft incessant clatter of rain.

The road out of Shuqba is a single strand of tarmac in the middle of the countryside that stretches out into the distance. Lined with half a dozen dead dogs, it's home to a boy racer who constantly zips back and forth, possibly looking for dogs to run over.

'This place is known for car-stealing,' says Mohammad, as the low-slung motor cruises towards us for the fourth time.

'You know there was one car thief …' Mohammed smiles and puts on a set of wide eyes before continuing ' … and he was really well known. He was famous!'

'A famous car thief?'

'Oh, yes. He would steal ten cars a day. He used to say, "I will make the Israelis ride donkeys."'

'So he only stole Israeli cars?'

'Of course … At least, that is what they say.'

The sun makes fleeting breaks through the clouds and the pace picks up again as we pass through the countryside. Nothing matters beyond getting to Ni'lin before nightfall, and time makes a route march of our ramble.

'Can we slow down a minute?' says Phil at one point, wanting to get some water.

'Catch us up,' I shout back, glancing at my watch and the map. Every delayed step is now an irritation, no matter what the reason. Phil puts the camera down and takes his bottle from his bag.

Mohammad asks, 'Shall I pause for a cigarette?'

'If you can't walk and smoke then you shouldn't smoke,' I say ungraciously.

'Better obey the colonel,' sniggers Phil.

'We're late,' I snap, and walk on.

We hurry through the village of Qibya and then Budrus. Qibya was the site of a massacre in 1953 when, led by Ariel Sharon, Israeli troops murdered about seventy civilians. Outside the mosque, Mohammad talks to an old man in a crumpled jacket.

'Did you live here in '53?'

'Yes,' snaps the old man. 'And I have told my story to journalists many times before. And do you know,' he says with a dismissive stare, 'I have not had so much as one cigarette out of it.'

Quick as a flash, Mohammad pulls a cigarette from his pocket and says, 'Please smoke and tell us your story.'

The old man laughs, gruffly says, 'Give me a light,' then, after inhaling deeply, rolls up his jacket sleeve to show us the bullet scars on his arms, talks of his best friend being killed, and hiding from the Israelis.

Cigarette finished, he says, 'I must get to prayers,' before shaking hands and leaving us.

'That was fascinating to meet such a person,' says Mohammad in genuine respect.

'Right,' I reply morosely. 'And now that he's finished we should walk.'

In Budrus, the local council gathers to explain their campaign against the Barrier, of how they fought and organised, and yet such is my anxiety that I can only return their courtesy by trying to be discreet when I look at my watch.

At the edge of the village the road runs out. A man has kindly brought us to a sheep track and he stands on the slope above it, lifting his head as if expecting rain. The sky is a mass of low, dark clouds hurrying over the grey. The wind is gathering, too, and the grass is bending on the hills; barley that twists and rustles the signs of the coming storm.

'You want to walk to Ni'lin?' he asks.

'Yes. We should make it.'

'Hang on a minute, let's just ask if this is possible,' cautions Phil.

I turn to reassure him, saying, 'We won't go if it looks too difficult.' But I have not the slightest intention of stopping the walk.

'We have fifty minutes, maybe an hour, before darkness,' says Phil.

'Maybe less ...' starts the man.

'Roughly speaking ...' I jump in.

He looks to the sky and sighs. 'There is path on the top of that hill. Stick to the path and it will take you to Ni'lin.'

'Great. We should make it if we hurry. Yes?'

No one lifts their eyes, which is all the consent I need.

'Right then, come on. It will be fine if we get a move on.'

The sheep track broadens to a lane that gently rises to the hills, above which is nothing but dusk and clouds. Glimpsing parts of the Barrier's fencing and wire, Mohammad issues a cheery warning: 'We must not get too near the Wall. They are more likely to shoot at night.' There is little concern in his voice, but he feels he should add, 'If the army stop us, do not worry about me.'

'I'll just tell them the truth; that you are our translator.'

'Exactly. There is no problem.'

It starts to rain as we're walking through long grass that knots and tugs at out boots. It is slow and heavy drops: sporadic rain that lands on the waterproofs with a muffled *clump*.

'This way?'

'We will find the path up there ... that is what he said.'

Leaving what is left of the lane, we strike upwards. We quickly find ourselves on trails that are only wide enough for one foot at a time, and weave around thorn bushes and jagged rocks almost on tiptoe. Fifteen minutes later we reach the top but can find no path. There is nothing here but the brow of another rise and the sudden realisation that it is dark; the day finished without us noticing. Not so the rain, which tips into a deluge with such suddenness that it is impossible to ignore. We hurry to a large olive tree, huddling underneath it while the rain hisses down onto the canopy above us.

'Take this,' says Phil, handing Mohammad a headband with a torch on it.

Mohammad slips it on and a beam shines from his forehead.

'You look like a coal miner,' I say.

Phil slips on a luminous waistcoat.

'I've got a torch,' I say, and produce a small Maglite that possibly came out of a Christmas cracker.

'Right,' says Phil. 'I want to be seen and I want to see where I am going. Luckily we have got this night light.'

He holds up a rectangular halogen lamp that buzzes slightly as he switches it on, illuminating the tree and everything under it in harsh, bright light. 'OK. Let's stay together.'

'Yes, let's take our time and get down safely,' I say.

In total silence, Mohammad's headlight and Phil's arc-light turn on me for a moment, temporarily blinding me before they turn away with a sense of timing that I can only describe as contemptuous.

At the field's edge, thin pathways rise above the mud of the furrows. These are firmer to walk but come to abrupt ends and force us into the sodden soil all too often. The terraces make descending the slopes awkward. The rocks are slippery and the walls are either crumbling or drop dangerously away on the other side. So we crawl over them, lowering ourselves into the mud and onto the rocks below. Old bits of fencing are perilously rotten and leave strands of barbed wire dangling to catch us, but we keep moving slowly on, shouting warnings of holes, ruts, roots and dangling branches, waiting for each other when we separate, turning the lights to obstacles and dangers. Rain flickers like scratches in the beam of the lamps. Steam issues from our mouths and our hands have lost all feeling. But all the while we keep an eye on the two dark shades that have become the horizon.

As Phil stands on a ridge of terracing, reaching out for my hand while I use a tree stump to haul myself up to him, a sudden cry goes up across the night. We stand stock-still. Slowly I ask, 'What the fuck was that?'

Mohammad is standing on the pathway below, his light shining in the direction of the cry.

Eventually he says, 'I don't know.'

Then the wail goes up again, like a chorus of feral children howling into the night.

'The Wall is not far, so maybe it is soldiers,' offers Mohammad.

'Soldiers making noises for a laugh?'

'Sounded like kids, could be kids,' says Phil.

'A pack of kids ... No, it's dogs,' I say.

Mohammad hunches his shoulders as the rain rolls from his jacket. 'It could be,' he says, and for the first time he sounds worried. When it comes again, the clamouring yell of feral dogs sounds nearer this time.

'We should keep moving,' says Mohammad.

Instead, Phil laughs. His hair is ragged and damp, his goatee looks as though it is barely clinging onto his chin. 'Oh, bollocks. It's raining, I'm soaked, it's dark, we don't know where we are going and we have wild dogs on our arses. What else can go wrong?'

And with that he slips and suddenly disappears from sight, along with his light.

All is silent, even the dogs. The shock stuns us, then Mohammad and I both scream, 'Phil!'

'I'm all right,' a voice calls out from somewhere below us, 'I'm fine.'

On the other side of the ridge, Phil stands rubbing his hands on his knees, the light still intact, blasting a patch of bright light on the ground in front of him.

'I slipped,' he laughs. 'I'm OK.'

And behind him is Ni'lin. The familiar green lights of a mosque shine from the minaret, houses dot the land around it and in the distance cars are made visible by their headlamps following the curving roads.

'Brilliant,' I gasp. 'Brilliant! Ten ... fifteen minutes' walk, Phil, then a cup of tea. Brilliant.' I laugh with him in relief.

'We still have a climb to get down, so let's be careful,' he cautions.

'Noooo,' says Mohammad in the midst of a realisation. 'This is bad.'

'What?'

'Look. Look at the lights! The village will see the lights up here.'

'I should hope so,' says Phil, holding his lamp in the air so we stand in a cone of light.

'Nooo, the village will think we are settlers or the army ... Oh, fuck.'

'I don't understand.'

'If they think we are settlers they will defend themselves. They might come for us. Oh God. We need to get off the hill very quickly.'

The only way down is straight down, over the terracing. Clambering over the walls is our only option, so we start looking for lower jumps onto the steps below, searching under the blank glare of the lamps for gaps in the cactus hedgerows and dodging low tree branches. Phil and I move slowly as the starkness of the light robs us of the ability to judge depth and distance.

'Keep together,' says Phil, as Mohammad jumps from the precipice of stones and mud into the dark, lit only by the headlamp that spills across the ground as he lands.

'I'm going to phone the police,' Mohammad calls to us. 'I'll explain to them we are internationals coming down the mountain and we are friendly.' He is clearly rattled and stands punching numbers as rain splashes and his goatee drips water onto the keypad of his phone. Phil and I slide over the stone walls on our backsides, looking for rocks on the other side to step onto. Rivulets flow around us and I hear Mohammad's frustration when he snaps, 'Oh my God.'

'What?'

'The police are on answer machine.'

'Stay together,' shouts Phil. 'Mohammad, wait a sec.'

But he is already on his next call, phone fixed to his ear, trudging through mud and over puddles and stones, heading to the next wall. He shouts in Arabic then in English: 'Internationals. We are internationals.' Then stands on a ledge of rubble and calls back to us, 'Shit, man, I told them we are internationals, and to send some police out to meet us and they say they have no one there.'

'Well, someone is coming to meet us.'

Phil has spotted a set of car headlights driving from the village towards the hill. The beams lollop from side to side as the car bumps on the track below. With no one else here, the car is definitely coming for us, slowly and relentlessly. There is no need for them to hurry as there is nowhere for us to go, and we have lit up the hillside.

'Wave at them,' says Mohammad, and he starts to call out in Arabic, his arms frantically flapping.

'Let them know we're friendly,' calls Phil.

The car has stopped. Figures emerge from the doors. Phil resolutely holds the lamp high as he moves cautiously over the shale and mud. I hold my tiny beam aloft, peering out from the hillside to see four men and a car, and I am struck by the incongruousness of a lynch mob in a hatchback.

Standing in mud up to my ankles, on a terrace, up a hill, I am pondering modernity when I notice Mohammad has stopped yelling. He has stopped moving, too. Instead, he is holding his hands up. He is twenty metres ahead of us and on the lower slopes, but he is frozen to the spot. I feel the rain running from my hair behind my ears and watch the men. They are pointing at him. Pointing something at him. It is only when Mohammad shuffles to one side, grins and calls to us, 'Watch out here, guys,' that I realise they are pointing torches up the hill to stop him breaking his neck. He is, it transpires, very near a gully and a considerable drop. The 'lynch mob' is talking him down the terraces, showing him where the safe pathway lies.

Once we are all at the car, explanations are carried out. We had been walking over the men's farmland when they saw our lights on the hillside. Thinking we were thieves coming to steal their equipment, they had set out to deal with us, little realising they would end up giving us a lift.

'*Shokran*,' I say, as we squash into the back of the car.

'*Shokran*,' adds Phil.

'Mohammad,' I say, 'would you please tell them we are really grateful for their help and sorry to cause them any inconvenience making them come out in this weather.'

'*Shokran* ...' begins Mohammad. The driver listens and stares at us as the windscreen wipers scrape backwards and forwards on the screen in front of him.

In Ariel on the Israeli side of the Barrier, Phil had accused me of being 'seduced by the comfort of the settlement'. I had been drinking coffee, eating toast and looking at Snow White when he had said it, so he had at least half a point. On the Israeli side, the roads are smooth, the checkpoints wave you through and soldiers are immeasurably more polite. Life is certainly harder here on the Palestinian side. Everything takes longer, things unravel more quickly, and people do not expect the best outcomes. But as I look at the view of Ni'lin through the smeary, misted window of the car, this is where I want to be more than anywhere else.

Mohammad turns from speaking to the driver to address Phil and me in the back seat. 'He said we should be careful. There have been thieves around here and problems with the army, too, so we should start our walk earlier tomorrow morning.'

Sitting on my lap, Phil nods, then says quietly, 'Let's not have another day like this.'

'Sorry, mate,' I say, but in my mud-covered clothes, tired and wet through, I am not sorry at all. I am delighted.

chapter 12
HAPPY BIRTHDAY

On paper, the ramble is a simple affair: moving from A to B and following the line of the Barrier. Each morning we start walking from the point we had finished at the night before, and so we go on.

The exception is Bil'in. We have broken from our route and come to Bil'in a week ahead of schedule, because today is a special day in the village's life.

Bil'in has had many famous visitors, from anti-apartheid leader Archbishop Desmond Tutu and US president Jimmy Carter. But, with the exception of its reputation, nothing about the village of Bil'in could be described as big. The village square barely has room for all four corners, and the main road through the village is not 'main' in any sense; although it is in every sense the 'only'. If you were to arrive here on a Wednesday or a Thursday, knowing nothing of the place, you'd be forgiven for thinking it sleepy or nondescript. However, come Friday, things change dramatically. Friday is protest day.

Today is the fifth anniversary of the weekly protests. Bil'in might be small, it might even be a hot, windless suntrap, but today it is packed with protesters. Literally in fact, as flag-waving young Palestinians cover the flat roofs surrounding the square for a view of the speakers. Swarms of journalists move around, poking cameras with improbable lenses into everything and everyone's way; an *Al Jazeera* satellite truck broadcasts the event live, and the prime minister of the Palestinian National Authority, Salaam Fayyad, appears, flanked by men in shades and earpieces with wires running into their collars. Today is a big day in a small village. It is a big day for the Israeli protestors, too, who gather a few metres from the square, waiting for the demonstration after the speeches. New arrivals pour out of taxi buses, cars unload, there's shouting, waving and general mayhem as comrades and friends are hugged and greeted. The blocked street is a hub of pre-protest activity: leaflets are handed out, suncream applied and students in Che T-shirts pose for camera phones. Anarchists mingle with young Palestinians, leaning against the cemetery wall chatting and smoking. The socialists assemble a banner, those protest props that are essentially tracts written in shouting font. One begins: 'ONLY AN INTERNATIONAL SOCIALIST WORKERS STRUGGLE CAN DISMANTLE THE WALL, CHECKPOINTS, SETTLEMENTS AND END THE OCCUPATION!'

Socialists, I think. *Even the slogans need sub-editing,* although the familiarity is cheering. Likewise, it is the similarities to home that draw me to the older peaceniks and liberals. Wherever you are in the world, they will always dress like they have turned up for a spot of gardening. Perhaps this is my constituency: liberals who fancy a walk after lunch.

A woman called Anat looks to be one of my fellow constituents.

'This is the first time I have been here,' she says. 'I was frightened of coming, but my daughter persuaded me.'

'Is she here?'

'Yes, there,' she says, waving at someone behind me. Turning, I see a young woman with a *keffiyeh* round her shoulders, clutching a can of Coke and waving back. Phil lifts his stills camera to photograph her, but she shakes her head, covering up the can's logo with a guilty and cheerful grin.

'So why did you come here?' I ask, turning back to Anat.

She stops and fills a pause with a deep breath before sighing, 'I am ashamed.' She lets the words hang in the light of the sun, as if resting from their journey. 'I am an Israeli. All of this is done in my name and it is … shameful.'

*

Earlier in the day, while the podium was being assembled in the square, I had spoken to the coordinator of the Bil'in Popular Committee. Mohammad Khatib is a thin man with a quick mind and a lot on it, and is in the midst of organising the public-address system while we chat. The Barrier took sixty per cent of Bil'in's land; land the settlement on the other side of the Barrier promptly set about building on.

'There was a legal action where you forced the army to reroute the Barrier …'

'Yes, it cancelled 1,500 apartments the settlement wanted to build, but there's 1,500 already built.'

The existing apartments are illegal under Israeli planning law and furthermore are built on Palestinian land, but neither fact was enough to get the Israeli courts to remove the settlers and demolish the apartments. Bil'in's land seems lost for ever. However, the villagers' legal actions did force the authorities to reroute the Barrier, and cancelled the building of an additional 1,500 planned apartments.[23]

'So how much land did you get back?'

Mohammad Khatib points a lad with a pile of plastic chairs in the right direction and says, 'They must give back about 700 *dunum*s.'

'So is it a partial victory?'

'It is good. It gives hope to continue the struggle but it is not enough. We are still a long way from what we want. We want the Wall demolished.' He breaks off to yell at someone to stop testing the loudspeaker and then indicates I might want to quickly ask another question.

'How important is it to have the Israeli activists with you?'

'The Israelis and the internationals are a main part in our struggle,' he says, ignoring his phone that has started to ring. 'This is a Palestinian leadership, it is our agenda and the Israelis are here in solidarity. But when I, as a Palestinian, see an Israeli arrested the same as me, it strengthens my belief in them. And I welcome that solidarity.' Someone shouts a question at him and he turns to quickly answer, then carries on, 'When it is just Palestinians on the demonstration, the soldiers have different orders, and they use different weapons. But, importantly, the soldiers behave differently when Israelis and internationals are with us.'

With an almost inevitable sense of timing volunteers are starting to hang a commemorative banner on the side of a house. It is a stencilled image of a man with his arms open, on a red backdrop. Written in black letters are the words, 'Goodbye, Bassem' and underneath, 'You were a friend to us all'.

'That was Bassem, one of our organisers. He was killed during a demonstration: he was talking to a soldier saying, "Don't shoot," and they killed him.'

When the speeches finish and the last cheer has gone up for the last rousing slogan, the Palestinians move from the square to join the Israelis waiting by the cemetery. The intended march route is a simple one: walk through the village, down a hillside track and up to the agricultural crossing gate at the Barrier. What will occur at this point is uncertain, to me at least, though everyone else seems to know for a fact that when we reach the Barrier the army will tear-gas us all. Mohammad Khatib appears with a surgical mask dangling under his chin, the anarchists have gas masks hanging off their rucksacks, the internationals from the solidarity brigades have scarves and even the rambling liberals have their Palestinian *keffiyehs* ready to be pulled up over their faces. Everyone has something to breathe through, except me. All I have is my asthma inhaler, and it unlikely the Israeli army will defer military action because someone has a note from their mum excusing them from games.

The clatter of massing marchers builds to a pitch, and with all the banners and flags, the chanting, chatting and singing, the steward shouting instructions through a megaphone, and the piercing sound of a lorry alarm as it reverses out of the crowd, I nearly miss the Boy Scout marching band getting into formation. They have snare drums, a bass drum and a drum major complete with twirling baton, and are all dressed in their best kit: shirts, berets, pressed red scarves and woggles. This Scout band is part of the protest and is about to be marched into tear gas along with the rest of us. If only Wilfred Owen could see this. Suddenly, a clown's face pops out from behind the bass drum. A rather furtive clown in full make-up, a red nose and massive bright boots; then three more appear – clowns rarely work alone, particularly Israeli ones in the West Bank. Here, I suppose, to provide a bit of creative chaos and emphasise the non-violent nature of the event (or someone's agent has made the worst children's party booking ever), the clowns playfully dash through the crowd.

As I move to watch them, a woman's voice with an American accent says from behind me: 'Have you got your onion?'

Sitting on the cemetery wall is a young woman wearing pigtails, and round glasses that match her face.

'Always carry an onion to a protest,' she says precociously.

'Sorry?'

'It eases the effects of tear gas. When they fire the gas smell your onion; shove it right under your nose and breathe. It helps.'

She says this with total authority, yet it transpires she is only eighteen, a Jew from Brooklyn, and has never been to a demo before.

'How do you know about this?'

'I read about it on the internet. There's lots of good advice on there about demonstrations. So I read up on it before I came.'

Looking around, I start to spot the onions in the crowd. People are cutting them in half, putting them in their pockets, wrapping them in hankies and sharing them. It is as if I am on the trading floor of the onion exchange.

'That sounds like an urban myth,' I say with confidence, but when I nip into a nearby shop, I discover there has been a run on onions. Not a single one is to be found, not even the pickled variety.

The sight of an ambulance on a demonstration like this has all the reassurance of a hearse at a care home. In fact, there are two, and I also notice that the Scouts have been sent back. The rest of the marchers, however, head unarmed towards the soldiers.

One of the ambulances takes up pole position by the protest leaders in anticipation of the inevitable confrontation, while the other sits on the hilltop as most of the village files past on the narrow track: young and old, men and women; nearly the whole of Bil'in is out today. From the hillside it looks almost biblical, this tide flowing down the slope and up the other side. Families walk together, some still wearing their best from Friday prayers; others are in T-shirts and baseball hats, balancing their kids on their shoulders while mums in *chadors* and young women in their *hijabs* hold the smaller ones' hands.

The young men, the Palestinian youth alongside the Israeli anarchos and activists, are the first to the Barrier; the ambulance right alongside them. Camera crews in gas masks, helmets and flak jackets run among them, seeking the best frontline shots. Figures mass by the gates. Shouts are heard, the wire is gripped and the mesh pulled back and forth, back and forth, in a sudden mass effort. Each heave drags the wire lower until the protesters wrench the wretched iron from the earth and, before the army can react, the Barrier is down. Masked figures pour onto the other side of the Barrier, running through the gap. Palestinian flags wave in an almighty fluster as protestors hurl themselves across the hill with the army in full chase. The event is remarkable not so much for the fencing coming down, but for the sight of Palestinians running on their own land. The masked flag-wavers dodge the soldiers and a military tanker starts spraying jets of 'skunk water'; a massive stream of stinking liquid that falls from the sky like a fountain of filth onto the crowd below. It smells like shit: gag-inducing, stinking chemical shit. Out of the corner of my eye I see a clown holding his red nose. Then, as the skunk water stops, the tear gas begins. The valley fills with the sound of thumps and cracks. Vapour trails of gas arc high then drop like rips in the sky and the air is now a stinging cloud. The ambulance disappears from view. The hillside is covered by gas mist, and half the protestors run as more gas bursts over them and descends. More vapour trails appear in the air, their trajectory moving rapidly towards us. The clown and I duck under the olive trees for shelter but in seconds, the canisters start to fall among the boughs. The gas rolls towards us, the dark fumes engulfing the branches, and we turn and scarper back up the hill, the clown's boots flapping wildly as he retreats. The track is full of coughing, spluttering marchers returning to the village. A crying student takes the arm of an Israeli woman clutching a shawl over her face. Children and mums go by hand in hand. A man leans over, holding a finger against one nostril and expelling a stream of snot from the other. The air no longer carries the sound of exploding canisters but the hacking and hawking of a crowd of protesters making their way home.

At first I'm convinced the gas missed me, which is really stupid. For that to have happened, the tear gas would need to be sentient, directional and programmed to avoid English dads of a certain girth. The thought is not only irrational but quickly dispelled by the first signs of pain. My eyes start to sting, making me blink. I twitch and shake my head, but the irritation intensifies. My nose starts to run, my throat rasps and rattles, my lungs are numb and heavy. I can't feel myself breathe, I don't even know if I am breathing. I want to gasp for air but am terrified of gulping down more of the stuff. A wave of fear washes over me. Head down, eyes streaming, I stumble and spit, concentrating on keeping up with the rest of the retching mass. We plod upwards, past the political officials and their retinue of security clasping clean white paper towels, and past a home with its washing left hanging out in the chemical breeze. In the middle of the phlegm and the gagging, a small woman in an old, oversized biker's helmet, a pair of science-lab goggles and a scarf tied tightly around her face, approaches me.

'Do you want some onion?' she says in a broad Brooklyn accent.

'Thank you.'

Pressing it under my nostrils and inhaling with a freakish gusto, the raw acidic zing cuts up my nose and through my panic. It works, the onion works! I have no idea if there is a scientific reason behind it, or if it is just a relief to smell something other than gas, but the onion smells great and I feel I can breathe again.

'That *is* better.'

'See?' she says, taking the onion back with a smile.

'What made you come here today?'

'Well, I actually came over as part of a Zionist teen camp thing.' Playing, she looks around furtively and says, 'Don't tell anyone.'

'How does that work?'

'I'm eighteen, and I've never really been out of the States before, but the camp pays your airfare and takes you on a Zionist camp so you can "experience Israel". But it's an open return ticket, so when I finished the camp I thought I'd experience this, too.'

'That is quite adventurous.'

'I did my homework. On the internet.' She smiles, holding up the onion.

We join some of the Israeli anarchists, gas masks dangling, still in the throes of excitement and adrenalin. They gabble through the events: 'That was amazing at the Wall.'

'I know, I know … the fence coming down!'

I venture a question: 'Apart from the fence coming down, though, this is a bit of a routine, isn't it?'

The replies are short and blunt: 'It is.'

'We get to the Wall and they gas us.'

'A ritual, almost,' I suggest.

'Look,' a short chap with shorter hair and a crooked grin says. 'The army know we are coming; the demo takes place every Friday. They know. We know they know. They know we know they know … It is a matter of showing resistance.'

'So is that your reason for coming?' I ask.

'Yes,' he says, and then his smile drops. 'And Bassem was my friend.'

chapter 13
MARK IN WONDERLAND

One week later Phil and I are on the other side of the Barrier, opposite Bil'in. We are back on schedule and set to go past the village once again, also on Friday, but this time on the Israeli side.

Our day's route takes us around the city of Modi'in Illit, an ultra-religious city and the source of Bil'in's problems. It is just about everything Bil'in is not: new, large and Israeli. It is also different from many places in Israel, too, as this city is for ultra-orthodox Jews: a religious city, built for religious folk – a bit like Utah but without the hedonistic underbelly.

Though there might be an absence of drugs, rock 'n' roll and, in many cases, television, there is a lot of sex in Modi'in Illit, as the yearly population growth of ten per cent will testify, making it the largest illegal settlement in the West Bank. It is this phenomenal growth rate that requires the settlement to expand; except the land it intends to use belongs to the Palestinian village of Bil'in, conveniently annexed by the Barrier.

The Israeli city was started in 1982 but it feels like the builders were paid before they finished. Roads occasionally run out of pavement, piles of rubble appear in the street and roundabouts wait to be landscaped. I don't know the correct architectural term for this place but I suspect it might be 'urban sprawl' or 'urban sprawl … with a very long snagging list'. Palm trees sporadically line the roads or sit by bus shelters, but it is tower blocks that dominate the city, stacked side by side in pale brown and grey brick, block after block after block. Essentially, the settlement is a nice religious council estate.

Our Hebrew translator is a wiry chap with a close-cut crop of ginger hair. He is an Israeli ex-soldier and a political activist involved in refugee rights. He is young, fit and in possession of a pair of waterproof trousers, detailed maps of the area and a lunch packed by his mum. I would be lying if I said I wasn't envious of all of those things, especially the trousers.

'Hi, I'm Zohar,' he says.

'Mark.'

'Phil.'

Hands are shaken, heads nodded and we set off through the settlement.

'So, Zohar, how old are you then?'

'Twenty-six.'

'Twenty-six! Good Lord, you're but a babe,' I say in mock plummy tones.

This casual remark was meant to highlight my age rather than his, but Zohar says, 'A babe, am I?'

'That sounded patronising.'

'A babe,' he repeats slowly.

'So, what's the route?' Phil says, changing the subject, but my stupid remark will stay with Zohar.

It is 9 a.m. and to celebrate the holiday of Purim, kids are wearing fancy dress to school. It is often the small differences that mark out uniformity, so the sight of a boy dressed as a policeman and another as an astronaut serves to highlight the fact that most kids are dressed as biblical characters complete with crowns, robes, sepulchres and scrolls. Mini-kings and half-pint prophets clutch their parents' hands and hurry through the grey morning. It is clear we, too, are one of those small differences. Most people stare at us and when it comes to staring, these folk really do put the effort in. They have turned staring into a form of aerobic exercise. A car slows and comes to a stop right next to me while the driver burns a good few calories just looking me up and down. There is no sense of threat or malice in the interest shown, just intense curiosity; nonetheless, it is slightly unnerving.

'At what point do we consider this rude?' I ask Zohar.

'No, no, it is not rudeness; they just want to know who you are.'

And so, to the next car that slows I say: 'Hi, I'm Mark.'

The family in the car are very friendly: the driver smiles and natters while kids pile off the back seat in Purim party clothes. One girl is not wearing a costume: no robes, no tablets of stone, not even a staff of any description; just leggings, a dress and a floppy hat.

'Have you not got a costume?' I ask the child.

'This *is* her costume,' says her mother.

'Yes,' says the girl.

'Tell him what you have come as.'

'I'm a tourist.'

'Well, you look fantastic,' I say, noticing the sunglasses resting on her head.

'Thank you.' The young girl waves giddily, tilts her head like a starlet and giggles.

A group of men has assembled by the now-vacated car and in time-honoured ritual have lifted up the bonnet and begun pointing at engine parts. The conversation is in Hebrew and I can barely speak a few words of the language but I am fluent in bullshit and know the car-engine ritual backwards. 'Could be the distributor ...' I pipe up to the group.

The settlers look round. Fortunately they speak bullshit too, recognise the word 'distributor' and nod wisely at my suggestion. This is a form of acceptance, so when the ritual finishes with the traditional conclusion of, 'You'd best get that looked at,' it is my cue to ask about the settlement. These are pleasant folk and our twenty-minute chat is full of the smiles, shrugs, beard tugging and hand gestures that make for a friendly conversation, but it boils down to this: 'How do you feel about Bil'in and living here?'

'We would rather not be so near the fence but what choice do we have?'

'Might the settlement's presence here be a cause of conflict?'

'No.'

'How do you feel about the settlement being illegal under international law?'

'There is a higher law: God's law.'

'Does it bother you that the settlement is over the Green Line?'

'This is our land and we just need a home.'

There is nothing to keep us here and we walk, moving from the kerbside to the countryside, through the stages of the city's development, as it begins to rain once again. At the edge of the settlement the apartment blocks are in stasis, surrounded by scaffolding: concrete awaiting cladding, windows awaiting frames; all awaiting the settlement freeze to end and building to start again. Beyond this lies a series of builders' yards full of supplies. The ones nearest the unfinished estate have Portakabins and barbed-wire compounds to guard the diggers, 'dozers and assorted mechanical machinery. Next comes a series of goods yards stacked with coils of plastic piping, pre-cast concrete beams and palettes full of tiles wrapped with straps. Then follows valleys of aggregate: huge mounds of building materials; sand and gravel hills three or four storeys high. They have their own geography: some are lined neatly in rows with cones and peaks, some form mountainous ranges. There are escarpments of sharp sand, ridgeways of gravel and you can walk under cliffs of ballast or climb mounds so tall they deserve to be named. There is no one but us in these impromptu chasms and it is easy to imagine we have wandered onto a 1970s *Dr Who* filming location.

'We can climb this one,' I call to Phil.

'Are you sure?'

'Sort of …'

The slope is steep and very high but it's ballast, a mix of sand and stone, so it should be easy to dig my boots in and traverse across. I am halfway up when the entire edifice suddenly starts to slip from under me, every step crumbling as my foot lands. The side of the hill starts to shift away and instinctively I run and skip my way desperately upwards, across the collapsing sand, with all the grace and agility of a stilt-walking pig. I only just make the gallop to the firm ground of the peak and safety, and fall on my hands and knees, watching my breath steaming from me, listening to the white noise of the rain and the sound of Phil snorting his face off in laughter. On the far side of the builders' supplies lie mountains of builders' waste. Officially it's landscaping, though some call it 'infilling' and a few might dare say it is 'fly-tipping'; the differences being a matter of perception and permits.

Wet and scuffed, we walk from the rubble to arrive at the green pastures of Bil'in's captured land. On the brow of the hill sits the Barrier and behind it sits the village of Bil'in. Exactly opposite us is the road we marched down just a week before, and we are in the spot where the soldiers tear-gassed us from.

Zohar reminds us that today is Friday, the day of the weekly demonstration. 'The army will be here soon to prepare for the protest.'

The prospect of watching the army tear-gas the very people I marched alongside only a week ago is not an appealing one. But we agree that we should try and see the protest from where the army stand. With impeccable timing, an Israeli military transporter drives into view, winding along the Barrier. The transporter is big, armour-plated and deserves its own entrance music, preferably the 'Imperial March' from *Star Wars*. As it draws to a halt, the side doors open, though without a sci-fi hiss or a striding villain in a cloak. Instead, a handful of conscripts alight with a slouch born of institutional boredom.

'Would you mind if I hand out some leaflets?' Zohar suddenly asks me.

'Pardon?'

'To the soldiers ... I have leaflets in my bag.'

'Well, that depends on the leaflets. If it's "2 for 1" pizza offers you want to give the soldiers that would be a little odd ...'

'No, it's not. They are about war crimes and how Israeli soldiers are committing them.'

'Leafleting soldiers about war crimes is fine.'

'Yes?'

'Why not, it's your walk, too,' I say, trying to be inclusive and make amends for calling him a 'babe' earlier.

The squad spilling out of the transporter is straight from central casting: an abnormally large soldier unloads riot shields; a couple of ordinary Joes carry helmets stacked like cardboard cups; the officer is tall and dashing; while the corporal is small and yappy. Sauntering towards them, I wave and shout, 'Hi. How are you? My name is Mark Thomas. I'm writing about the Barrier and was wondering what time the demonstration is due to start?'

The corporal spots I'm holding a digital sound recorder, which isn't difficult: it's silver, has a red 'recording' light which is on, and I am holding it in his general direction.

'Look out, he has a recorder!' With the instincts of a bodyguard he dramatically thrusts himself between his commander and the recorder, almost pushing his boss over at the same time. 'Is that recording?' he barks, arms stretched wide.

'Yes.'

'You can't record!' he snaps. Then he simultaneously tries to slap the machine from my hand while backing away. Everyone goes quiet and looks at him, even his officer. It is the kind of silent stare that if you listen carefully, sighs the word, 'Twat'.

Now would be the perfect moment for Zohar to say, 'Can I give you a leaflet about war crimes?' but he keeps them in his rucksack, perhaps sensing that any attempt to hand them out would be met by the corporal leaping into the leaflets' path.

'Please don't hit the equipment,' I say in a tired, dad voice.

'You can't record!'

'Why not?'

178

The officer steps round the corporal, exasperatedly holding up his hands. 'If you want to protest you must go to the other side.'

'We don't want to protest, we just want to observe the protest; we are press,' I say, holding out my press card. The corporal twitches, resisting the urge to jump in front of it.

'If you want to report the demonstration you must go to the other side,' says the officer. 'This is a closed military area. You must go.'

'What bit exactly is the closed military area?' I ask slowly.

'All of it,' he replies, equally slowly.

'Where does the closed military area end, then?'

'It doesn't.'

'So where can we go?'

'Back.'

We do not go back; instead, we follow the Barrier across the hills as it moves south, away from the soldiers and the protest. Once we are far enough away and as the clouds blow away to leave a clear sky, we take the chance to share lunch. Earlier we had picked up some snacks from a small settlement 'corner shop', the type that stocks everything and smells of soap and bread. As we wandered the aisles I had stopped dead in my tracks by the nectarines.

'Hang on a minute, listen to that.'

'Bloody hell,' Phil had gasped in amazement. 'It isn't, is it?'

'It bloody is.'

The piped in-store music playing for the good, religious folk of Modi'in Illit was instantly recognisable: 'Smoke on the Water!' exclaimed Phil. 'Smoke on the bloody Water.'

The familiar plodding bass line – learnt by any male of my generation who ventured near a guitar as a boy – droned its incongruous way out of the tannoy above the men in homburg hats and women in wigs who were going about their last-minute Friday shop before Shabbat.

'You'll notice the music played in the shop only has men singing; they will not play music with women singing,' Zohar had commented.

'But Deep Purple! That's the real issue. Wow! Nothing exemplifies a fear of the future quite like seventies rock.'

Zohar had smiled, 'For the religious community, clinging to the past isn't a problem.'

As we eat the oranges and nuts bought under the wailing chorus of '*Smoke on the water, fire in the sky*', I ask Zohar a question that has been with me all morning. 'This community is quite insular, isn't it?'

'No,' he says calmly.

'Really?'

'Really. It is not quite insular. It is very insular.'

'OK, then, do you think this makes the idea of the Barrier, the separation of Arabs and Jews, easier for them? I mean, they are separate, anyway.'

'Yes, of course. Here basically men study; they don't work.'

'What do they study?'

'The Torah. It is very inward-looking. It is not that they dislike other people. The best way of looking at it is that non-Jews only have seven *mitzvahs* ...'

'*Mitzvahs?*'

'Duties, obligations to God, tasks. A Jew has hundreds of *mitzvahs*: 613, in fact. These are simply things they must do. That is what concerns them. They are not much interested in anyone else.'

'Do you know what I find very cool about being an orthodox Jew?'

Phil and Zohar look at me.

'Seriously.'

'Go on,' says Phil.

'It is the complete absence of fashion pressure.' Zohar grins and Phil shakes his head. 'A man can wake up every day of his life knowing he needs a black suit, white shirt and a hat. That's it.

Brilliant. Every day is Blues Brothers Day. I bet no religious Jewish male has ever said the words, "That is soo last year." Never.'

'There might be a bit more to the religion than that,' says Zohar.

'That is not the point. I'm nearly forty-seven, and a dad, and those two things change who I am; everything, from my relationships to my clothes. Old dads in designer T-shirts are cringingly trendy; if the T-shirts have slogans, the dad is doing a sponsored walk; in Fred Perry T-shirts, we still think telling stories about seeing The Clash in '77 is interesting. Short-sleeve shirts are just expensive paunch-concealers. Long sleeves yell, "City-wanker-on-the-weekend". Jeans can't be straight or tight. Baggy makes me older. Cords are tasteless. Slacks sound bad from the off. Trainers take me back to trendy dad. Deck shoes are for yuppies. Flip-flops are just no. Jackets are dull. Leather jackets are for mid-life crises. Overcoats are for funerals.'

'Wow!'

'Exactly. When I was a young man I got up and slung on anything and looked fine, because I was young and scruffy and thought I was hip. Now I wake up and spend half an hour just aiming for neutral. Thirty minutes each morning trying not to look like a twat.'

'What has this got to do with orthodox Judaism?' says Zohar.

'I envy the consistency of their identity.'

Phil takes a deep breath and a slug of water from his bottle before he says, 'Have you ever thought of speaking to someone about this on a professional basis?'

After lunch we trek on in a burst of sunshine. The pathways are old networks of tracks and easy to follow. Small groups of ibex bound over the slopes ahead and for a short while the walking is good.

A few miles south and the Barrier's route crosses a highway and a checkpoint, which looks like a militarised road toll. We have no intention of crossing the checkpoint. We want to cross over the road it sits upon and as we do so we pass a solitary booth in the middle of the traffic, I resist the urge to say, 'Three for *Finding Nemo*, please.'

We attract the attention of the soldier.

'Hey, where are you going?' he shouts, leaning out of the booth, all crew cut and shades.

'Walking along the fence,' Zohar calls back.

'*Rega!*' he snaps, and makes a gesture of an outstretched hand jerking an imaginary length of string between pressed forefinger and thumb.

'That means wait here,' says Zohar.

'The word or the gesture?'

'Both.'

Stepping over to us, the soldier says, 'Enjoy the protest?'

'We didn't go,' Zohar replies.

The soldier points at our feet and says, 'Muddy boots!' in expectant triumph, as if this not only clinches his argument but means that we will instantly gasp, 'My God, Holmes, how did you do that?' Instead, he is met with a casual wave of cynicism, a snort of derision, a shake of the head and a muttered, 'Did somebody fail profiling class?'

Still smiling, the soldier says, 'You want to walk along the Barrier?'

'Yes,' says Zohar sharply, 'that is where we are going.'

'You can't go down there.'

'Well, we are going there,' Zohar replies, turning his back on the conversation and heading for the road. We confidently follow his lead onto the highway, before dashing, stopping, waving and screaming 'STOP!' at the on-coming traffic, with all the dignity of walking road-kill.

Having crossed the road (remaining on the Israeli side), we stop to examine our options. These are to follow the highway back to where we started this morning, or ignore the soldier and follow the Barrier. The second route is, on paper at least, shorter and nicer, taking us down a narrow strip of land that runs between the Barrier and the Israeli town of Maccabim. Looking over Zohar's shoulder at the map, I say, 'The gap between the Barrier and Maccabim is fairly narrow ...'

'But we will be able to walk this, I think, and it looks like there is open land at the end. We should be able to do this,' muses Zohar.

Climbing the crash barrier, we leave the highway, clamber down an embankment and almost immediately enter a totally different environment from the roaring cars above us. Weeds and plants come up to our chests, the ground quickly becomes a marsh and the marsh a stream. As the rain starts to pour we can see Maccabim beyond a clump of trees, its houses visible through the leaves; the emergence of a small pavement to guide us through the mire would not go amiss. Instead, Phil finds the words, 'Oh, fuck' while I find the words, 'Double bollocky fuck', and all of us find a yellow sign with the words, 'DANGER: ELECTRIC FENCE'. We are effectively in a corridor between the coiled barbed wire of the Barrier and some high-voltage chicken wire. This no-man's land is our only pathway, however, and with that realisation, a lightning bolt cracks dramatically across the dark sky, a thundering boom rolling in moments later. *If anyone in Maccabim has a spooky old church organ*, I think, *now would be an appropriate time to start playing.*

'OK, everyone just stay away from the wire and we will be fine,' says Phil, whose ability to state the obvious is borne of a desire to remain positive in all things, though not in a circuitry sense.

'You're right,' I add.

'Just keep on to the field at the end.'

This weird corridor of land runs downhill, a series of pylons spanning its length. Crammed under these power cables is a slalom course of sodden earth dotted with terraced olive groves, bushes, brambles and large lumps of jagged stone. Terraces come to abrupt ends, but the thickets under them give no indication as to the drop, so our legs either stop suddenly with juddering jolts or fall through space leaving us perilously spatchcocked. For a couple of kilometres we slip and sink, stumble and wade our way across this narrow, waterlogged way.

'Coffee,' shouts Phil. 'I'm having hot coffee when we finish.'

'Yes,' I luxuriate, 'coffee!'

'Proper Arabic coffee with loads of sugar.'

'From a proper cup, too!'

Then it starts to hail. Balls of ice pelt our jackets, their mini-thuds reverberating inside our hoods like peas dropped on a drum. More lightning swipes the air and the hail bounces off our jackets. We hold out our hands to catch it.

'This couldn't get any more biblical,' shouts Phil, laughing above the noise of pelting ice.

'It could,' says Zohar. 'Frogs next, I think.'

We shelter under an olive tree until the hail stops, then venture further into the ever-narrowing corridor. The pathway is barely a metre wide now, with the electric fence right next to us, and barbed-wire razor coils stacked in a tangle to our other side. Dark green leaves push through the electric wire, dripping with the day's downpours, and nettles spring high around us, poised and indifferent. Ahead, though, is the end: the open field and our destination. Except it isn't.

Two steps more reveal that the path is entirely wrapped in razor wire, metres from the open land. We are stuck, surrounded by overgrown undergrowth, jagged metal and signs warning us of imminent death. It is a crushing moment.

'We have to go back, then,' I say.

'Yes, we do,' sighs Zohar.

'Fuck, fuck, *fuck*. Two or three kilometres back uphill in this,' rages Phil.

'Unless …' says Zohar, 'I seem to remember seeing some-thing …'

Five minutes later we gaze at a hole in the razor wire. This is what Zohar had seen. The hole is a portal that leads straight onto the Barrier. It is precisely cut, so we would only need to stoop to pass through; indeed, loose strands have been neatly tucked away to one side to avoid catching on anyone, or anything, passing through.

'Who do you think did this?' I ask, slightly nervously.

'I have no idea,' says Zohar, 'but it is here.'

'It is a very neat job,' says Phil.

Lying next to the hole is the familiar red sign: MORTAL DANGER: MILITARY ZONE. ANY PERSON WHO PASSES OR DAMAGES THIS FENCE ENDANGERS HIS LIFE.

'I think we should go through,' says Zohar.

'Onto the Wall?'

'Yes. It will be a lot easier walking there than walking through this. What can happen to us?'

'That,' I reply, pointing to the sign.

'No,' he says, dismissively. 'Nothing will happen. We will get off the Wall when we find a place that's easier to walk.'

'Are you nuts?'

'What? Are you worried about the army?'

'YES!'

Then Zohar says, 'Perhaps they will give us a lift ...'

'Oh, fuck off. The Israeli army will give us a lift?'

'You don't know,' he says calmly.

'That is true, I don't know. But I do know the Israeli army's global notoriety is not based on its taxi service.'

It is also true we had walked on the Barrier in Ariel and got away with it, but in Ariel the army were not tear-gassing Palestinian protestors on a weekly basis.

'Bil'in is just up the road,' I protest to Zohar. 'Aren't they going to be on edge around here?'

'That's miles away.'

He stands by the gaping hole in the wire like an attendant, waiting to guide us through. 'I think we should do it,' he says, almost daring me.

I look at Phil, whose eyebrows are raised so high with concern you could backcomb them, then turn back to Zohar and ask him, 'Is all this about me calling you a babe earlier?'

'It could be.' He shrugs.

'OK, let's go through,' I say.

Zohar shouts, 'Fuck it!' and we lunge through the gap, leaving the Israeli side behind, run down a concrete slope, scrabble up the other side and stand in the middle of the Barrier.

We are exposed on the road's broad expanse as it tracks downhill and onto the plain below, and immediately I regret doing this. The confidence we had moments ago has vanished. Even Zohar looks uncomfortable and we walk in silence. It is a muffled kind of quiet, broken only by the sound of our own heartbeats and our wet boots, whose clumps underline our anxiety as our strides beat quick and long. We are slightly delirious with foreboding, a dread born of the knowledge that our actions have set off a chain of events that we are as yet unaware of.

Perhaps the army won't see us, I think. *Or perhaps we can find another hole in the wire and clamber through.* In truth, I have become stupid with fear.

Quite suddenly, we arrive at an agricultural crossing gate, next to the open fields we had tried to reach. The gates are oddly plain and the barbed wire that rests along the top of the frame has fallen away at one side.

'We could climb over here.'

My words sound strange after so intense a silence.

'Why?' says Zohar.

'Because we need to get off the Wall, and if we hurry, we might make it without being seen.'

'They will see us.'

'Then they will have seen us already, and it doesn't matter … Phil? I want to get off the Wall, what about you?'

'Yeah, I want out, so I'm for it.'

'Zohar?'

'I don't know, but OK.'

Fear grants me the delusion of agility and with graceless speed I straddle the gate, hoist both legs over and drop to the other side, back into Israel. Zohar lands behind me, then Phil. We smile and nod at each other, then walk along an old tarmac path with increasing relief.

'Well,' says Zohar after fifty metres or so. 'I think we have a success. It was a good plan to go on the Wall and it was a good plan to leave it. So, well done to all of us.'

The thing about the Israeli army is that it really does have impeccable timing. Phil hears the Hummer first. 'Er, guys ...?' he says, and all of us turn at the whine of the tyres and rumble of the engine.

The squat armoured vehicle passes through the gate we have just climbed over and revs towards us. As it pulls up, Zohar, waving his arms, walks towards it. Instantly, a soldier holding a rifle leaps out, shouting, 'Stay where you are!' It is the small yappy corporal.

I respond to the four soldiers who now surround us at gunpoint in a way that only the British middle classes can: I bellow the solitary word, 'Sorry.' It is uttered in the traditional way, cringingly, and more sung than spoken; as much a sign of embarrassment as an apology.

'Sorry.'

'Yes,' says Phil, 'we are very sorry.'

'Sorry, for putting you to such trouble.' I offer my hand to a man holding something that looks like it fires tear gas.

For good measure Phil says, 'Sorry!' again.

And I do too: 'Sorry. We're really sorry.'

'Genuinely.'

'Genuinely sorry.'

'Sorry,' repeats Phil.

The soldier with the biggest gun lifts his finger to his lips and hisses, 'Shhh.' Phil hunches in contrition and whispers, 'Sorry.'

'Passports,' barks the corporal, and goes to scan them on an in-vehicle computer of some kind.

'Form a line,' says another soldier, 'and turn around.'

'Pardon?'

'Turn around.'

Compliantly, we turn away from the road full of troops to face the hills ahead of us.

'Lift your heads up, please.'

'What is this for?' I ask.

The soldier puts an arm on my shoulder and points to an extremely tall communications tower in the distance. 'They want to take your photo.'

'They can photograph us from there?' says Phil.

'That is what filmed you climbing over the fence,' says the soldier.

'That's miles away!' says Phil as with a mix of awe and outrage, I splutter, 'That's incredible,' before my performer's DNA kicks in and I instinctively pose for the camera.

In the midst of crackling radio static, flashing lights, the arrival of another Hummer, yet more soldiers and a gun that, we learn later, fires very large, rubber-coated steel bullets, our sporadic attempts to explain who we are, what we are doing and how we came to be on the Barrier, are interspersed with talk of our imminent arrest.

It's no longer raining but Phil and I are soaked, and our wet clothes cling coldly as we stand there. Phil had once told me that he had attended a 'hostile environment training course', which insurers normally insist foreign correspondents and journos complete before covering them. 'Basically,' he had said, 'you pay for ex-soldiers to role-play hostage situations so they can train you on how to handle yourself.'

'What did your training teach you?'

'If taken hostage, you should behave in a friendly manner and try not to provoke your kidnappers.'

'So if I have this correctly, the current thinking among experts is that when kidnapped, don't tell the man with the AK-47 you shagged his mum.'

'Basically.'

'Money well spent, Phil.'

'But … if stopped by the Israeli army, the advice was to be polite and try and establish a friendly relationship by chatting to the soldiers about subjects like football.'

So, shivering slightly by the Hummer, I ask our guard, 'What football team do you follow? Chelsea? Liverpool?'

The soldier shakes his head.

'What, then, Arsenal or Manchester United? Not Man U!'

'No talking,' says the soldier, shaking his head. 'Another time.'

It is at *this* moment that Zohar, as a former soldier in the Israeli forces, displays his own impeccable timing: he starts to hand out leaflets on Israeli war crimes. One of the leaflets ends up in the hands of no less a man than the district commander, to whom I am summoned to plead our case. He sits in the front of a Hummer staring out of the front windscreen with a foot casually perched on the doorframe. He is a vision of the boredom of power.

'Sorry. British!' I blurt out. 'I really am most terribly sorry to have dragged you out and caused so much inconvenience. We have made a terribly silly mistake and you've had to expend time and energy upon our stupidity. I can only assure you of two things: I am British and this is a cock-up on our part. With us lot if it's cock-up or conspiracy, go for cock-up every time. I only hope you will forgive this stupidity on our part and see we had no malicious intent in any …'

He holds up his hand, stopping me short.

'You are British,' he says slowly, 'so you know the importance of procedure.' He grants himself a smile. 'We must all follow the procedure. Where would we be without it?'

'You're absolutely right,' I say, mistakenly responding to the rhetorical question.

' … And the procedure in this instance takes the matter out of my hands. I am powerless,' he says disingenuously.

'Oh.'

'I must transfer you to the police, who will arrest you.'

*

I rejoin Phil and realise the walk is over. Not just this section of it; the entire ramble ends here.

The small corporal approaches. 'Two of you come with me. One will wait here.'

'Why is one of us to stay?'

'There is room for two of you in the vehicle: one waits with my men and we will come back for them after taking the other two to the checkpoint.'

'I'll wait,' volunteers Phil.

'You OK with that?'

'Yeah, but wait for me there, right?' says Phil.

'Yeah, of course,' I say and am led to the armoured car.

The heater has warmed the Hummer, but the floor in the back has a puddle of water in which my feet sit, and my seat has broken one side having loosened itself from its frame. On a shelf behind me, a rifle lies unattended and within reach, its availability a reminder of our total lack of control in this car.

'Seat belt,' says the corporal, insisting I strap into the wobbling chair. The air momentarily smells of cigarette smoke as the driver only partially exhales out of the window, then the Hummer accelerates onto the road and I sit in the wobbling chair jiggling around like a dashboard toy.

Zohar looks up with a glum face and says, 'See, we did get a lift.'

Dumped at the checkpoint and ordered to wait until the corporal returns with Phil, a revelation occurs to me. Putting my hand in my coat pocket I find my mobile phone and instantly remember that Nava, our Israeli fixer, had said, 'If you get into trouble, you call me straight away.'

Scurrying to one side, keeping out of sight, my fingers jab at the keypad of my phone. 'Nava,' I whisper when she answers, 'it's Mark. Sorry to call you on a Friday night.'

Instantly she says, 'Where are you and what has happened?'

'I have fucked up really badly ...' I start to tell the tale.

After listening Nava replies, 'I don't know if I can do anything. It's Friday night, and people will be difficult to reach. But pass the phone to the guy you were walking with; I need him to find out some information.'

'Zohar?'

'If that's his name, yes.'

While Zohar speaks to Nava, Phil returns bedraggled, his coat clinging wetly to his rakish frame.

'You OK?'

Phil nods. 'What now?'

'Don't know. Wait for the police to pick us up, I suppose. But I think we're in jail for the weekend.'

'Really?'

'It's Friday. No one is going to process us before Sunday morning. But if we are charged and it goes to court ... a fine? Jail? Deportation? I don't know.'

Zohar returns, handing me the phone. Overhearing my last comment, he says, 'Let's see.'

While we wait, the sun sets. Shabbat has arrived and traffic into the checkpoint has all but stopped. Lights are on in the inspection booth, and the corporal has arrived with a pizza tray to general applause. I feel numb with resignation. This is how the ramble will finish: watching conscripts eat pizza. I am certain we will be charged as we were so clearly in the wrong, and jail will mean deportation, and deportation will mean never being able to return to take this route again. I feel the shame of defeat and its hollow sting. I wish we had never gone through the wire. I wish I had said no. I wish I had not called Zohar a 'babe'. I wish failure could be more spectacular. I wish the last moments of this walk aren't the sight of a squaddy burning his lips on hot mozzarella.

*

The night is colder and the lights brighter when two soldiers come over and immediately start a heated discussion in Hebrew with Zohar.

'What's this?' I call.

'Hold on,' Zohar says, before returning to the fray: the soldiers pointing and shouting.

I know any interruption I make will merely add to the confusion but instinctively I blurt out, 'I want to know what they are saying.'

Flustered, Zohar says, 'They say we were warned.'

'Warned?' and suddenly I find myself shouting: 'That is shit! Utter shit!'

'Stop.'

'Bollocks to this shit.'

'Please stop,' pleads Zohar.

'Fuck this!'

'No, stop!' he shouts, and I do stop, finally. Then with a terse, quiet voice he says, 'They are releasing us.'

'Releasing us?'

'Yes. They are not happy about it but they are letting us go.'

I swallow and in a small voice say, 'Sorry.'

Zohar continues with the soldiers while I phone Nava.

'Nava, what happened?'

'Ah, good. You are free.'

'What did you do?' I laugh in sheer relief.

Nava quickly recites the litany of events: 'I got Zohar to find out the name of the unit and the commander: I find his number, I phone him, I explain who I am and who you are. I said, "They fucked up, they know they fucked up and they are very sorry, so let them go." I told him, "This walk is officially recognised, so let them go. They have serious interviews with high-ranking security people next week." I said, "It's Friday, let them go so we can get on with the weekend."'

'What did he say?'

'Well, we argue a lot. But in the end he said, "I don't need this. I have a Palestinian caught cutting the wire and I have to deal with him, but this I don't need. So I will let them go." And now you are free.'

'Thank you.'

'So now you will buy lunch when I see you in Jerusalem.'

'Anywhere and anything. Thank you, thank you, thank you, Nava!'

'OK.'

'I'll let you get back to your weekend.'

'Yes ... and Mark?'

'Yes?'

'Don't fuck up any more. I know this army, I know how they work, and you won't get away with this again.'

'I know.'

'Don't fuck with them.'

'Yes.'

'Goodnight.'

She is right of course, but before leaving I can't help approaching the checkpoint soldiers to ask, 'I wonder if you could call my friends and me a taxi to take us home?'

'Leave here and go,' they shout.

And we do, casually forgetting that the Palestinian wire-cutter does not have an Israeli fixer who can phone the right person and argue on their behalf.

chapter 14
HARD TRAVELLIN'

Phil has developed a new habit, that of waking each morning briefly convinced he is a children's TV presenter. He sits bolt upright and with a croaking falsetto sings out, 'Morning!' then, gripped by an as yet unidentified syndrome, he walks to the window and lists all the things he can see: 'Sun. Ah, sun. Birds. Goats. Nice birds and trees. Lovely trees.' After thirty seconds it finishes suddenly, and he completely crashes. 'Right,' he will say, '... coffee.'

It is like having a bipolar Elton John alarm clock. Yesterday, though, he stood at the window completely silently. Something had happened, and that something was the weather. Outside were mud slides, flash floods and slow floods, coupled with road blocks and a lot of work absenteeism. Yesterday was spent waiting to walk, sitting in empty coffee shops in Ramallah listening to news reports of, 'the worst storms in a decade'. We sipped our way through the day till evening came, then we watched the cops directing traffic in the mist and cloud using the red stick lights that are normally reserved for use on runways by men with headphones and luminous jackets.

This morning, however, Phil stands by the window and says, '... Minaret ... er, garage ... er, cloud ... fuck it. Coffee.'

This is about as good a weather report as we could hope for and, given we are behind schedule, today's walk is on. Rain is expected so I have packed all our phones, snacks and first-aid equipment into one Tupperware sandwich box. True, the dates may take on a slight taste of Germolene, but I have wedged the route map firmly at the bottom of the box, so if we get lost we need only turn over the plastic container to navigate.

Out by the Barrier, the countryside looks battered and bruised from the storms: roads are blocked and paths are all but washed away in some places. Mohammad from Qalqilya is walking with us again, and has turned up wearing his leather jacket and his one concession to the bad weather: a standard issue ethnic woolly hat, giving him the appearance of a Tibetan rockabilly.

'Which way are we going?'

'Well, we have a tight schedule...'

'We wouldn't be walking in this if we didn't,' adds Phil.

In front of us a tractor is driving through the flooded fields, spraying great muddy fountains in its wake and it is obvious that we will not be able to walk in the fields immediately alongside the Barrier. Instead, we must take the roads that run parallel to it.

' ... and it is going to be very hilly today,' I say, looking at the Tupperware. 'It begins flat but there is a big range of hills to climb. At least, it looks like a range of hills.'

'Yeah,' says Phil, 'though you could be trying to map-read a pitta crust.'

The clouds burst above us as we reach the bottom of the hills with five kilometres to go to the next village. There is just one road up: steep and narrow, the constant rain cascades down it like a water slide. It flows in a fast, steady torrent, complete with small waves that lap at our feet, our boots spraying droplets as we tramp upwards. The stone gully next to the road burbles and gushes, any detritus long since washed away, leaving the water running fast and clear. The weather has us surrounded: dense clouds shroud the road, covering everything beyond twenty-five metres ahead in grey oblivion. We walk through a mire of cloud. The wind and rain turns our faces raw but when it finally abates, the clinging mist covers us in cold. I trudge on, my lungs puffing like a model in the Science Museum and my calf muscles stretched out of tune. But there is a vague pleasure in clomping steadily up the steep climb, and there are rewards. A small owl shelters in a roadside crag near enough for us to watch it shake the wet from its wings and reset its ruffled feathers. And the mist may have a bitter bite but, up on the hilltops, we take time to stand and watch how the close clouds move, marvelling at the wisps and tendrils that glide right by us.

Two hours after starting up the foothills we wander into Beit Anan, a village at the summit. It's windy and the streets are empty but for a couple of kids and the grocer.

'I need tea,' says Phil.

'Yes,' says Mohammad emphatically. 'I need tea and I want to stop feeling wet through.' The three of us are so drenched that children could plant cress seeds on us as a science project.

Thankfully there is a tea shop in the village, with condensation invitingly misting the view through its windows. Inside, the room is packed with men playing cards, smoking and sipping tea, most of them wrapped in their winter coats. There is a wooden serving bar at the far end and a couple of paintings of the village hang on the otherwise bare walls: imagine a very popular working men's club run in a garage and you'll be close to a picture of the place. As we wait, cautiously dripping rain onto the floor, the entire room looks up idly, assessing us, before returning to the game in hand.

'Come,' says the appearing waiter and he ushers us round the tables, straight to a large, cylindrical stove standing in the middle of the room. It is brilliantly utilitarian: half a dozen small, wrought-iron prongs are splayed around a blackened chimney pipe that runs to the roof and disappears. The soot-smeared glass hatch is opened, fuel thrown into the flames and space made for us at the nearest table by customers insistent on giving up their seats. A tray of tea appears in thin, fluted glasses, hot and sweet.

'They do not have any food,' says Mohammad, 'but they are happy for us to eat what we have bought.'

So the pittas are fished out of the Tupperware pharmacy and the waiter spears them on the wrought-iron spikes to warm the bread on the stove. We huddle by the fire, our hands held out to it, feeling the cold slowly leave our clothes. Standing there we start to steam. Wisps of smoke rise from our wet trousers, chased away by the heat; we smoulder like we are about to spontaneously combust. The vapors rise in a constant flow, sitting surrounded by complete strangers in a room at the top of a steep, just-conquered ridge, steaming before their very eyes, I declare to Phil and Mohammad, 'This is the best tea room in the world.'

Over tea, Mohammad shoots me a wink and a nod and says, 'Someone has gone to fetch a councillor for you to talk to.'

I sag visibly at the prospect. 'We have spoken to a lot of councillors; what would I ask him that we have not asked already?'

'You could ask why there are so many men in this room playing cards at two o' clock in the afternoon and not working.'

'It'll just be more stories about farmers and how the Israelis took their land and shot their donkeys,' I sigh.

'OK, it is your walk and that is fine,' he says evenly, 'but I am curious why you do not want to just listen to what he says.'

'Because we have to keep to the schedule. When we fall behind the schedule, we make mistakes.'

'Oh, come on,' laughs Mohammad. 'You make enough mistakes even on schedule; what difference will a few more make?'

'No, we stick to the schedule.'

Mohammad shrugs and then says the worst thing anyone could possibly say to me in this situation. 'OK, you're the boss.'

'I am no one's boss,' I spit angrily. 'And I'll fire anyone who says I am.'

Mohammad laughs and my contrition is quick. 'You're right, I'm sorry, I should talk to him.'

'OK.'

But Mohammad's remark has stung me. He might as well have said: 'I'm a powerless Palestinian, just happy to be in the presence of a British man who has seen so little of my country and yet knows so much more about it than anyone else.' I am humiliated by my own pomposity and dismissive attitude. Feeling shame, I want to say, 'You've got me wrong. Please don't stereotype me. I'm not a colonialist. I'm not a racist. I'm just an arrogant bastard. Just an ordinary, run-of-the-mill cunt.'

Mamoon, the councillor, cuts a distinctive figure when he enters the tea shop: jacket collar pulled up against the wind, he stamps his feet at the doorway before coming inside. He has the air of local politician with a dash of matinée idol: his hair is lustrous and his chin jutting, but his eyes are soft and seem to say, 'I have never knowingly run over an animal.' In common with so many Palestinian men, however, it transpires that he has been in prison on four occasions.

Introductions are made, a quiet spot located and Mohammad says, 'I will ask a question, if you don't mind, about unemployment ...'

Before he can finish, Mamoon says, 'Look around you, look how many men are sitting here who should be working. Some are farmers, but many are workers who used to work in Israel before the Wall.'

'What about Jerusalem?' Mohammad continues. 'Lots of people used to work there, I think?'

Mamoon nods with eyes wide: 'Of course, this village is very close to Jerusalem. Maybe eight hundred men used to work there before the Wall.'

Given that any Palestinian wanting to work in Israel has to get a permit to cross the checkpoint, I ask, 'Currently, how many men have permits to work in Jerusalem?'

'Around twenty.'

'Only twenty?'

'Most workers did not get permits. There were a few attempts by people to climb over the fence into Israel, but most of these guys got arrested because there are cameras everywhere ...'

'We know.'

' ... while there were some who tried to hide in the garbage trucks to smuggle themselves across.'

'Really?'

'Sometimes, they even try to get into Jerusalem using the sewage tunnels. They go underground, from Beit Hanina.'

'They crawl through sewage tunnels!' I repeat in disbelief.

Mamoon looks round the room. 'All of these men have families and they have to earn money. They have to get to Israel any way they can.'

We sip tea for a moment. Mohammad looks at his watch, aware that time is ticking on, when I ask, 'Could you arrange for us to talk to some of them?'

'Pardon?'

'The men who have tried to cross the Wall, could we speak to some of them?'

Mohammad looks at me. 'The schedule?'

'Not right away. It will take time to arrange,' nods Mamoon.

'Then we can come back later,' I say, as Mohammad almost imperceptibly shakes his head.

Later, when the rain has stopped and the evening has a brief hour of sun, we return to meet Mamoon and a dozen men. Our meeting point is a half-decorated rooftop patio littered with plastic seats and paint pots.

'Is everyone OK with talking about crossing into Israel?' I ask the crowd, and Mohammad translates to this mini-mob of all ages.

'It is fine,' says Mamoon.

'Well, can I ask who worked in Israel before the Wall?'

'We all did,' say half a dozen voices.

'And how many of you have permits to cross into Israel for work?'

They all shake their heads to a man, moaning, laughing, waving their hands and grumbling, 'None of us.'

'So do you cross into Israel illegally?'

Eyebrows and voices are raised to answer. 'Yes, of course,' shouts one.

'What other choice do we have?' says another.

'Maybe *you* could take us in your car next time,' suggests a voice from the back.

'But how do you cross? Where do you cross?'

The group answer as a chorus: 'Beit Iksa.'

Mamoon explains, 'Beit Iksa is a place to the east of here where they have not built the Wall.'

'There is a gap,' someone says.

'There is a valley and trees at Beit Iksa,' Mamoon continues, 'and at about 2 a.m., they try to cross using the trees to hide. It is only a few hundred metres into Israel.'

A man with stubble like black sandpaper and a collarless leather jacket says, 'The soldiers are there every night, too, trying to catch you. If they catch you, you could get two months in jail and they fine you, too. Maybe 1000 shekels.'

'Sometimes if the soldiers catch someone, they will not bother with court.' A balding man with his hands stuffed deep into the pockets of his fleece picks up the tale. 'They will take him into the trees and break his hands or legs.'

'Really?' I say, more in shock than questioning mode.

And the mini-mob nods its collective head and sighs.

'But getting across is just the first part of the problem,' says Mamoon. 'Once across you have to get a bus or a taxi, but if the driver thinks you are an Arab they will call the police. Soldiers get on the buses, too, and the driver might tell them, "There is an Arab in seat twenty," or whatever. Or the driver will flash his headlights at an army jeep and the soldiers will come on and take you.'

'I heard people hide in tankers and garbage trucks to cross; have any of you done that?'

Nearly everyone laughs with the chuckle of the guilty; even the smokers at the railings turn to smile.

'Yes,' someone says. 'And cars, too.'

'Who has crossed in a car?'

'I have,' says one young man, shaking his head in embarrassment. 'I was caught in the boot of a car at the checkpoint. My friend was driving and he was released, which is unusual, but they kept me at the checkpoint the whole day. Every time a soldier walked past me they would kick me or slap me. They kept me there until evening and then let me go.'

'Didn't they jail you or take it to court?'

'No, I was lucky.'

Time has passed and the men start to break away. It is time to finish.

'Well, thanks for your time ...' I start.

'There is one more thing,' says Mamoon. 'Once you have crossed into Israel and got the bus without being caught, you can work all day and when you have finished the employer might say, "I have no money, I am not going to pay you," and you can do nothing. They will say, "If you do not go, I will call the police."'

'Is this common?' I ask, sensing the communal response. 'Yes,' says the depleted mob.

The oldest man points to the man with the stubble: 'He is taking his ex-employer to court to get his money. And that was with a permit!'

'I worked for eleven years,' explains the man with the stubble, 'and one day there was a suicide bomb that went off somewhere and I arrive at work and the Israeli employer says, "I don't want you, I don't need you; you are fired and I am not going to pay you."'

His testimony finishes this strange rooftop meeting, and we say our thanks and leave. The encounter with Mamoon has gripped me, hearing about the risks Palestinians take just to earn a living.

It has been one of the most compelling days on the walk: unexpected and intriguing. Best of all, Mohammad is gracious enough never to mention my fit of pique and the abandonment of my beloved schedule.

The next morning Phil chimes at the window like a man restored his sight: 'Chickens. Sun. Trees, lovely trees. Mosque. More trees. Cloud. Fluffy cloud.' In layman's terms, this means the storm has passed but we should expect an overcast and breezy day.

Better weather is welcome, not least because we are scheduled to walk with Samia, a university lecturer and co-founder of Ramallah's only group of ramblers – the past few days' weather has kept everyone else indoors, including her, but today we have agreed to meet under the fabulously named 'Star and Bucks' in Ramallah city square, then drive back to yesterday's finishing point to start the day's walk.

'How will I recognise you?' I had asked.

'I will be wearing my walking jacket.'

A walking jacket in Ramallah is, it turns out, a distinctive item and Samia is easy to spot, particularly as the jacket is accompanied by a woolly hat, walking boots and nothing less than a lightweight aluminium hiking pole.

'Samia.'

'Mark,' she replies, and I immediately feel a bond of rambling kinship.

We quickly leave the city and return to the pathways and goat trails of the hills. Samia is a lecturer in Economics in Birzeit University and walking is her passion.

'Do you have a name for the group, like the "Ramallah Ramblers" or something?'

'Nearly,' she laughs. 'We are called "Shat-ha", which means "a walk in the wilderness".'

'Hiking seems a rare Palestinian pastime, so what made you start the group?'

Samia answers with the thoroughness of her profession, 'Well ... One of the reasons is that the space we live in is contracting, due to the building of the settlements, the Wall, the checkpoints, et cetera: you can't drive for more than twenty-five minutes in the West Bank without hitting a checkpoint. So the space is suffocating. We live in enclaves surrounded by either the Israeli army or the settlements or the Wall. And we thought, one day, that one way of expanding the space is to walk, because when you walk you can walk for hours in the hills and stretch this very suffocating limited space to make it seem bigger. So we're trying to create the illusion of a more free and open space for ourselves. A way of trying to dodge reality, really, and ... Oh, hold on.'

We have walked onto some boggy ground and she steps to the side, avoiding the small mire before us.

'I think we can cross it,' I say, attempting to daintily tread through the sinking mud and grass the way only men my age and size can – namely, by failing.

'There. Just a little mud on our boots.' I say on the other side.
'Ah,' says Samia. 'Now the hike is baptised.'

For all of my fondness of Phil and Mohammad, it is great to be
walking with a walker. The experience is just different. She has a
similar manner to Fadhi, our guide from the start of the walk back
in the Jordan Valley: she is keen to halt a discussion on divestment
politics to find wild asparagus growing between cacti, and happy
to resume again once we have eaten. But, most of all, she has given
thought to the whys and wherefores of rambling.

'Do you ever walk near the Wall?' I ask.

'Never,' she replies, immediately. 'This is the first time I've
walked by the Wall around here. The purpose of our hikes is to
relax and enjoy ourselves. Thus the first criteria is to try to avoid
the settlements, settlers, the army, the Wall and the checkpoints.
Of course, we are not always successful; we found even when we
used the maps we would sometimes run into "outposts" ...'

The best way to describe an outpost is this: all Israeli settlements on the West Bank are illegal under international law, while
'outposts' are also illegal under *Israeli* law, too. When Israeli law
says an Israeli settler is acting illegally, you really need to watch
out, and so 'outposts' are 'unplanned' and 'unapproved' settlement expansions, and are thus uncharted on maps.

' ... and once we walked upon an outpost by mistake and the
settlers attacked us, pointed guns at us and brought in the army.
They accused us of spying, of taking pictures because we wanted
to bomb them. The cameras were confiscated and it was a big
mess. So you don't want a close encounter with settlers or the
army because the consequences could be very grave. So, really,
we walk to escape.'

At the mention of escaping, I tell Samia of the stories Mamoon
and the workers had told me about trying to cross the Barrier.

'It is something many of us have had to do.'

'Have you crossed the Wall illegally?' I say, surprised that a lecturer would need to do so.

Samia nods. 'I was invited to speak at an American university and had to get a visa from the US embassy in Israel. But there was some security alert and the Israelis were not giving permits to cross the checkpoint. So I paid someone to take me across. There are Palestinians, Israeli Arabs, with Israeli cars and number plates and you pay them a fee and they will drive you across.'

'Didn't the soldiers stop you at the checkpoint?'

'Not if you look Israeli. So that is what we did: we had to dress up to look Israeli. They hung a Star of David from the rear-view mirror, put a copy of an Israeli right-wing newspaper on the dashboard and the woman in the front seat dressed like a young Israeli soldier. So she had on tight jeans and a T-shirt, trainers, and bunched her hair into a ponytail. She was wearing shades and she put her feet up on the dashboard, with her arm leaning out the window, and chewed gum. She looked really arrogant. And when we drove up to the checkpoint, the soldiers just waved us through. They didn't stop us or ask for our ID. They just waved us through. This is what the soldiers think their fellow Israelis look like.'

I am not sure we have managed to escape the reality of life under the Occupation and the Barrier today. The arrival of a border patrol jeep, blaring its siren at us, intruded upon our reverie. But the day has been full of good moments: the fun of the four of us sharing a picnic by a natural spring; of wandering on a hillside of scrub and finding a place covered in orchids, and marvelling at their pink and white petals. I am not sure if it is possible to lose oneself in a 'perfect walk' here; to experience the feelings of freedom that brings. But, as we cross the rim of a valley on descending pathways, along the fields and crops lush and fresh from the stormy rains, deep green on the red-brown soil, Samia breaks the discussion suddenly with a hushed, urgent hiss of, 'There!' as a deer breaks cover, dashing through streaks of sunlight across the terraces. We stand in silence as it disappears at a clip.

'I think I will suggest that the hiking group make an exception and walk here, near the Wall,' she says.

chapter 15
THE TUNNEL OF HUMAN SHIT

The next morning, as Phil scratches his goatee with morning rigour and recites his list of seen objects at the window, I randomly swear at misplaced equipment. The past two days have been damp and sweaty enough for me to grumble, 'I will be so pissed off if I am the only rambler to go to the Middle East and get trench foot.' Added to this, the pile of dirty washing in the corner of the guest house room has started to attract fruit flies and I cover yesterday's T-shirt with talcum powder in the belief that while it won't mask the smell, it might sow the seeds of doubt in the nostrils of the inhaler.

It's the fourteenth day of the second walk and our route starts where we had left it the night before, in a village north-west of Jerusalem called At Tira. At the edge of the village is Road 443, a four-lane highway that links Tel Aviv to Jerusalem by passing through the West Bank. Although it is built on confiscated Palestinian land, this road is not for Palestinians. It is for Israelis and those with Jerusalem IDs only: a club-class settler road not for the likes of the native hoi polloi. It has been shut to Palestinians since 2000 when a spate of attacks on the road left six Israelis dead. To ensure that Palestinians didn't sneak back onto the road to enjoy the tarmac privileges and rights reserved for Israeli drivers, the army blocked all access roads from any Palestinian villages that led to Road 443. This effectively sealed in the communities – all that the Palestinians now have to connect with the rest of their home-land is an old, single-lane hill road, which means that what was a twelve-minute drive into Ramallah now takes an hour and a half; longer if the weather is bad.[24]

Phil, Mohammad and I stand looking down at Road 443 with Issa, the ex-mayor of At Tira. He has recently stood down but was one of the group of local village mayors who led the legal battle against the Israeli-only road.

On the other side of the highway is the village's boys' school. For the Israeli architects, the school presented a major problem: how to allow the Barrier to surround the neighbouring Israeli settlement of Beit Horon, maintain an Israeli-only road, and still allow the Palestinian children access to their school. How could the children cross the road if they were not allowed to set foot upon it? How could they cross a barrier they weren't allowed within 150 metres of? The Israelis very kindly built them a tunnel.

Issa, all straight back and hands clasped in front, regards the kids meandering to school with a patrician eye. Some run and play, a couple share crisps from a bag, another is reading last night's homework; all of them wrapped up against the morning chill. The kids walk from the village to the hillside, scramble down a dirt track, walk along the edge of Road 443 and take a stone stairway down to the tunnel that leads under the road.

'We should walk with the children,' says Phil.

'You want to go to the school? That is not a problem; I will arrange this,' Issa says, then calls to two youngsters who happen to be walking past: 'I want you to take these with you to the school; don't worry, they are friends. Show them the tunnel. You are in charge. OK?'

The kids are self-conscious with concerned faces, red fleeces and light blue rucksacks donated by UNICEF. One looks up as if he wants to say, 'I'm only nine.' The other wants to say, 'I can't do double bows in my shoelaces yet.' But they both nod.

When Mohammad asks, 'Is this the way you always come to school?' they look up at him, wide-eyed and alert, and say, 'Yes,' with quiet voices.

Along with a growing crowd of children, they lead us along the dirt track at the side of the road, which is busy with on-coming rush-hour traffic, and down the stone stairs to the tunnel under Road 443. It is not a grand affair this tunnel, nor a friendly one. There is no consideration that children walk through here on their way to school: there are no tiles, murals or even lights; it is merely a concrete hole with less finesse than a council inspection point. It is small and dark and I can touch the roof with my hand easily, and both sides if I stretch out my arms. The tunnel is divided in half by two narrow channels – the one raised slightly above the other is where the children walk. No one walks in the lower channel.

'What happens there?' Mohammad asks, pointing at the lower channel.

A child with a black woollen hat answers, 'Water. This is for drainage. But when it rains sewage comes down, too; sewage from the settlement.'

'The sewage just runs down here,' adds his friend, who is wearing a baseball cap.

'Sewage,' I find myself repeating out loud.

'It smells really bad,' says Woolly Hat.

'In the summer it stinks,' says Baseball Cap.

We walk through and the cars above us drive on. Emerging onto a narrow path, it is a matter of metres to the school itself, and we are met by teachers who had seen us coming down the hillside. Introductions are made and tea is drunk, while the headmaster explains that the Israeli army has placed a demolition order on the school toilets.[25] Apparently, the Israeli authorities are happy for the kids to walk in a tunnel next to human shit but not to let them have a toilet.

Returning via the tunnel to the village side of the highway, Issa takes us to the access road from the village onto Road 443; or it would be an access road, if it were not for large and incredibly heavy concrete cubes placed in a line on the tarmac. Each one is one metre across and there are two lines of nine blocks across the road.

'This once was the main road in and out of the village,' says Issa.

The immediate area carries the detritus of no-man's land: charred remains of a small fire, soot marks against the concrete, empty bottles, blue plastic bags and cigarette butts. The army was not able to line the blocks on the grass verge next to the road, presumably because they could sink or slip in the rain or be dug out, so the verge is well used as a path, judging by the dirt line around it.

Along with five other villages, Issa, who was then mayor, took legal action in June 2007 against the army's decision to shut the road to Palestinians, and in 2009 they won: the High Court declared the army should open the road.

'It is a great feeling to win but I knew in advance they would not listen to us,' says Issa. 'The soldiers refused to open it.'[26]

The peculiar thing about this deserted road is that, for a dead end, it is remarkably alive. As we talk, a car with yellow Israeli plates lurches with alacrity towards us; it looks like it has turned off Road 443 by mistake. It gets halfway up the access road, realises what it has done and stops sharply near the barrier. *Ha*, I think, *well, that's one Israeli who didn't know about the Israelis-only rule.* The car U-turns with a scrunch and gives one short beep of its horn. Seemingly from nowhere, two Palestinians suddenly dash through a gap on the muddy verge. With casual haste they half walk to the car, glance around, jump in and slam the doors as it revs quickly away, turns onto the highway and is lost in traffic, all in the time it takes for me to blurt out, 'Whoa, those guys must be busting into Israel!'

'Probably,' says Issa calmly. 'Or they will if they don't get stopped at the checkpoint.'

'Does that happen often?'

'All the time. This has become a kind of unofficial customs checkpoint.'

With that, two white vans pull up, one on either side of the blocks. Men start to unload kitchen cabinets and cupboards from the village side, stacking them on the blocks, while men from the highway side load them into the other van, that has Israeli plates. Deftly, they move with the same cautious haste as the workers who sped away only moments before.

Hands in the pockets of his camel-hair coat, Issa moves confidently among the men, chatting to them. 'He is a carpenter from the village,' Issa explains. 'He has done this work for someone in the Ramallah area, but he cannot take the work there himself because the road is sealed. So he has to pay for this man' – pointing to the Israeli van driver – 'to deliver it for him.'

'How much does that cost him?'

'I have asked him and he said it doubles his costs, but he has to work and what can he do? So he has to drive here, unload and reload, and if the army comes they will stop him. That is why they hurry.'

For a closed road, it is an exceptionally busy one. More men lurk near the edge of it, smoking quietly with their eyes on the road. Another car arrives and two of them slip by and drive off. Then a pick-up truck eases itself past the army barrier. With a scramble of spinning wheels it heaves its way onto the Palestinian road and into the village. No sooner than it has gone, than a massive lorry parks up on the highway side with a pneumatic hiss and a metallic squawk. Leaving the engine running, the driver gets out for a cigarette.

'Are you delivering or collecting?' I ask over the rumble of the ticking-over motor.

'Delivering. Dates.'

"What?'

'Dates.' he mimes eating the fruit.

'Ah. OK, dates. How often do you deliver here?'

'Depends – once a week, twice; sometimes once a month.'

'Do you worry about the police?'

'If they come it'll be bad for me, of course.' He shrugs but seems relaxed. It's business as usual at this informal customs point. A grocer's van arrives to collect the dates: both vehicles fling their doors open and, with shrill reversing alarms bleeping wildly, back right up to the blocks, the Israeli lorry practically mounts them. Standing on the barrier between the two vehicles, a man starts loading the dates straight onto the back of the Palestinian van. The grocer waits by the cab, and while his son loads the fruit I ask, 'How is this organised? Who do you organise it with?'

'Simple. I phone the factory where they pack the dates, tell them what I want, give them the time and place, and they send the lorry over.'

'You arrange this with the factory?' I say, amazed that the Israeli company has organised a drop-off at a road block.

'Yes. They are in Tel Aviv. We are dependent on them. And today they put up the price of dates by six shekels a kilo,' he says indignantly. 'Why? Because they can do it and I can do nothing. Last month they put up the price by five shekels. If I complain they say, "Go somewhere else."'

With that, he goes to sign for his fruit, finish the paperwork and get his receipt; like he would for a normal transaction. We stay for a further forty minutes watching cars go, people arrive, lorries unload and pack; we even see an army jeep appear, though it veers away onto the highway at the last moment. Eventually, however, I look at my watch and say to Phil, 'We really should get going.'

'Yes, but what a weird place.'

'OK, let's go,' says Mohammad, clapping his hands together.

'We've got to get to Jerusalem in two days,' I say, pulling out the map.

Phil picks his bag up and says, 'Couldn't we just hitch a lift?'

'Here we definitely could,' says Mohammad. 'Do you want me to ask?'

'No, we have to walk …'

' … and we have to keep to the schedule,' says Mohammad. 'But sometimes things happen. You can't plan everything.'

'One thing I am going to plan,' I reply, 'is that when the next person tells me the Barrier stops suicide bombers, I will tell them how many people I have seen cross into Israel, easily and under the radar.'

'Of course,' says Mohammad. 'If you are determined and desperate enough, you can always get across.'

It occurs to me that suicide bombers might have those qualities.

Each day, a chance encounter yields another story, which is both exciting and frustrating as we are held hostage by the schedule. I worry we will never complete the ramble with the time lost to offers of coffee and the tales told while drinking it. Equally, I regret the stories we have missed, the tales half heard and my ill-mannered haste in the face of hospitality, dashing in panic to reach the day's destination. There are too many times when the momentum of the walk leaves these stories echoing in our footfalls.

From At Tira, we leave the unofficial customs point and the tunnel of waste to catch up with ourselves again. We watch the Barrier tumble over the hills like a roller-coaster, the tarmac and wire riding the bumps in a long, smooth line. One thing is for sure: when this Wall comes down, the Palestinians will have one hell of a skate park on their hands.

We wander by it into Beitunia, a town nearly named after a flower. In this instance, a miss is as good as a mile. Along the valley, a lake sits calmly, flatly, and long, a vast expanse of flood-water between two shores of houses. Field after field is flooded, along with a handful of blackened trees standing leafless and forlorn in their midst, while patches of dark, thin reeds break the water's reflection like stubble.

Across this impromptu lagoon is a single road, raised and somewhat lonely. Mohammad, Phil and I wander across it beneath a sky that is clear and blue after having emptied its contents upon the land. We meander over the path enjoying the eerie sense of space.

Once we are on the opposite shore, we return to the Barrier. We are walking to a village called Rafat to meet a man called Fadhi, who has experienced the situation of not being able to cross the Barrier despite his daughter being ill.

In some ways, this is a story we have half heard on earlier parts of the walk. Back up north, for example, on the first ramble, we heard it when we stayed with the local mayor, in the small village called Anin. His living room had been full of men from the village and I had been sitting next to a charming though frayed-looking and tired man, who had introduced himself as a doctor.

'What happened to your friend in the corner?' I had nodded to a patient on a makeshift bed.

'He was working very high up on a building and he fell and broke his shoulder.'

'Ouch.'

'He is my cousin.'

'Well, he is lucky to have a doctor for a cousin,' I had said, smiling. 'It must be very useful and comforting.'

He had paused expertly before saying, 'I am a gynaecologist.'

'Oh,' I had said, stumped for an instant, but then his warm smile had broken out beneath his moustache, inviting me to laugh. After we had drunk tea, he said, 'We run clinics here, and they have to be good; the hospitals are far away and if there are complications, sometimes women cannot get across the Wall for hospital.' He had paused, and then continued: 'You know, we must be the only place in the world that has three sets of statistics for childbirth.'

'Really?'

'We have figures for home births, hospital births and births at checkpoints.'

'That is astounding,' I had said with genuine shock, but as the evening had run on, and as our start the next morning was early, I had forgotten, among the plethora of other stories, the doctor's words. It was only later, when I checked the statistics from the Red Crescent Society, that they had sunk in. Pregnant women needing hospital treatment on the other side of the Barrier are subject to delays, and often prevented from crossing. Since the beginning of the Second *Intifada* in 2000, more than sixty women have been forced to give birth at checkpoints, with five women and thirty-nine babies dying as a result.

We heard another echo of this story, of how the Barrier affects public health, in Jayyus, the village where the children had been rounded up at night. We had walked to the Barrier where the slopes were steep and rocky, and had met an old man called Osman. He lived twenty metres from the familiar wire and military road, his home perched on the hillside.

'You must come and have tea,' he had said, as he slouched against the wind, his thick, grey hair protruding from under his woollen hat. He was a cracking chap with more smiles than teeth, and hands that were big and worn like tree roots. We had walked down to his hut, which had a corrugated roof covered in rocks to keep it from blowing off, when suddenly soldiers had quickly arrived on the Barrier, metres from us, and shouting, 'What are you doing?'

'I live here,' Osman had shouted back.

'What are they doing?'

'They are having tea with me,' he said, with a dismissive wave of his gnarled hand. After the soldiers departed, we had stood looking at the hills, and Osman had told us: 'This land is my land, and on the other side of the Wall. But if I want to go to work on it I need permission and I have to cross through the agricultural crossing gate, which is a long way from here.' The gates are opened by the army at certain set times: normally, an hour in the morning, shut, and then reopened in the evening. So at certain times and only with permission can Osman use the agricultural crossing gates to work on their own land.

'You know, a few years ago, my father was working on the other side of the Wall. He was eighty-five, and he had permission – he was planting trees and picking olives – and he fell. My older brother saw him; he is metres away but on the other side of the Barrier; what can he do? He can do nothing. My father, he crawled slowly to the gate and asked the soldiers to open it and they refused. They did not open the gate until the official time in the evening. We took him to hospital; he had broken his legs and back.'

'How long was your father waiting before they opened the gate?'

'About three hours.'

I'd forgotten about this story, too, because an hour later I was interviewing a twelve-year-old about his arrest by the army, checking his story with various accounts from around the village and, two days after that, I was home for Christmas. But walking over the tarmac track that runs across the mass of floodwater at Beitunia, I remember these stories as we go in silence. Having left them behind, these tales have caught up with me as we move across the water to the shore, to the Barrier and then on. Our destination is the village of Rafat, on the outskirts of the city of Ramallah, a city home to politicians, NGOs, aid workers and the West Bank's metropolitan elite. As we get nearer to Ramallah, you can sense the disposable income level rise with the increase in billboard sites. The Barrier here reverts to a concrete wall, but Rafat is small and far enough from the city to be a quiet place.

At a typical Palestinian home, a single storey house of not-quite-white stone blocks, Fadhi is waiting for us in a small conservatory attached to its side. The sunlight comes in through the glass and he sits, perched on the sofa, as children hurry to fetch tea. He is a youngish man, a teacher, with glasses and a soft wispy beard.

'So, tell me about your daughter,' I say.

'Well, when she was born there was a problem,' he replies in a soft voice.

'Sorry, but could you speak up a little?'

He mutters slightly flustered, 'Two weeks after she was born, she was transferred to hospital in Jerusalem. It was very bad; the doctor said she was in a serious condition and she might die. But I was not allowed to see her. They would not let me cross the checkpoint to get to the hospital in Jerusalem.'

'How did you feel about that?'

His eyes widen and Fadhi shakes his head. 'I was so worried I couldn't work, I couldn't eat. For fifteen days she was in hospital.'

'Did you apply for permission?'

'Yes, of course. Now my daughter is six months old and still has to go to hospital; I have applied five times to the authorities and they have refused each time. I even went for a meeting with Israeli intelligence and still they refused to give permission.'

'She still has to go to hospital ...?'

'Once a month, at least.'

'Who takes her?'

'My wife, but she has to get a permit to get through the check-point each time.'

Sitting on the edge of the sofa, Fadhi beckons me to drink. Tea has arrived, brought out by one of his other children, a six-year-old boy who stands straight and silent, holding an oversized tray that is covered in small glasses full of steaming tea. He stands patiently as he has no doubt been told to do so. Like any father of a newborn, Fadhi looks tired but he flashes the child a small smile. His story is a small tale, one of many.

After tea the urgency of our schedule dictates we leave. Farewells are exchanged and hands shaken, and once again I leave too hastily. Later, I find out that the international NGO *Medicin du Monde* estimates one-third of the villages in the West Bank do not have open and free access to medical facilities.

As we return to the Barrier to follow its path into the city, I say to Phil and Mohammad, 'You know what gets me? That all of this is done in the name of security.'

'Ah, they call it security, yes,' says Mohammad.

Well I reckon they are right. Because when you make kids walk through tunnels of human shit and stop a father seeing his sick baby, then I reckon you will probably need that security.

chapter 16
SINLESS AND CASTING

Have you ever wondered what a militarised meat-packing plant might look like? No? Nor me, to be honest, but on the off-chance anyone should ask, point them in the direction of the biggest checkpoint on the West Bank, Qalandiya.

'If you want to get into East Jerusalem at that checkpoint, allow yourself between forty minutes to an hour to cross,' Palestinian friends had told me, although they could have added, 'Prepare for the crush, don't take anything more fragile than a brick, and make sure you floss, out of politeness.'

The main street from Ramallah leads to the concrete watch-tower, splattered with paint and scorch marks, that overlooks the queues of traffic into the checkpoint and the massive shed through which most have to cross by foot. Inside, Palestinians press into numbered pens, each with a single caged turnstile at one end allowing one person through at a time to have their ID checked and belongings scanned.

I work my way into a pen and hover at the edge of the fray. When the light above the turnstile turns green, a buzzer sounds, and everyone heaves forward. I am instantly pulled into the crush. The light returns to red again and folk reassemble their limbs at the appropriate angles. We are all wedged against each other, pressed into a close proximity that is somewhere between a January sale and sex. I spend much of the next forty minutes looking at a builder's face. He is taller than I am, with two missing upper incisors, a lot of ear hair and a Real Madrid bobble hat. At one point, the warmth of this squeezed mass makes me sleepy and I rest my head on his chest for a second, before snapping bolt upright, reddening, muttering 'Sorry' and checking his fleece for drool. Just near the bars of the caged turnstile the builder and I are forced to separate. I find my torso going in one direction and my legs in another, caught awkwardly between two people and the gate. A young man kindly eases himself out of the way to allow me through, twisting to make room for me and therefore forfeiting his place. It is a moment of civility in the enforced brutishness of the checkpoint. 'Thank you,' I say to him in English and Arabic.

He nods his head politely and says, 'You are British?'

'Yes,' I reply to his face, barely six inches from my own.

Smiling warmly, he says, 'Are you aware of the Balfour Declaration ...'

'I'm Scottish! I'm Scottish!' I cry, but it is too late.

Waiting for us on the other side of the checkpoint are Fred and Itamar, who we walked with earlier in Ariel. They are nice folk, but frankly neither of them look good on paper. Itamar is ex-army and an obsessive *Monty Python* fan and I can see why, for some, the only thing worse than an ex-Israeli soldier is an ex-Israeli soldier who constantly says, 'He's not the Messiah, he's a very naughty boy.' Fred runs an alternative tour guide company, a good one too, but before that he was a street act, a juggler. Let me tell you, people: juggling is the hobby of the friendless. It is watched by the dull and performed by the more dull; the only form of entertainment where the performer has less creative imagination than the audience. There is no oxymoron quite like 'circus skills'; none comes close, not 'civil war', 'progressive cuts' or even 'supermodel'.

Fortunately, Fred and Itamar are better in the flesh and it is a good two hours into the walk before anyone says, '"We are the knights who say 'Ni'."'

The journey today will go from the Palestinian side of the Barrier, to the Israeli side, and then back again. Leaving Qalandiya, we come into East Jerusalem and skirt the Palestinian area of

Ar Ram, the homes of which are all painted white with black water tanks on them. The road follows the Barrier here, and cuts left and right in short, sharp bursts. The demarcation lines, too, are close here and, at a set of crossroads, the area changes from a Palestinian neighbourhood into an Israeli settlement. In a matter of metres, houses turn from white to brick brown; *hijabs* give way to wigs; and graffiti turns from Arabic to Hebrew.

One good thing about illegal Israeli settlements is that the bigger ones normally have decent bakeries, and we wander into the nearest shopping precinct in search of one. The settlement of Newe Ya'akov was until recently known as an area where new immigrants came to settle, though there is an increasing ultra-orthodox presence. These are not rich folk so we don't expect a lavish affair in the precinct; nor do we get it. We find a grocer: a purveyor of unmemorable croissants and fine scowls. As we leave the shop he says loudly, 'After we kick out the Arabs, we should throw out the rubbish.'

'I think they mean us,' I say to Phil. 'I think we're the rubbish.'

'Maybe. Or he could just be an eco-racist.'

'Green racists? "Recycle Prejudice, Fuck the Arabs"?'

'Bigotry recycling!'

'That's the only kind there is, Phil.'

'You would need to have different bins, though; one where you put your homophobia, one for misogyny and one for racism ...'

'Those could be different colours.'

'They would have to be.'

'But there'll always someone who'll put their misogyny and homophobia in the racism bin.'

'That'll be the orthodox.'

'Or the fundamentalists.'

Leaving the precinct, we skirt the settlement along clean kerbs, passing apartment blocks and peering drivers, along kindergarten playgrounds wrapped in barbed wire and on, to parkland. A track veers from the road onto a strip of woodland where a group of hyrax sit on some rubble, looking at us. These are odd rodents: bigger than a guinea pig and smaller than a hare, they look like a rat got lucky with a rabbit. We take a moment to return their stare before we move on through the footpaths along the edge of pine glades. A few folk are out tramping the path, too. In tracksuits and trainers, they look like they have been told to walk by their doctor, and move with a begrudging stride.

The paths soon give way to hills and after a gentle hike to the top of the hill, Itamar unpacks his coffee pot and gas stove to make proper Arabic coffee, while we look over the Barrier, now concrete, in the near distance. While he boils the water, he tells us about the first time he killed a man, which is not something you normally hear from a Caffé Nero barista. In the army, Itamar had shot a Palestinian in a fire fight. Crawling past the body, he had said to himself: 'I should look at his face; I should at least remember the face of the man I killed.'

'What did he look like?' I ask him.

'Oh, I don't remember – some guy with a moustache. But I remember thinking I should remember.'

'Is that what you envisaged when you were conscripted?'

'Yes, pretty much. I envisaged not only killing but being distraught as a consequence, being emotionally damaged by my actions. We would watch *Platoon* and *Fourth of July* all the time.'

'Really?'

'Yes, really. That's the Zionist left for you; always fighting and crying.'

'You really envisaged all of this before you joined?'

'Yes. I also thought it would help get me girls, too.'

'Seriously?'

'Yes, it is true. I thought they would be attracted to the masculinity and the emotional damage. And it works sometimes, too; mainly with international girls,' says Itamar, in a matter-of-fact way. Then, pondering, he adds, 'But I'm working on that.'

*

Much has changed in our surroundings over the past two days and it's not just the cessation of the rain: we have moved from rural fields to urban alleyways, and the Barrier has changed from barbed wire and electric fences to the grey concrete slabs familiar to the world's collective imagination. However, in Jerusalem's municipal sprawl you can move through communities and changes in the space of a corner or a matter of steps. Today has seen us move through Palestinian areas in East Jerusalem into illegal Israeli settlements, back across the Barrier at Hizma and finally following the concrete line of the Barrier into the Palestinian town of Anata. This is where we meet Wael, a Palestinian friend of Itamar's.

Wael is a rounding man; he's short, too, and has cropped black hair cut close to his skull, with a pair of killer '77 sunglasses perched on it. Wael has bright, white, clean trainers and a smile as wry as it is warm. Above all else, he has presence, in spades; it is entirely complimentary when I say he's a little bit punk rock.

'Come, I will walk with you round the Wall,' he says, as if it is his (Wael tells me his family lost some 101 *dunams* of land when it was confiscated by the Israeli authorities, so he does have a claim to some of it).

The Barrier is close by here, built right next to the town's homes. Anata spills from the top of a hill but never gets far down the slopes before the Barrier catches it, constricting it in a concrete grip that seems to almost physically force the apartment buildings up into the air. On the rise above the Barrier, there is a clear view of the concrete structure curving along the valley ridge, tilting and twisting along the roll of the hills, but always running tight to Anata's homes, hemming them in. Just over the other side is a valley, an empty expanse stretching down the hill from the concrete, all the way across to the illegal settlement of Pisgat Ze'ev.

'I have asked Israeli officials, "Why does the Barrier come so close to the houses of Anata; why is it not in the valley?"'

'What did they say?' asks Wael.

'They said this route was for security.'

Wael snorts, 'Huh! If I had my machine gun I could shoot any settler in Pisgat Ze'ev from here. It is absolutely not for security; it is to steal the land.'

Wael's use of the word 'my' in reference to the words 'machine gun' is curious. But I am nearly certain he doesn't actually have one. Very nearly.

We walk into the gully, the slim space between the back end of Anata's outlying homes and the Barrier. To our right are the concrete slabs of the Barrier itself, about eight metres tall, each with a round hole at the top where the crane hooks lowered each section into place. The ground next to the Barrier is just rough concrete poured for the foundations – rather than having any thoughts for a pedestrian thoroughfare in mind – but it creates a passageway with room to walk two abreast, rarely more. The town's steep slopes are immediately to our left. We have entered a ravine, caught between the hillside and the Barrier, and it's soon apparent that the only way out is to walk the entire length of it.

The slopes of Anata are steep, sometimes sheer, cliffs, covered in tall weeds, shrubs and debris. Rocks scatter the sides, sewage pipes appear from nowhere to run down the length of the hill, and half-finished apartments top the hill's horizon in complementary concrete grey. Rubbish is everywhere.

'This is like a no-man's land,' I say.

'It is,' laughs Wael. 'This is the first time I have been to the Wall in Anata. People do not come here. It is ugly and miserable.'

Mere metres later the gully fills with the stench of sewage and the rocks give way to a blanket of mud and shit, which lies pristine, smooth and shiny; an uncracked bed of crap drying in the sun. The mud is more firm directly against the Barrier and Fred, clutching his rolled umbrella, tiptoes on the compact shit, his circus skills coming into their own. Wael and I are caught on the other side of the gully, but find a sea of plastic bottles in the ocean of crap to use as stepping stones. Coke bottles, turps bottles, green ones, clear ones, one litre, two litres, ones with handles on the side, bleach bottles, water bottles, bottle tops and bottle caps all crunch and fold as we scurry and lollop over them.

'Wael,' I start, when we are safely on concrete again, 'you are involved in Combatants for Peace …'

'I am a founder!'

'So you were a combatant, a fighter?'

'Yes,' he explains. 'First, we as a people have a right to fight the occupation: this is under international law; the right to defend yourself, and to fight to liberate your land and people.'

It comes as little surprise that Wael treads lightly on the theory and, it transpires, did actually have a machine gun, or at least trained with one. In 1990, he was arrested attempting to blow up an Israeli police station with a car bomb.

'There was a massacre. An Israeli soldier, he lined up seven Palestinians and killed them. It was a massacre. I was so angry. I talked to my commander. I said we have to do something to teach the Israelis our Palestinian blood is not so cheap. We cannot do nothing. I told him, "I can put a car bomb beside the government quarters."' He was caught at the Allenby Bridge moving equipment to make the bomb.

'Do you regret trying to plant the car bomb?'

'I would be a liar if I said I was sorry. I chose that target because it was not civilian: all of them are police or security services, no civilians, and if you are going to fight, you have to fight others who are armed.'

'So do you think those people who target children with suicide bombs are terrorists?'

'Absolutely, yes. We are against terrorism: it is not of our religion, it is not our tradition.'

'Does the subject get debated much in Palestinian society?'

'Yes, of course.' He sounds mildly surprised that I might think it's not. 'If there is bombing in a nightclub, for example, some might say the bomber is *shahid*, a martyr, but I say, "No, he is a terrorist; he is going to kill civilians!"' Wael repeats his conviction:

'If you have an armed struggle, you have to fight people who are armed … Until now. Now we chose a non-violent way to get our freedom.'

We walk for a moment in silence, both using sticks to press on as the gully moves uphill. An armchair sits in the middle of the concrete path with shards of broken glass scattered around it. A makeshift ladder is leaning against the Barrier. Walking under it, Wael says, 'For sixty-five years we have been fighting each other, and our blood and Israeli blood is still running, so we have to be a little bit wise to end the conflict.'

Above us, kids have appeared on the ridges. Standing over us, looking down as we wander along the gully, they are following us, running ahead, disappearing behind boulders only to pop up later, sometimes higher, sometimes nearer, but always there.

The conversation moves on to Combatants for Peace, the campaigning group of ex-Israeli soldiers and ex-Palestinian fighters, where Wael and Itamar met.

'I met Itamar at the third ever meeting,' says Wael.

'No, I wasn't at that one,' replies Itamar, who is alongside us. 'You are thinking of my brother.'

'His two brothers are founders of Combatants for Peace, too,' Wael says, smiling and shrugging at his own confusion. 'I heard about the second ever meeting from friends: I said to them, "Where are you going?" and they said, "To meet Israeli soldiers!" I thought they were mad but I went to the next meeting.'

A pebble hits the Barrier behind us, then another lands with a hollow clack, clicking eerily along the rough concrete.

'Hey,' Wael shouts up at the ridge above us, then calls out in Arabic till a handful of kids walk to the edge and with some trepidation make themselves known. When another pebble scuttles by, Wael calls out again, and two of the smallest children point at someone over the brow. A sheepish child joins the others, dropping a stone from his hand as he does so. They must be nine years old, at most.

'They think you will bring soldiers to them by walking here,' says Wael.

'Will we?'

'No,' he says with confidence, and he calls to the kids who are still following us. They have moved down the hill to be nearer to us, and are listening to our conversation.

Itamar gets us back to the first Combatants for Peace meetings, where Israeli and Palestinian fighters gathered to discuss the conflict. 'It was very strange,' he says. 'You are going to meet someone who was ready to kill you. You're going to shake hands with him.'

'"You are crazy meeting Israelis!"' says Wael, mimicking his friends' initial disapproval. 'But that third meeting ran for three hours. We are enemies from military backgrounds but we found a chance to sit down and talk peace.'

Suddenly, with an almighty *crack!* a rock slams into the Barrier behind Phil, then one above Fred. Instinctively we duck, looking in panic at the hillside. *Crack!* Another lands.

'Watch out,' someone calls.

'What the fuck?'

Crack! Crack!

'Up there,' points Itamar.

At the very top of the ridge, standing on the roof of a half-built house, four masked youths, much older than those nearby, are hurling rocks at us.

'Don't run, and keep your eyes on the rocks!' shouts Itamar.

Crack!

The rooftop is a distance up the hill and the height gives the rocks incredible velocity. These are no pebbles; these are big, the size of a fist. But the distance gives us about three seconds to spot the rock, see its trajectory and dodge it.

'Fucking hell,' I shout, thinking if one connects it will take someone's head off. There is nowhere to go. We are trapped in the gully. All we can do is huddle on.

Suddenly, the air fills with even more black shapes flying towards us.

Crack! Crack! Crack! Phil runs for cover.

'Stay calm,' calls Fred.

To my astonishment, Wael is standing upright, holding his arms out like a prophet, clutching his walking stick and shouting at the stone throwers.

'What are you doing, I am a Palestinian! These are our guests!'

By way of reply, the air fills again as the youths redouble their efforts and still Wael stands, moving slightly this way and telling them off, berating them as an elder spokesman. Like I said, the man has presence.

'Keep walking,' says Fred, and he calmly leads us out of the immediate range of the stones. I am as terrified as it is possible to be without physically shaking.

'I'm sorry about that,' says Wael, when we are clear. 'They probably thought you were the secret police or the army. But you must judge the situation, not them.'

Lying, I agree, saying, 'I don't judge them.' But of course I do. There have been many discussions about stone throwing on the walk. Mohammad with the goatee beard had said, 'A stone is a symbolic gesture of our struggle,' just as the Israeli anarchists at Bil'in had said stone throwing was unarmed resistance. But for all the symbolism and theory, it is simply fucking terrifying being on the receiving end of them. One of those stones could have easily split a head open, and we could not have escaped or called in medical help. It is entirely possible someone could have had a serious injury or died. So fuck the little bastards.

Then something occurs to me. When Wael went to meet the Israeli soldiers it must have been a real moment for him: going to meet the people who had killed his comrades and might even have tried to have killed him. So while I judge the stone-throwing youths, he is clearly the bigger man.

Some ten metres ahead, Fred and Itamar are surrounded by the younger kids, who have come down from the slopes and are now gabbling and playing around the tour guide and the ex-Israeli soldier.

'Jesus, it's like the Pied Piper over there,' I say to Phil.

'I don't know what they are doing, but as long as the kids stay around us, the older ones won't risk ambushing us again,' he says.

As we walk on, both of us keep a wary eye on the hills. Up in the slopes, a broken pipe flows as a sewage waterfall, cascading down ledges, burbling over stones, down gulches and falling through broken metal frames. The sides of the waterfall are marked by tatty shreds of plastic hanging forlornly from discarded wire and branches.

'So I joined Combatants for Peace, and our main goals are to end the Occupation and for a Palestinian state to be built along the 1967 border. This is what the PLO wanted, but this time we are doing it with non-violent methods. This is different. Before, it was the armed struggle, but we learn from the Indian experience and the South African experience; they use the non-violent way and they succeed.'

'And those who want another *intifada*? The kids?'

'We try to convince them that the non-violent way is more effective.'

The walk ends by a checkpoint, right by Shufat refugee camp, and the kids drift off. We say our thanks and farewells to Wael, promising to keep in contact. His shades have not moved a millimetre, though his trainers are not quite as white as they were at the start. When he departs with his rock and roll presence, he leaves me with a tiny crush on him.

Dusk has begun to fall and the camp's street lights start to glimmer, and we all start to relax a bit. I say to Itamar, 'You know, when we were being stoned, I did feel for the Israeli soldiers who have to face that.'

'They *are* protected, with helmets and shields.' He smiles.

'Yes, but one of those things could cause serious damage.'

'And they do, but the soldiers have much more fire power. Plus they are better equipped and better trained. Don't feel too sorry for them.'

'What do you think stopped them chucking the rocks?' asks Phil.

'Well, in part it was Wael and in part we walked out of range ...' I begin.

'But they could easily have run along to another place and started again. We were completely trapped, we were sitting ducks,' interrupts Phil.

'It was because the younger kids were walking with us. They wouldn't risk hitting one of the younger children,' says Fred.

'It was nearly *Life of Brian*,' Itamar says, then in a falsetto voice declares, '"Stone him! Stone him!"'

Turning to Fred, I say, 'Well done for keeping them walking with you. Seriously, it was amazing. I mean, they walked all that way.'

'You know what kept them interested?' asks Fred.

'No.'

He picks up three pebbles and throws them into a cascade. 'Juggling. Kids love juggling.'

'My God,' says Phil, 'you've been saved by juggling.'

PART THREE
JERUSALEM AND
THE FINAL DAYS

ODEH

*Odeh Salameh waits on the busy main road to guide us to his home.
He is easy to spot in a crowd: he is six foot five inches tall, dressed in
a neat and orderly manner with a pen in the top pocket of his shirt.
While he laughs, he sways slightly from side to side like Ray Charles
when he sings.*

*He leads us through light, clean lanes and alleys, past halted foot-
ball games that resume once we're through, to his apartment block
near the Barrier.*

'Here,' he says, at the front steps.

*I know little of Odeh's case, save it is to do with maps and bound-
aries, so insert the sum total of my knowledge into one sentence: 'Your
house is on the edge of some boundary lines ...'*

'This is the problem right here,' he says, pointing to the lane we
have just walked down. 'Between these two buildings runs the
Jerusalem municipal boundary. If you look at the map, it will show
you the boundary line comes up to the doorsteps here.'

'Even though it is on the West Bank side of the Wall?'

'Yes. The Wall went over it.' *So, on this occasion, the Barrier has
trapped a small bit of Jerusalem on the West Bank side.*

'Therefore, technically, I am standing in Jerusalem now.'

'Yes,' *smiles Odeh, allowing himself a chuckle and a sway.*

'So where does the boundary line run from here, then?'

'Straight through this part,' he says, turning to point to the side
of his apartment block. 'The balcony, the living room and part of the
dining room are in Jerusalem as they are over the municipal line...'

'And the rest of the apartment?'

' ... the toilet, kitchen and bedrooms are in the West Bank.'

'So part of your home is in Israel, but you only have a West Bank
ID card?'

'Yes.'

'Well, I can see that's a problem when you want to watch TV ...'

As the Israeli authorities are not known for their laissez-faire attitude, I ask, 'What did the Israelis do?' with a certain sense of dread.

The police and army raided the apartment block one night and charged everyone with the crime of illegally entering Israel. For using their family living rooms.

'Because you went to the living room!'

'And the dining room.'

'They raided you!'

'And the balcony in the summer.'

'What did they say?'

'They said we need permission to enter Israel and we should apply for permission to the Israeli authorities.'

' To use your own living room!'

'They showed us the court documents that said we were illegal.'

'Court documents?'

'Yes.'

Court documents? That must mean an Israeli judge (and I use the term loosely) saw a map of the boundary line and the Barrier and thought, 'The cunning bastards! Sneaking into Israel under the cover of a house!' and signed the court papers.

'There are eight families in the apartment block,' says Odeh. 'The police arrested about one hundred and twenty of us and took us to the station. We were interviewed separately and they wanted me to sign a piece of paper saying I was living in Israel illegally. They were saying that I should leave.'

'What did you do?'

'I didn't sign, and so after twenty-four hours they released me but they said, "OK, we don't care; we shall put it on the computer that you entered Israel illegally."'

'What does that mean for you?'

'I work in Jerusalem and have a permit to get across the checkpoint. But when I came to renew it the authorities refused, saying, "You have illegally entered Israel." The police had put it on the main

ODEH

computer. So I was not allowed permission. And this was not just for me, but others in the building, too.'

'So the police put a group of you on the computer?'

'Yes, so we could not go to work in Jerusalem. But I have to look after my family, so we had to get a lawyer to go to court and get it taken off the computer. It cost $1,000 and took six months to change it, all so I can get a permit to go to work.' He shrugs and smiles and says, 'Come, we should go inside for tea.'

Nationalist Israelis will be pleased to know the living room is the best room in the house. The coffee table is decorated with an embroidered white cloth and an ornate fruit bowl. The display cupboards boast tea sets behind their glass fronts, and the sofa has cushions that are plumped to perfection. It is a delightful place to sit with Odeh while he rifles through a box file holding his family's paperwork: deeds of ownership of land now taken; notices from the government of land expropriated; and the usual certificates children collect. The kids politely fetch and carry trays, then silently join us on the sofa, which I have a suspicion might be in part of the room that sits in the West Bank.

After tea and thanks, we exit the living room and Israel, enter the West Bank at the toilet, re-enter Israel via the dining room, go into the West Bank at the stairwell, return to Israel at the doorsteps and are back in the West Bank by the end of the lane.

chapter 17
OUR MAN

The British Consul General in East Jerusalem, the aptly named Richard Makepeace, has agreed to come for a walk along the route of the Barrier. 'Sounds like a good idea,' he said. In order to make time for us in his schedule, we are to meet at the British Consulate, drive to the start of the walk, walk the route, and then the Consul General will be picked up at the finishing point and whisked back to his diplomatic duties.

Phil and I, not entirely knowing what to expect, arrive at the appointed time and wait with security until Richard Makepeace walks through the door. He could not be anything but British, and the appellation 'Our Man in Jerusalem' is tailor-made to fit. In a jacket bordering on a blazer and with a British accent that can only be described as 'formal wear', Richard Makepeace shakes our hands, says, 'Right then, let's be off,' and cheerfully leads us outside, adding, 'I thought we'd take the Consular car.'

The 'Consular car' is a silver, chauffer-driven, armour-plated BMW with tinted, bullet-proof windows and a small Union Jack flying at the bonnet. It is enormous, must weigh a ton figuratively and literally, and in it we stand no chance of blending in anywhere except at a Bond villain car rally. On the plus side no one is going to cut us up and if they did we would barely notice: we might hear a faint metallic crump but would just keep gliding onwards. Getting in and sliding onto one of the back seats, I would be lying if I said I wasn't just a teensy bit excited and I whisper to Phil, 'I've got armchairs smaller than this.'

'My sofa is smaller than this,' he says, bouncing slightly.

'It is very expensive,' says the driver. 'Very expensive.'

'Welcome to the Consulate,' says Richard Makepeace, climbing into the back with us. 'You'll note this is a Consulate not an Embassy,' he adds, 'as that would recognise Israel as having legal sovereignty over East Jerusalem. Though we do hope one day that this will be the Embassy for a future Palestinian state. Right then, we should go.'

The car pulls out and roars into the Jerusalem traffic with the Union Jack fluttering before us. This is not what I had expected at all. Diplomats, in the popular imagination – or mine, at least – are people who avoid causing offence; they are discreet, tactful people, they are mannered, they are ... diplomatic. So the Consul General's willingness to talk so directly is confounding.

'Jerusalem is unique, even in my line of business,' he says. 'Normally every ambassador goes and presents their credentials to a government. I don't. I can't present credentials to the government of Israel because we don't regard the government of Israel as sovereign in law over Jerusalem, and there isn't a government for a Palestinian state with sovereignty in Jerusalem.'

The UN's plans for the partition of Palestine and the creation of Israel in 1947 originally designated Jerusalem as a *corpus separatum* – an international city under UN control. However, the Arab-Israeli War of 1948, which followed Israel's declaration of independence, saw the city bitterly fought over and the 1949 Armistice Agreement divided the city into a Jewish area, West Jerusalem, and an Arab area, East Jerusalem, under Jordanian rule. The situation remained like that until the Six Day War in 1967 when Israel captured East Jerusalem from Jordan and 'reunified' it or, to be more technically correct, annexed it

The word 'annex' sounds innocent enough but it derives from the Latin *annexus* meaning 'to nick'. I made that up. The word is actually a formal legal term for taking over someone else's territory and incorporating it into your own: highly organised, ideologically motivated nicking. The international community do not recognise

Israel as the rightful government of East Jerusalem and to emphasise the point, the Consular General adds, 'Every country's
embassy in Israel remains in Tel Aviv, which is clearly a very strong
international recognition of the legality of the situation here.'

I nod sagely as if he is repeating something I have oft thought
myself. But while this may seem obscure, it is significant, as it
shows how the rest of the world officially sees Israel's take-over
of East Jerusalem: as a take-over.

We move through the traffic or rather the traffic moves around
us, and quickly we leave the city for the narrower village roads,
where cars stop completely and wait for us to pass.

'There was a book festival in East Jerusalem,' I begin, turning
to the Consul General, 'in 2009, I think?'

'Oh, yes, it was a writers' festival. The year Jerusalem was Arab
Capital of Culture. The Israelis decided this was not acceptable so
they closed down the book fair.'

'I heard you held the fair in the gardens of the British
Consulate. Is that right?'

'Well, the opening ceremony was held by the French and the
closing one held in the British Consulate, yes,' agrees Richard
Makepeace. The idea of hosting a banned book fair in the
Consulate's gardens is joyously British. It may not make up for
the Balfour Declaration but the notion of cucumber sandwiches
and discussions about dissident literature over the azaleas conjures
up a national image of fair play and subversion that is frequently
lost and often merely mythical. 'British writers who came out for
the event were left wondering what threat was posed to Israel by
a book fair and readings from children's books, among other
things,' he muses wryly.

Crossing to the Palestine side of the Barrier at a fly-blown
checkpoint south of Jerusalem, we leave the soldiers staring after
the diplomat's car as it pulls away to join us later. In a matter of
minutes we are in the hills, and once again I am forced to stop
by the sheer wonder of them. It is impossible not to think them

glorious, impossible to stop your gaze being drawn into the sky's endless blue and lose yourself for a moment. It almost feels rude when we break the silence.

'Everyone thought I was crazy when I came here because I was so excited ... because of the hills,' says the Consul General as we take a moment to marvel. 'It was the idea of vistas like this. Every house has a view.'

'Do you get out walking much?'

'Not nearly as much as I would like. But I have just about fulfilled my ambition, to wander around the old city without getting lost. I spent one very wet Christmas with a tattered guide-book. But it paid off.'

As the British Consul General to 'those parts known as East and West Jerusalem, the West Bank and Gaza', Richard Makepeace is a fluent Arabic speaker and clearly loves the place. It also transpires that this charming and precise man has a sense of humour drier than the Swiss Navy. I mentioned that I thought Palestinians 'naturally regard their politicians in much the same manner as we regard ours', to which he replied, 'Absolutely,' paused perfectly and added, ' ... with deep respect.' At times it seems as if he just can't help himself offering insights and thoughts, is happy to discuss the growing non-violent movement on the Palestinian side and the importance of 'nation building', and shares his observations freely: 'I am very often asked questions about who are the moderates and who are the extremists,' he says, as he walks with his hands behind his back. 'I say, "I am not sure these are different people." If someone has just pointed a gun at your child at a check-point you're probably feeling pretty extreme as you drive into the office. Maybe by the afternoon, with some good news on how they've done at school, you're in a more longer-term frame of mind.' Most of all we talk about Jerusalem, trying to answer the simple question of why Jerusalem is so important.

'Well, it is particularly the competition over the holy site, the *al-Haram al-Sharif* according to the Muslim narrative, and the

Temple Mount according to the Jewish narrative,' muses Our Man. 'It is the competition for Jerusalem between Islam and Judaism which I think has made it such a touchstone for conflict over the years, and it still is. When there is violence in Jerusalem, it has that additional quality.'

'A totemic quality?'

'Exactly; it touches very deep, deep religious beliefs. If something happens in the holy site in Jerusalem it is seen throughout not just the Arab world but around the Islamic world.'

Coming to a particularly steep path down, a goat track full of loose stones and scree, we contemplate the options before us. 'Hang on a second, I'll try and find you a stick,' I say, as I start to look among some bushes.

'Don't worry, I'll survive,' he says. Then, chuckling, quips, 'Famous last words. At this point HM Consul General goes tumbling down the hill ... I'll say I was pushed, of course.'

Phil and I descend slowly, sideways, using the length of our boots for greater grip, and hiking poles to control our speed and stop us falling. The British Consul General, meanwhile, in blazer and gold-rimmed Ray-Bans, hands still clasped behind him, calmly leans back, aims straight down the path and perambulates gently to its end admiring the view.

We stop for a moment. 'Water?'

'No, thanks ... oh, actually, it is pretty hot so I'll take a little. Thank you.'

'So Jerusalem ...'

The Consul General passes the bottle back and says, 'I just don't see stability in the region without a state of Palestine ... Palestine is quoted by everybody, whether it is Tehran or Afghanistan or Pakistan or indeed the UK, as an example of the failure of international action, of the fact that the Occupation continues. The issue will remain a running sore internationally until there is a just solution.'

'OK, but why is Jerusalem so important, in terms of any kind of peace process?'

'The two most difficult issues for both parties are refugees and Jerusalem. Refugees because it involves some sort of assessment being made of what actually happened in 1948: how did these Palestinian refugees come to be refugees?[27] And Jerusalem, well, I don't think anyone internationally believes that there is going to be a Palestinian state without a capital in East Jerusalem. And clearly there are very many on the Israeli side who seem to think a solution can be reached without any concession on the city. A few years ago, Israel celebrated the fortieth anniversary of the "Unification of Jerusalem", as they put it. Israel is just not thinking in terms of an occupation any longer.'

'So one side doesn't accept they are an occupying force.'

'Exactly. Israel has staked out their claim to Jerusalem in a way they haven't done anywhere else in the West Bank.'

Over valleys, up steep climbs, under trees and through groves we wander. Through villages where the Consul General chats in fluent Arabic with inquisitive drivers who stop alongside us, or to politely turn down offers of coffee from Palestinians whose homes we pass. Finally, we come to our arranged meeting point where the silver car sits waiting for us.

'Thanks for walking with us,' I say to the Consul General.

'Oh, a pleasure. I would happily do it again.'

'I've found it a genuinely enlightening walk.'

'I'll give you a lift over the checkpoint if you'd like,' he offers.

Speaking from this experience, I can vouch that there is only one way to approach an Israeli checkpoint in the Occupied Territories. That is, in a silver, bullet-proof BWM with the Union Jack flying at the bonnet. The soldiers start staring from 150 metres away.

'Now, because the windows are bullet-proof they don't open, so you have to hold your ID up at the window,' says the Consul General.

Slowing to a halt we press our passports up against the window and watch the soldiers gawp before waving us through. It is tempting to shout, 'Yaarghhhh!' and do the wanker sign. But I settle on sitting back and humming 'A Modern Major General' from *The Pirates of Penzance*.

There are many occasions when the UK government's behaviour makes me hang my head, like selling military equipment to Israel[28] or refusing to condemn Israel's actions in the Security Council of the UN. But I remember the conversation about the banned book fair in the Consulate garden, and the odd sensation I had while discussing it. Initially I thought the swelling feeling was indigestion, but then I realised it was in fact an emotional feeling, one of rightness and belonging. It was, it turns out, a passing moment of national pride. *Bloody hell*, I thought. *This is what patriotism feels like. I had forgotten.* One of the fantastic things about individual identity is that some of it is set while much of it changes, but we always have a degree of choice about who we are. So today I'm not going to be English, not a Londoner nor even a South Londoner. Today I am going to be British. Just to give it a go. Who knows, I might be a moderate by the afternoon.

chapter 18
SHEIKH JARRAH

Back in East Jerusalem! And not a moment too soon. Phil and I have had quite enough of each other. We have walked, eaten and slept together for far too long; often in conditions so cramped I've seen things even doctors wince at. Don't get me wrong, we're not splitting up, but there's only so many times you can watch someone scrub their smalls in travel wash before the magic starts wearing off. At the start of the ramble, we had been eager to accommodate and compromise, but now everything is annoying: he doesn't shave, can't tie his boots correctly and he breathes funny, too.

'No offence,' Phil says. 'But maybe we should start walking with other people.'

'We just need some time apart,' I agree.

We have fallen behind with our plans and need to reorganise, so will stay in East Jerusalem for a few days. I can make a new schedule, coordinate the final push south, sort out walkers, translators, beds, route logistics and assessments, and Phil can go anywhere I am not. He can find a bar or go to Tel Aviv; he can do nearly anything as there are a lot of places where I am not.

In truth, reorganising is only one factor in the decision to stay in East Jerusalem. The other is the chance to stay in a hotel. I have fixated on this luxury for the past week now, unable to even utter the word 'hotel' without sounding like Barry White. So, Phil might say, 'I'm looking forward to East Jerusalem,' and I would respond, 'Oh, yeah. I'm gonna be in a hoe-tell, that's right, baby. All. Night.

Long. A hoe-tell, baby, like I said I would.' This would then roll into a tuneless rendition of the great man's classic, '"I'm qualified to satisfy you ... In any way you want me too."'

'Shut up, shut up,' Phil would laugh. Although I think I may be imagining his laughter.

The hotel, run by a Palestinian family, is friendly, clean and quirky. Bolted to the corridor wall, right by my room, is a small loudspeaker that constantly pipes out music; not just any old hotel lobby music, oh no, this plays ambient harp music. Relaxation music! Is there any music more infuriating than relaxation music? Never in my dullest dreams have I imagined I might ever have to phone a hotel reception at 2 a.m. and shout, 'Can you kill the bloody harp, please!' But despite the New Age tinkling, the place is perfect and I have got exactly what I wanted: privacy. The chance to sit alone in a room each evening, not listening to anyone else's voice and best of all not hearing my own. The harp is small beer.

The days are spent in cafés and offices with a cast of activists, NGOs, guides and Nava the Israeli fixer; meetings are attended, coffee is drunk, maps are toiled over and a new schedule rises from the ashes of the old.

'I need to speak to more Israelis,' I say to Nava over yet more coffee

'You have the meeting with the commander of the Border Police ...'

'We need the mayor of Jerusalem.'

'He won't interview.'

'Could we ask again?'

'Mark, don't you follow the news?' Nava crossly rattles through her reasoning: 'The vice-president of the US visits Israel tomorrow. An official visit. In Israel, this is big news. Israel wants to keep building settlements; the US wants Israel to stop, to keep the settlement freeze. So what does the mayor of Jerusalem do? He announces that 1,600 new homes will be built in East Jerusalem. Just before the visit.'

'This is exactly why I need to talk him.'

'Mark! The whole world wants to talk to him. Bibi Netanyahu can't get an interview with the mayor! You think he will say, "Wait a minute, Bibi, wait a minute Mr Vice-President, I have first to talk to a comedian from Britain"? Mark, the mayor is a little bit too busy right now to talk to you.'

'Oh, sure, he'll use that excuse ...'

We might not have the mayor or indeed any muncipal official to interview, but we can visit the heart of Israel's plans for East Jerusalem. Tomorrow, we are going to see Sheikh Jarrah, a Palestinian district elevated, by the fate of twenty-eight homes, to status of international *cause célèbre*. It is the epicentre of Jewish settlers' attempts to demographically transform the predominantly Palestinian city of East Jerusalem into an Israeli city, a Jewish city, and they are doing this by removing Palestinians one home at a time.

The rather splendid British Consul General mentioned Sheikh Jarrah when we had walked together: 'A lot of this is due to the fact that this Occupation should not have been allowed to go on for so long ... Humanitarian law isn't designed to cope with the situation in Sheikh Jarrah, where people expelled from one home then find themselves expelled from another. They end up expelled from the very home in which they find themselves as refugees.'

This is the case for many in Sheikh Jarrah: they had fled the events of 1948, the *Nakba* (the Catastrophe), arrived in East Jerusalem as refugees, and were given land by the United Nations Relief and Works Agency (UNRWA) and the Jordanian Mandate. Here, they had made their homes. Israel, contrary to international law, then annexed the city in 1967, and Israeli settlers set about using the courts to evict the community, claiming Jews had lived there before 1948 and thus the land and homes should 'return' to Jewish ownership. One by one, the settlers are evicting the Palestinians using any and every means, leaving the families destitute and making them refugees for the second time.[29]

Tomorrow's visit will not be the first time I have been to Sheikh Jarrah: before the ramble started, I had done a recce and on my first ever evening in East Jerusalem had been taken there by Ray Dolphin from the UN Office for the Coordination of Humanitarian Affairs. Ray covers Jerusalem and the Barrier for the United Nations. He is tall, with swept-back hair and, being Irish, speaks with the appropriate accent. He is also one of those chaps who is in danger of giving the UN a good name.

It had been late, cold and dark when Ray and I had arrived at Sheikh Jarrah. A small group of people, the Ghawi family, had been sitting around a brazier in the street, opposite the home they once lived in. A settler organisation had had the family evicted, arguing that the land had originally belonged to Jews. As soon as this was done, the settlers moved in, while the family erected a tent in the street opposite.

'The family belongings were thrown out by the settlers when they took over the house,' said Ray, taking a chair offered by one of the group.

'Did you not call the police?' I asked the family as I joined them around the fire. Those that spoke English had chuckled first, others with the translation.

'It was the police who evicted them,' Ray said.

'They helped the settlers take over the house? Wow.'

'So the family live out here in a tent.'

'As a protest?'

'Where else should we go?' someone said. 'There is nowhere for us.'

'But this is winter,' I spluttered. 'Have the Israeli social services not got involved?'

The chuckle was hollow this time.

'Surely they have an obligation to house the family?'

'No,' said Ray.

'What about the children? The Israeli social services must have some provision of care for the children; they must be able to find a shelter or hostel for the mother and children at least?'

These questions were barely met with a shrug. Perplexed and confused, I turned to Ray. 'What about school, doesn't the school raise the issue with the authorities about the kids being homeless? Surely the school would intervene in some way to get help, wouldn't they?'

'The police did actually come round ...'

'And?'

'They took down the tent. They said it was illegal.'

'The tent is illegal!'

'The tent.'

'But this is absolutely nuts. How can all these people get thrown out of their home, get no support, no rehousing, no help for the kids and then they are the criminals for living in a tent!'

Ray had leant closer to the brazier and talked to the family in Arabic. Then he sat back and looked at me, saying: 'I was just explaining this is your first day in East Jerusalem.' The family had nodded and smiled in an understanding way.

'These are all perfectly reasonable questions,' said Ray, 'and you are right to ask them. But you're reacting the way you would do at home in England. This, however, is Israel. It all seems mad at first but it makes perfect sense if you remember the Israelis *modus operandi* to achieve, "Maximum land with minimum Arabs". That's what they want: "Maximum land with minimum Arabs". Understand that and the madness does at least have a purpose to it.'

So how does this apply to Sheikh Jarrah? Well, the settlers have plans to build a 200-home settlement on the site of the neighbourhood, and the second part of that equation means the Arabs have to go. It's all part of creating an 'undivided Jerusalem', and preventing East Jerusalem from becoming the capital of a future Palestinian state.

It's the morning of our visit to Sheikh Jarrah. Phil has had a shave and I've stopped singing Barry White. The ambient harp music *is* playing again, but you can't have everything.

Phil's on good form and is full of stories about Tel Aviv. 'Oh, man,' he says, 'compared to this place it's like another country …'

'I think it might actually be that.'

'And guess what? That demographics professor …'

'Professor Soffer?'

'Yes, well, he was right. The place is full of croissants and small dogs. There are loads of bakeries and loads of small dogs. Hundreds of them! It's like being in the south of France but less polite.'

The walk from the hotel to the occupied houses takes twenty minutes, starting in the quieter streets, passing low stone homes and gardens, onto the road by the foreign consulates where drivers test their horns in the early traffic, then down the sloping road that leads to the Old City and turning left at a car dealer's forecourt. There we enter the street I had come to with Ray Dolphin only four months ago. The neighbourhood is waking up, birds chirrup from gardens and an old man emerges through an iron gate overhung with palms and cordylines, framed in pointed greenery. At the far end of the street a handful of women sit in the shade of a fig tree, on a roughly fashioned wooden bench.

'I guess that's the settlers, then.' Phil gestures to a building that is draped in Israeli flags: one hangs down the side of the wall, two stick out from the first floor balcony, one flies from the roof and a string of blue and white bunting flaps gently on the parapet.

'How do you do it, Holmes? Was it the flags?'

'If you look closely up on the roof, Watson,' says Phil in a plummy tone, 'you'll see a twenty-foot sculpture of a nine-branched candleholder.'

'Ahhh, the giant Jewish candles on the roof.'

'Indeed.'

'That's a fuck-off birthday cake.'

With the massive menorah on its roof, the occupied home has the appearance of a religious squat: green tarpaulin sheets hang over the wrought-iron balcony; the windows are blacked out and barred; there's a lean-to made from a patchwork of assorted materials; the fencing is irregular and broken; and the metal gates are locked with fist-sized padlocks. It would be fair to say the settlers aren't much interested in blending in.

It seems calm out here, however, and in other circumstances it would be a fine thing to sit under a fig tree or enjoy the lazy morning sun. The women at the bench nod as we approach but, just as I start to introduce myself, something happens back up the street near the car dealer. Things are about to heat up, and quickly, too.

We turn to stare as a large group of Israelis enters the street from the main road. They have hit the street as a coordinated pack, sticking to the middle of the road and striding quickly. A core group is flanked by armed security, who are all guns, wrap-around shades and earpieces. In the middle of the phalanx are two settlers, walking on either side of a politician of some sort, talking to him and attempting to appear casual. The politician sticks out a mile. I don't know who he is as I've never seen him before in my life, and have no proof of his profession other than the fact that he is in the middle, he's in a suit and has the brisk swagger of a man who expects gratitude and thinks he shits wisdom. He's a politician.

The group have planned exactly where they are going and arrive abruptly at a house not far from where we are standing. A wail goes up from the group, this is the al-Kurd family home. The security guards with their machine guns fan out and enter the garden doorway. The Israeli politician turns to his *yarmulke*-wearing escorts and, nodding at the Palestinian colours painted on the outside wall, says in Hebrew, 'If this is ours, why is this flag here?' He doesn't wait for an answer but strides into the al-Kurd family's property.

'Phil!' I call as I dash towards the group, who are disappearing into the garden.

'I'm there!' calls Phil from behind me and I hear him running too. We have no idea of who has just arrived at that house, but it's too early for the post and it sure ain't Ocado. All I know is that the politician thinks highly enough of himself for me to be interested.

By the entrance to the home now stand two guards who eat way too much protein and need to cut out the supplement shakes. I can feel that Phil is still next to me as we slip past them and through the entrance. Inside, the garden bristles with men, guns and media opportunities. The press pack is small and so is the garden, so they form a line descending in importance from the politician, who stands at the bungalow door. There is the photographer, the cameraman and lastly a radio reporter. Oh, and then me and Phil.

The door is covered in graffiti and the windows are barred. This is the al-Kurd family home, and right next to it, a small tent. The story here is that the Palestinian family had built a two-room extension on to it – the part of the house the politician is currently inspecting – for their son and his growing family. The courts, however, declared the two rooms illegal as it had no building permit, and then evicted the occupants and sealed the extension. In December 2009, a settler got in, occupied the extension and has stayed there ever since, like some weird colonialist cuckoo living on the other side of the wall, inches from the family who built it. The tent was put up so the al-Kurds could guard against more settlers occupying their rooms.

Nudging up next to the radio reporter, I whisper, 'Who is this guy?'

'The deputy mayor of Jerusalem, David Hadari,'

'The deputy mayor!'

'One of them, yes.'

'What's he here for?'

'Ask him.'

'You can be sure I will,' I say happily. He might not be *the* mayor, but he is a deputy mayor, and he has just walked into one of the city's biggest controversies.

Phil winks that the camera is rolling. David Hadari has wire glasses, red cheeks and a *yarmulke* in a faded black colour to match his hair, which matches his suit. It transpires he is from the political party, Jewish Home (they used to be called the National Religious Party, which will give you a hint as to which end of the spectrum they sit). He's not far right, but not far from it either.

'I'm here to express our rights and sovereignty in Jerusalem,' he starts as the radio reporter waits next to him. 'Some very courageous and idealistic settlers came here to strengthen Jerusalem and we are very proud of them.'

It is an understatement to say his manner is unfortunate. He has a small man's habit of sticking his chin in the air, either compensating for lack of height or inviting someone to punch it. As a politician, he has yet to master a simple, standard smile and appears to either gloat or smirk like a sidekick.

'Why is it important for Israel to have East and West Jerusalem?' I ask, slipping in next to him, aware that people from the street are beginning to come into the garden.

'This is my home, this is my house,' he says, sounding shocked that I even asked, though quite clearly it isn't his home at all. 'This is my city; it belongs to me and all of my country.'

'But there are Palestinians that live here.'

'No, no ...'

'So you dispute that Palestinians live here?'

'It belongs to us. It was Jewish land before 1948; it was the first land Jewish people ever bought in Jerusalem.'

'OK, so if Israelis can claim homes that were occupied by Jews before 1948 in East Jerusalem, can Palestinian families come to West Jerusalem and get houses that used to belong to them?'

'Excuse me.' He holds up his arm indicating the conversation is about to end. 'It is our country. It is our city. It belongs to us. That's it.'

He has finished, so he pauses, possibly waiting for someone to fetch a hook to pull his chin down. As he moves to leave, the deputy mayor is deftly blocked by the Israeli radio reporter. 'What are you saying to these people, these Arabs?' the reporter begins, pointing to the small and now teeming garden. 'Look how they are. Look how they live.'

'I am saying ...' starts Deputy Mayor David Hadari, but he is drowned out with shouts and denunciations from a clutch of Palestinian women next to him. 'I am saying,' he starts again, but the next-door neighbour is now leaning over the wall by the rose bushes, shouting into his ear. Raising his voice to be heard over the cacophony, David Hadari leans into the mic. 'I am saying that we are in one whole united city' – news of that unity has yet to reach this particular garden, but he continues – 'Jerusalem is part of the Jewish state and belongs to Israel ...'

'No, it belongs to the Palestinians. It belongs to us,' shouts an old woman in Hebrew, interrupting the deputy mayor in mid-flow.

Her name is Rifka al-Kurd. She is eighty-eight, and was born in Haifa; her family lost their home there in 1948. For a split second, David Hadari looks affronted at the rudeness of being interrupted by this woman, but it is her garden that we are all standing in. The deputy mayor ignores her. He doesn't respond to her or address her in anyway; he seems to look right through her to the canvas shelter the family erected next to the rooms the settler has taken over.

'Look!' he appeals to the reporter. 'Look how liberal the settlers are! They allow them to put a tent up in the garden. I have never seen settlers like that!' He gestures at the canvas shelter as if giving a character reference. Can we not see the human kindness the settler is displaying in allowing Rifka al-Kurd a tent in her own garden, next to her house that he has squatted?

David Hadari leaves this fracas of his own making and steps onto the road to talk to the settlers outside the occupied home belonging to the Ghawi family, the family under the fig tree. The hunched figure of Rifka al-Kurd pursues him from the garden to the road, standing in the middle of the street screaming and raising her hand with each outburst. The settlers, surrounded by security and police, ignore her. Still, Rifka steps forward, screaming at them. Her daughter, Maysa, runs to her side and takes her arm, leading her to a taxi. Maysa shuts the door on her mother then her own anger spills over and she too screams in fury. She smacks her outstretched arm at the elbow, a universal 'Fuck you!', takes a step forward, catches herself and spins away to the taxi, only to find that her elderly aunt who was in the car with her mother has now got out. As her aunt shrieks at the settlers, Maysa shepherds her back to the car that, once full, speeds away down the street. Deputy Mayor David Hadari simply walks through the iron gates of the occupied home to greet the settlers. He can be heard saluting them: 'With your life and your actions you strengthen us! Well done! Well done!'

Back in the al-Kurd family garden, one of the neighbours stands by the canvas shelter watching over the property for them. He is an older gentleman and lives across the road.

'Whenever a big US official visits, they start coming into the area and pressuring us,' he says. 'It is not a coincidence that the deputy mayor comes today.'

'During the US vice-president's visit?'

'Yes. The settlers want to show everyone that they are the power.'

In the garden by the small beds and borders next to the rose bush, we chat for a while of other homes targeted by the settlers, of the campaign to evict them that has gone on for over thirty years, and the weekly demonstrations in support of the Palestinian residents.

Then, through the entrance, Phil spots the deputy mayor again. Emerging into a street quieter than when he left it, Deputy Mayor David Hadari starts to the main road.

I hurry after him, in time for us to hear him say in Hebrew to the settler leaders: 'I don't think he is a proper journalist.' I doubt he realises he has made his one accurate comment of the day.

'Deputy Mayor, can you just answer one quick question? If it is OK for Israelis to claim homes in East Jerusalem but not OK for Palestinians to claim homes in West Jerusalem, does that mean there is one law for one and one law for another?'

'No, no, no, there is only one law in Israel, but this is the Jewish country.' Then he shrugs and says something remarkable considering he is an elected law-maker and a powerful man. He says, 'What can I do?'

What can he do? It is tempting to start on a long list but then he adds, 'This is our country.' He says it without a quiver of doubt, as if it were an immutable law of physics.

'But if one group can claim homes and another can't because of race, you are creating law based on race, aren't you?

'This city belongs to us, OK?'

'But you're not actually answering the question.'

'So I don't answer it. I don't answer it.'

'But you can't create a law that only applies to one race of people and doesn't apply to another.'

'I spoke with you a lot,' he says, turning away. 'Thank you, bye bye.' With that Deputy Mayor David Hadari turns his back to me to finish his trip and bid farewell to his guides. Shaking hands with the settler leaders and the police, he says to them in Hebrew, 'You are doing God's work.'

God. Of course. That's why this is an immutable law: God. When someone is behaving this badly, mention of him is bound to make an appearance sooner or later.

JERUSALEM & E1 EXTENSION

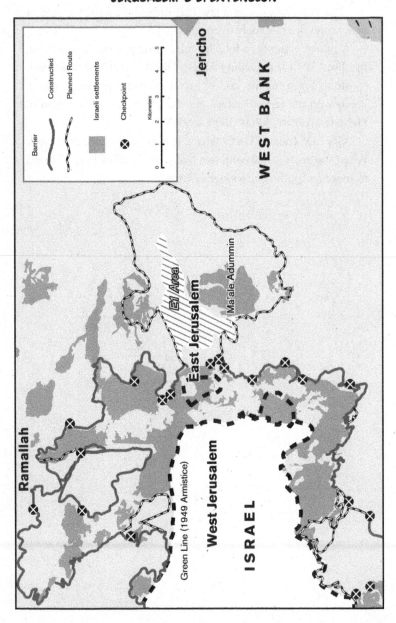

Legend:
- Barrier: Constructed
- Planned Route
- Israeli settlements
- Checkpoint

Kilometers
0 1 2 3 4 5

Ramallah

WEST BANK

Jericho

E1 Area

Ma'ale Adummim

East Jerusalem

West Jerusalem

Green Line (1949 Armistice)

ISRAEL

chapter 19
GOD'S ESTATE AGENT

Arieh King is a thirty-six-year-old estate agent and religious ideologue; a combination that makes him one of the more pushy zealots, the type the more moderate zealots shy away from, as he does bang on a bit.

There aren't many things worse than being an estate agent, but one of them is being a religious estate agent. Picture a Foxton's branded Mini Cooper. Now imagine it with a fish logo on the boot.

Admittedly, this is a crude stereotype and, in real life, Arieh King isn't remotely like this cartoon portrait. He's much worse, really much, much worse. He's powerful, dangerous, deluded, bigoted and a peddler of self-justifying showmanship. In many ways a fully rounded human being. Arieh King founded the Israel Land Fund (ILF) in 2007, after 'realising a need to disrupt the purchase of Jewish-owned land in Israel by hostile, non-Jewish and enemy sources'. Quite a task as, according to Arieh King, these hostile enemy sources are, 'Arabs and non-Jews'. Which narrows down the suspect list to mere billions. 'Arabs and non-Jews are living and owning land all over Israel,' King fearlessly announces. That is how big this is. You read it right: non-Jews are living in Israel! The fact that his vision of Israel includes the West Bank, Gaza and bits of Jordan and Syria only goes to prove how many non-Jews are involved. However, King offers folk a chance to join his endeavours: 'House by house, lot by lot, the Israel Land Fund is ensuring the land of Israel stays in the hands of the Jewish people for ever.' Naturally the offer is only open to Jews.

With pronouncements like these, it's not surprising that King is involved with evictions at Sheikh Jarrah. What *is* surprising is his willingness to meet me, and the manner of his arrival. When we get to the settler apartment block in East Jerusalem the afternoon sun is out and so is he. An armed settler stands guard by the off-road garage parking entrance. As I approach he confuses himself with a customs official and orders, 'Passport.'

I confuse myself with a smart Alec and reply, 'The Israeli visa should be good for your building.'

'Wait outside,' he says.

The Palestinian taxi driver, Phil and I do just that, parking on the side of the driveway, leaning on the bonnet and collecting stares from Arieh's neighbours.

Phil has taken to wearing a straw cowboy hat. 'It keeps the sun off and confuses the hell out of the soldiers,' he had said and he was right: it is hard to label someone in a straw hat as threatening. It doesn't, however, do anything for the settlers, whose stares are mainly a mixture of suspicion and hostility, no doubt having us down as either internationals or media, or worse, house-hunters.

After forty minutes I ask out loud, 'Do you think we should have a time limit on this? Another twenty minutes, and then home?'

Suddenly, a scooter brakes with a jolt next to us. It revs at a noisy teenage whine and a man in a T-shirt and sandals shouts over the putt-putting of the bike, 'Sorry, I am late; I will show you why. Come, come, come. Get in the car, follow me! Follow me! Don't wait! Come!' He twists and shoves on the scooter, looks over his shoulder and shouts again, 'Follow me!' then, hunching and leaning over the handles as if willing it faster, hares off into the traffic.

'That,' I laugh, jumping back into our taxi, 'is an entrance! He's definitely not what we expected.'

'Oh, fuck,' groans Phil from the back seat, shaking his head. 'What?'

'We've got an eccentric. That's what.'

'What's wrong with that?'

'Eccentrics are always so fucking dull.'

*

Minutes later, we stand with King opposite the hillside cemetery of the Mount of Olives, where hundreds of ultra-orthodox Jews are attending a funeral.

'Look. Look at all these Jews!' says Arieh proudly.

'I don't mean to be rude, but are these special Jews? Because we *are* in Jerusalem, and there *are* a lot of them about.'

'Nooo,' says Arieh, and the words chewed on his lisp but none the worse for wear, start to gush out of him. 'Look, look, *look* how many Jews are here. This is really incredible. They have walked from the centre of Jerusalem for the burial of a rabbi and not even one who is very high up …'

'You've bought us to a funeral?'

' …Thousands will come. You will see. Look, look at them. You must get the camera on them. You will see; this whole hill will be black with Jews. Wait and you will see. This is why I was late; I got caught in the traffic as they walk through Jerusalem…'

Fifteen minutes later, his enthusiasm suddenly vanishes and he snaps, 'Come, I will show you where to go for the interview. Follow me. In the car. Come. I will take you.'

He starts the putt-putting engine of his scooter again, points the front wheel into the traffic and whizzes off. Seeing him do this for the second time is not as impressive.

Our destination is a crop of hillside apartments forming a new and virtually deserted estate. Arieh parks, removes his helmet, slips on a jungle-green, floppy hat and bounds up the steps from the pavement to an empty children's playground. Mobile clutched to his ear, he natters away in his green hat and pale blue T-shirt in front of an orange slide, like a kids' TV presenter on a fag break.*

Phone conversation over, he begins with boyish enthusiasm. 'We are here in the heart of a battle between fundamentalism and the Western world. We have had Nazism and Communism and now we face fundamentalism. And at the heart of this battle is Jerusalem, the frontline is Jerusalem … So, if Jerusalem is divided,

---

* *Arieh doesn't smoke*

it is a threat to the whole state of Israel and is a threat on the future of every Jew in the world.'

'So it is your struggle to make Jerusalem a Jewish city?'

'Yes,' he says determinedly, 'I am going to do everything to protect this holy place, and to bring in more Jews.'

His mobile buzzes, in a snap he answers it, holding his finger up to indicate that I should wait. He converses in Hebrew for two minutes, then hangs up.

'That was the deputy mayor of Jerusalem, David Hadari.'

'The guy who was down in Sheikh Jarrah the other day?'

'Yes ... right ... Where were we?' Without need of a prompt, he finds his place in his spiel again, and explains his main reason for setting up the Israel Land Fund: 'I got a database that shows funds, *Arab* funds, coming from Saudi Arabia, Egypt, Arab banks. To buy land in Israel, for the Arab nation in Israel; what they call Palestine.' With his voice rising in intensity he goes on, 'I gave this information to the police, the government and Knesset members and they did nothing! Nobody cares. And they [the Arabs] are continuing! They are buying today wherever they want! It is a democratic state, so the Arabs can do what they want,' he says, sounding cheated. 'They are buying in the centre of town,' he rails. 'In King David Street, these buildings belong to Arabs! Why can Arabs buy anything they want in Israel? Including Jerusalem, central *and* west? Whatever they want! And I cannot buy in Jerusalem!'

His phone buzzes and he checks it, but this time ignores it.

'You can't buy land in Jerusalem?' I ask incredulously.

'I can,' he concedes, shrugging. 'Legally, I can, yes ... But why do I have to confront demonstrations like these anarchists in Sheikh Jarrah?' And he is off again.

For two hours, Arieh performs a series of rants where the best chance of my interjecting to ask a question would be for me to phone him. He also has a habit of speaking in headlines, only to row back on them. An example would be his explanation of the Israel Land Fund: 'People are buying land. And this is what we want. We [the ILF] don't want to become landowners. We want Jews from all over the world to come and be owners.'

'Do the buyers live in Israel?'

'Unfortunately, most of them prefer to buy and stay overseas.'

'But you get commission?'

'No,' he says quickly.

'Really? I read that you took commission.'

Then he rows back again and admits, yes. 'When we are dealing with Galilee, where we know the land going to be economical, then we take a commission. Not in Jerusalem. Jerusalem is ideological, one hundred per cent. We don't take any commission.'

'And then there are the evictions in Sheikh Jarrah.'

'No. I am not doing evictions. I am paying the people. I prefer them to take the money, go quiet. Check me. You can ask every Arab about that. This is not my way, to kick people out in the middle of the night.'

'But you do deliver eviction notices.'

'Of course.'

'In the middle of the night ... with the army. There is footage of you doing that on the BBC.'

'It is not my decision; it is the army's decision, unfortunately,' he says, rowing again.

He interrupts the interview continually to answer the phone to the deputy mayor and others. All this time he must be aware that he is being recorded and it can't have passed his notice that conversations in Hebrew can be translated, conversations that run: 'This morning I was there with the mayor ... Now I want the mayor to issue a demolition order ... If the mayor is issuing a municipal demolition order, the police have to escort the building inspectors ...'

It is difficult to know if Arieh King's relationship to these politicians is that of lobbyist, ally or leader, but it clearly helps to have some political connections in this game. Especially as King's plan is to build 200,000 new homes; all in Palestinian areas. King seems to suffer from a syndrome that I had thought a particularly

British strain of idiocy: the 'uberdog' syndrome, where the well off bemoan their lot, whinging on about how life is stacked against them. For example: 'These days, you can only get into Oxford or Cambridge if you went to a state school,' they will bray. 'If your children are privately educated, they just don't stand a chance. It is totally biased.' Arieh is a classic 'uberdog', and he fires off tirades and salvos of imagined injustices. He laments the fact the Israelis cannot enter certain Palestinian cities on the West Bank, which, while true, pales in comparison with the restrictions on Palestinian movement, not only into Israel but crucially within the West Bank itself.

'It is apartheid against Jews,' declares the man whose property transactions are based entirely on race.

'What is your objection to not being able to get in to these places?'

'I have properties ...' he begins. 'And it has bad effect on the Arab living behind the Wall' – for a moment he appears to be on the verge of empathy, about to show some emotional depth and see something from someone else's view point – 'and the result of this is the Arabs are moving from their neighbourhoods into the Jewish neighbourhoods,' says the man who has just complained about apartheid.

The Arieh King Show is a well-honed portrait of a put-upon settler, where everything is everyone else's fault: the media, the anarchists, the leftists, the soldiers, the government and the big bad Arabs, performed by an obsessive who can't quite make up his mind if he wants to be seen as powerful or humble. The finale is his boastful offer to take us to Sheikh Jarrah where settlers are occupying Palestinian homes, and he himself has appeared at night with the army and court papers. If we go with him, we will see, apparently, that he is actually well regarded.

'People will come up and say, "Look, it is him!" No one will shout at me. I tell you, you will see.'

'OK, brilliant. Let's go to Sheikh Jarrah then.'

Arieh gets on his scooter and drives off into the evening light, leading the way. Except we never get there. Instead, he leads us to a friendlier part of town, nearer his home, having phoned ahead to warn them of our arrival. His offer is a bluff.

The ambient harp music is still playing at the hotel when we get back.

'Did you have a good day?' asks the owner.

'Great,' I say.

'Tiring,' says Phil.

'I'll bring some tea,' the owner says, tiptoeing into the kitchen.

It is late and the small lobby is quiet, so we sink into the old easy chairs with a hushed 'hff'.

'It's New Age water torture,' I whisper.

'I don't mind, as long as I'm not near that odious man.'

'He is a piece of work,' I admit, 'but a character ...'

'He's a twat ...'

'Well, yes ...'

' ... and you can't change the facts. He might be a character but he's a twat.'

'I'm a performer and a person with no small ego myself, so I find him interesting. You have to admit it was quite a performance.'

'He's a bigot.'

'Yes, he is but ...'

'He's a complete bastard.'

'Then this might not be the best time to tell you that I have arranged to meet up with him later in the week.'

Phil snorts with laughter and, forgetting where we are or the hour of the night, shouts in disbelief, 'Oh, for fuck's sake! You're as fucking mad as him! I don't want to ever see that fucking bastard ... Oh, thank you for the tea ... and sorry about the language.'

'No problem,' says the owner, placing a tray on the table in front of us. 'Do not worry at all. I understand.'

'You must know who we're talking about then,' says Phil.

'I hope you don't,' I add, 'and I hope you never do.'

'Today!' I pronounce to Phil and the hotel owner over the harp music the following morning. 'Today I declare war on paper!'

'What?'

'Why not, Phil? We've had war on drugs ...'

'Which we lost,' he adds, looking like a true veteran from that particular conflict.

' ... I declare war on trees and all the derivatives thereof. My rucksack is stuffed with human rights reports and I get more every day. So no more documents, no more reports, no more paper.'

'A war on paper would make the acronym WOP.'

'What?'

'WOP. You'll be fighting WOP.'

'WOP.'

'It sounds racist.'

'OK, I declare a *jihad* against paper!'

'That still has its own problems ...'

'OK then. A battle against paper!'

'And that's BAP! You have gone from WOP to JAP to BAP.'

'Look, I just don't want any more paper. OK?'

'OK, but does that include maps?'

'Oh, fuck off.'

Maps are my weak spot. I love them. Phil once innocently suggested we use a TomTom, but only once. A good map is a thing of beauty, something to be gazed upon and stared into for meaning. None of it helps with direction and I still get hopelessly lost but that is not the point; what matters is the time spent dreaming over it. My favourite analysis of orienteering actually occurred on a wet family holiday in Cornwall, when my son said, 'Dad, you may know where you are going, you may not. But the best map-readers know when their families have had enough.' It is true that my family has had to endure more than its share of this pastime. When asked why the route of the ramble stuck to walking alongside the Barrier, my

wife had replied for me, saying, 'Because he's shit at map-reading.'
So I wonder if I am holding it upside down again when my map
shows a hole in the Barrier. Right at the back of East Jerusalem; a
serious hole too, a gap two kilometres wide, so it's obviously not
foxes. I phone the authorities to report it but they say they are
already aware of it. I phone Ray Dolphin and say, 'The UN map
shows a hole in the Wall.' Fortunately, working for the UN in the
West Bank isn't too demanding so he has some time to explain what
is going on. The hole looks to be a connecting point from Jerusalem
to a planned extension of the Barrier. On the map, its shape is that
of a speech bubble that starts at the gap and inflates deep into the
West Bank, gouging out a large chunk of territory and taking it for
Israel. *Is this another example of the Barrier being used to grab land?*
I wonder. *Or are my map-reading skills oversimplifying things?*

On a sunny afternoon, Ray drives me to the break in the
Barrier or, as Dr Seuss might call it, the 'gap in the map'. It is a
clear day and from the hillside vantage point the countryside
unfurls under a cloudless sky of perfect blues. It is the ideal spot
to compare the cartography to the reality.

'Right,' says Ray, as he flattens a UN map on the top of a parapet wall. 'The Barrier started in 2002, but there was no official
route for a whole year. Construction started but it was an entire
year before the route and plans were published, which is strange.'
Not for Lambeth Council it isn't, but I take the point. It does
seem odd that the Israeli government should employ thousands
of people to build a massive military barrier in order to surround
the West Bank and when asked to produce a plan of it responds
by hissing, 'Shhhh, it's a secret!'

Tapping the map in confirmation, Ray says, 'What we have
here is the latest map from June 2006, as approved by the Israeli
Parliament. This enormous bubble here wasn't in the first official
routes. This only appeared in 2005.'

'Three years after they started work on the Wall.'

'Yes. The proposed route of this bit of the Wall now encircles
an enormous amount of land, over fifty square kilometres. This

area is larger than the municipal area of Tel Aviv, and 30,000 settlers will effectively be brought into Israel, because this proposed bubble will join the settlement of Ma'ale Adumim to Israel.'

Ma'ale Adumim is a city settlement to the east of Jerusalem. Like the other illegal settlements, it will find itself encircled by the proposed Barrier, thus extracting it from deep within the West Bank and placing it on the Israeli side.

'It's over there,' says Ray, turning slightly and pointing to apartment blocks on the horizon. 'That's Ma'ale Adumim, over in the hills.' He points to the map once more, and an area called E1, a controversial development plan to extend from the north-east of Jerusalem, deep into the West Bank to the settlement of Ma'ale Adumim. Once completed, it will connect the two cities into one large urban sprawl extending across the West Bank. Not only will it ensure there is no room for natural growth for Palestinian areas of East Jerusalem; it will also irrevocably cut off East Jerusalem from the rest of the West Bank, and break the West Bank in two.

Richard Makepeace, the British Consul General, had explained one of the hazards of this type of expansion when we had walked with him earlier: 'Every additional settlement that is built, every settlement unit – whether it is in Jerusalem or elsewhere in the Occupied Territories – that is a problem that has to be overcome in reaching a final status deal.'

With its plans for 3,500 housing units, the super settlement of E1 has the potential to be the biggest of those problems and, as such, is opposed by the whole international community. Even George W. Bush, a man not noted for his caution or his love of Arabs, was opposed to it. It takes an exceptional plan for George W. Bush to be the voice of moderation. In fact, there has been so much international pressure and condemnation that the Israelis have been forced to freeze construction. But, as Ray explains, the Barrier provides the perfect solution to this problem: 'It doesn't really matter that E1 is on hold at the moment, because once this part of the Wall is complete, E1 can be in-filled at any time.'

I start to notice places across the hills where the foundations for the proposed route look to have been laid already. It will not take much to get the Barrier up once the orders are given.

Ray sighs as he goes on to explain how Palestinians will be totally hemmed in by the Barrier and settlements. 'And,' he stresses, 'this is a political problem because the idea of a two-state solution relies on having a Palestinian state living side by side in peace and security with Israel … *with* some kind of capital in East Jerusalem. Clearly it is going to be impossible to have a Palestinian capital if East Jerusalem is cut off from the rest of the West Bank.'

The fact that the proposed route is a land grab and brings 30,000 settlers onto the Israeli side is just the start of its purpose. If built, it will cut the West Bank virtually in two and will take East Jerusalem – a critical component to any peace process – off the negotiating table. No wonder the Israeli authorities did not publish its map until they were three years into the building work. It's a declaration of war.

It is perhaps ironic that in a country without formal or internationally recognised borders that everyone seems to have their own map. It is less surprising that Arieh King has two. One, a piece of photocopied paper, is a planner's drawing of property boundaries, while the other is a biblical map kept in his heart (and thus less true to scale). He clutches them both as we stand on one side of a valley somewhere just north of the hole in the Barrier. It is three days since we first met God's estate agent and he has taken us to a site he hopes to see developed. It is, rather chillingly, part of the E1 corridor. We are on the Israeli side, at the top of a hill. Directly behind us is the Barrier, a mere 100 metres or so away. In front of us, on the other side of the valley, lies French Hill, an Israeli settlement between East Jerusalem and Ma'ale Adumim. Between the Barrier and the settlement is a valley full of scrub and, I suspect, landfill. This land is Arieh's battlefield in his struggle to turn the Palestinian city of East Jerusalem into a Jewish city.

'You want to build from the other side of the valley up to here, right?'

'Yes.'

'A Jewish neighbourhood?'

'There is room for some Arabs,' he says kindly.

'How many: what percentage?'

'Eighty–twenty.'

'Eighty per cent Jewish, twenty per cent Palestinian.'

'Most of it Jewish and part of it Arab, because Arabs own part of the land.' Unfolding his piece of paper, Arieh goes through the racial ownership of the land around us: 'There are more than thirty plots, we have one plot there, one plot here, two plots there ... This one is owned by an ultra-orthodox family; they bought it twenty-five years ago as an investment thinking it would by now be a Jewish neighbourhood. This is owned by an Arab ...' Charming as it to sit and sift through the racial dynamics of property ownership, the real intrigue of this site lies to the east: 'This is the best place to connect Jerusalem to E1 and Ma'ale Adumim,' he says, pointing towards the Dead Sea and Jordan. 'This is the only way Jerusalem can be one urban area.'

'Why is it so important for Jerusalem to become this one urban area?'

Arieh looks at me, wide-eyed: 'Because we are in a struggle for the future of Jerusalem, and one of the ways to protect Jerusalem is to stop it being divided. One way to do this is to connect one hill to another, one neighbourhood to another neighbourhood. To connect Jerusalem to E1 and to the city of Ma'ale Adumim.' Then, lowering his voice almost as if he is worried others might hear, he confides, 'If we will not do that, the other side, the Arabs, *will*; they are trying to connect the Arab villages.'

The notion that his urban plan will effectively cut the West Bank in two and destroy any peace plan can only be a cause of joy to him. Arieh has no intention of seeing a Palestinian state, as such a thing would be, 'the end of a Jewish state'. Anyway, peace doesn't seem to be his bag: first and foremost, the land is his and Palestinians have no right to it.

'The Bible is your map, isn't it?' I ask him.

'Yes. What is yours?'

'The one cartographers drew.'

'No. I believe in what God tells us ...'

'OK, so where are Israel's borders, then?'

'The Hiddekel.' He shrugs.

'The Euphrates in Iraq; that is Israel's border?'

'It is where it should be. This is what God promised Abraham, Isaac and Jacob.'

'Well, good luck with that.'

'No, no, God will do it.'

'Do you seriously envisage a day when Israeli settlements will go all the way from here into Iraq?'

'Absolutely.'

And a part of me thinks, *Go on, do it! Off you go.* I'd like to see the Israel Land Fund open an office in Iraq. After a dictatorship, war with Iran, the Gulf war, the US and UK invasion, military occupation, mass privatisation, civil war and sectarian conflict, what Iraq could *really* do with is a Zionist estate agent. The image of Arieh King driving into Iraq with an Israeli flag flying from his scooter is an appealing one.

'Tell me,' I ask, 'if God promised you all this land and he wants you to have it, why did he put all these Arabs in the way?'

'It could be to encourage us to do something; could be to wake people up to think about the reason they are here,' he says, before conceding, 'I don't have answers to everything.' So it would appear that Palestinians are here to remind Zionists to remove them: a Post-it note for their own expulsion. 'They have a mission that God gave them,' he says, 'but I do not know their mission. I know that God gave us a mission and I know that I need to do the most that I can in order to complete this mission.'

In a city where property and planning laws are weapons, Arieh is not only on a mission from God, he is fully armed too.

chapter 20
THE TRAGIC
ROUNDABOUT

I have a confession. I missed the Barrier. Not in the literal sense, as it is hard to escape the nine-metre-high concrete wall that carves its way through neighbourhood after neighbourhood; but I felt stuck in Jerusalem. I missed the walk and most of all I missed the hills with the fleeting glimpses of freedom they promise. Jerusalem was cramped and weird. It was packed with tourists, traders, the devout, the deluded, the armed and variations thereof. The centre is crammed with yuppie shopping malls and Christian coach trips offering a chance to 'walk in the footsteps of the prophets' complete with a full-size crucifix with wheels on the bottom to hook over one shoulder and walk the stations of the cross. You can't hire a crucifix without leaving a deposit, which suggests someone got a little too fond of theirs and took it home (if you ever visit a Jerusalem swingers' club and find yourself strung up on something with wheels, you'll know where it came from). So it is great to be away from Jerusalem and out on the Barrier again. It is spring, the grass is bright, the birdsong clear, the sun is up and the boy hitting the donkey with a stick has reappeared.

'Suncream?'

'Yeah, I'm done,' says Phil.

'Water?'

'Two bottles.'

Everything feels right today.

'It's three days to get south of Bethlehem. We've got a full bar of Kendal Mint Cake, half a tube of suncream, it's light and I'm wearing sunglasses.'

'Hit it,' says Phil.

Perhaps one of these three days will be *the* walk, the perfect walk. The omens are good: an easy walk, through city and then country, and all in good company. Jamal Juma, the coordinator of Stop the Wall, is walking with us today and it's good to have him on the walk as he has not long been released from jail. His arrest at the end of our first ramble had shaken us and caused international stirrings, as he is a prominent organiser and non-violent campaigner.

Jamal has a tai chi class to get to tonight and he rambles like he is already in the class: with the concentration of a drunk and the coordination of the sober, exactly what you need for tai chi.

'Did you expect to get arrested?' I ask.

'Oh, yes. The Israelis had been targeting non-violent activists for six months: first the young activists in the villages by the Barrier, then the Popular Committee Organisers; then they arrested my colleague at Stop the Wall, and I expected they would come.'

Jamal has an infectious smile, a worn face and ears that are not afraid of coming forward. 'As soon as Intelligence took me, they said, "Jamal, we have watched you for a while and, look, now your file is this big."' He holds up his finger and thumb, three or four inches apart.

'If your mime is anything to go by, that is a big file.'

'They said, "We are going to keep you for a long time. Nine years. But if you cooperate you will get four."'

'What for?'

'They said I was in contact with terrorist groups.'

'Did they name them?'

'They said Hezbollah. I laughed so hard when they said this, and said, "What would I be doing with them; I am an atheist! How do you make this connection? Check my file, you know I started in politics as a communist." Then they named everyone! I was seeing Hezbollah. I was seeing ETA. I was even seeing the Zapatistas in Mexico! I said, "Wow! I am really an international terrorist!"'

'Did they charge you with anything else?'

'They charged me with incitement, of travelling abroad and threatening the reputation of Israel.'

'But Israel already has a terrible reputation: how can you threaten it? What could you have done? Say, "Israel is reasonable and pleasant"?'

'I said, "I am campaigning against the settlements and the Wall. These are illegal and threaten peace and security. So take me to court for this."'

Jamal was released without charge after twenty-seven days, but he believes that he and other peaceful activists have been targeted for a specific reason: 'Our struggle over the past three or four years has been non-violent and has attracted strong international solidarity, like the boycott, divestment and sanctions campaign.[30] We moved the argument. We said, "Israel doesn't want peace; the state is racist and isolates people from each other, and from their land." Israel thinks that by attacking the grassroots resistance, it will stop the international solidarity.'

We ramble on the concrete foundations of the Barrier into which the slabs are set. The Barrier flows over the countryside, through villages, onto main roads, up alleys and cutting across people's back gardens. As it flows so do we, climbing over makeshift fences and waving apologies at the residents. Some gardens grow flowers to the edge of the concrete footings, but they all erect their fences up to the Barrier itself, marking out their land in its shadow, as if to say, 'Enough! *Halas!* You have taken enough.' Our route is a tour of humiliations and attempts to normalise life alongside this most abnormal of structures. In the village of Nazeria, for example, a blue metal door suddenly appears in the Barrier.

'This is for the kindergarten,' explains Jamal.

The kindergarten is on the Israeli side, so children only have fifteen minutes each morning to cross here to get to the Lego.

Another section of the Barrier has knitted people's homes into the very fabric of Barrier: concrete slabs run up to an apartment block, which then becomes the next part of the Barrier. Every single window and opening is covered with grids and grills. Bars are bolted into the brickwork, the roof lined with wire.

'They forced them to be part of the Wall; to function as part of the military.' The Barrier moves from concrete slab to home and back again, a patchwork of cement and brick, using homes as military quilting.

This is a fractured and abnormal landscape, where homes become barriers, children play under watchtowers, and parliaments are stillborn: in Abu Dis, the magnificent stone building that was to be the Palestinian parliament sits in the midst of a compound behind locked gates, old newspapers and dust blowing around the empty space. Biblical in size and Arabic in design with its arches and towers, it is a suitable home for law-makers. But the Palestinian state never came. So it sat unfinished, unfurnished and empty until the local university bought the building.

All the while, Jamal moves carefully and calmly, with measured steps, over the concrete crust of the footings. Every few steps, however, he hits the Barrier with the side of his fist. *Bump*. A slow and deliberate hit, it hardly makes a sound at all, just a soft *bump*. He neither mentions nor draws any attention to this act, over and above the attention the act draws to itself. *Bump*. Then he walks on. *Bump* again. Each time he draws his fist back into the swing of his stride, then *bump*. There is no blood, cuts or apparent bruising, and I wonder if it is a mental tick. Or an affectation? Is this an act? I have come to think that Jamal simply refuses to accept the Barrier. He refuses to normalise it and refuses to live with it, and each blow is a reminder of that: with each bump he marked his failure to comply.

We finish the walk sitting in the street by a closed grocer's shop, while some kids go to find the owner. My head droops between my knees, dripping sweat into a pool: the final hills were too hard and the sun too hot for a perfect walk. Even the tai chi disciple Jamal seems to buckle and he says, 'I might have an ice cream,' as the shop owner appears. Phil has taken off his straw cowboy hat to wipe his brow with the back of his hand, and reveals his fading highlights. I am so sunburnt I could present a daytime quiz show, while removing my bag has revealed a salt outline on the back of my T-shirt in the shape of the rucksack.

'You've killed a tortoise!' calls Phil and, sure enough, it looks just like the crime-scene chalk marks for the murdered reptile. Over the course of the walk I have actually removed at least three tortoises from the middle of the road, saving them from certain grisly vehicular doom, while today Phil and I saw the tiniest tortoise we had ever seen: small enough to make two grown, sweaty men say, 'Ahhh, loooook!' These hills are covered with tortoises, and they're easy to spot in the scrub and thorn bushes. When I was being shown around Bil'in after an encounter with the Israeli army, the fields were full of empty, plastic, round, black tear-gas grenades. Going to kick a muddy one I realised just in time that it was a tortoise. Another time, our guide Fadhi had picked one up and, pointing at its central ridge on its shell, said, 'Say this section is the West Bank, and these sections around it are Lebanon, Syria and Jordan. We have five million Palestinian refugees in these countries. Now the Jordan Valley is on a geological fault line, so one earthquake and the refugees would flood home into the West Bank, and the issue of the refugees' right to return would be solved once and for all.' I prefer to think that his was a political lesson about refugees rather than one of geology or humanitarian relief but, nonetheless, it took place on the back of a tortoise shell.

The second of our three days on the trip south of Bethlehem takes us to the predominantly Christian village of Beit Sahour. 'I am really looking forward to meeting the manager of the YMCA,' I said to Phil, looking around to see if the words were coming out of someone else's mouth as I spoke them.

We meet Nidal Abu Zuluf on a country lane on the outskirts of Beit Sahour. He is polite and courteous and looks like a head of year teacher. He leads us up the lane to the hilltop compound of a deserted Israeli military base. It contains a handful of army buildings, old offices and barracks: long, low, hollow shells with no doors, frames or fittings, empty of everything but dust, dirt and bird droppings. The grubby white walls are sprayed with graffiti proclaiming, 'Israel belongs to the Jews' and, 'The Jews will keep this land.' But there has been work done here recently: a new path, rubbish tidied and the ground cleared.

'The army confiscated the land here in the seventies, built a military base and the entire area of Beit Sahour was shelled from here in the Second *Intifada*. Many buildings were totally destroyed, including the YMCA building.'

'Israel shelled the YMCA?!'

'We are part of the neighbourhood and they shelled the neighbourhood.'

'Why did they shell the neighbourhood?'

'To defend themselves,' he says dryly, rattling a bunch of keys in his hands.

The military left the base in 2006 and with support from the US government the local council built a recreation park on part of the site, just a short distance from the empty barracks and the graffiti. The park has AstroTurf football pitches, a restaurant, and spaces for people to bring their own barbecue, as well as a theatre. Everything was going well until 2008 when, one day out of nowhere, the settlers arrived.

'Now the whole place is under pressure from the settler movement, in particular from a group called the "Woman in Green",' says Nidal.

'They're settler activists?' I ask, to clarify.

'Yes,' he says. 'The settlers have been here, claiming the land is theirs, and we have had demonstrations against this. If it becomes a settlement they will want the entire area, because settlers need buffer zones and natural extensions and watchtowers and such like.' Holding his arm out to lead us away, Nidal says, 'Come,' and jangles his keys again like a caretaker.

This is not an unfamiliar story in the West Bank: the army confiscates land and, on leaving, settlers take the land over.

At first, soldiers kept the settlers away from the old base, but then they started to give them escorts as the settlers tidied up in preparation for the day when they move in: in February 2010, the military declared their old base in Beit Sahour a closed military zone and therefore out of bounds to Palestinians. This removed any impediment to a new settlement being created.

The settlers might claim the Bible gives them this land, but Nidal is part of a significant Church movement that challenges that ideology and, sitting in the shade of a fig tree, he explains a little of Beit Sahour's history: 'As Christian Palestinians, we have always been involved in the national struggle for freedom, peace and justice.' In 1988, nearly a hundred people of Beit Sahour threw away their Israeli-issue ID cards, handing them to the mayor and demanding he give them back to the Israelis. 'We said we don't recognise the Occupation and will not be identified by ID cards given by Israel. A year later we went on tax strike.'

'Who did?'

'Beit Sahour.'

'All of Beit Sahour?'

'All of Beit Sahour. We said we would not pay tax so they can buy bullets and tear gas. We are not going to pay for the Occupation.'

'How did the Israeli authorities react?'

'They placed us under siege for forty-one days. They entered our houses taking TVs and fridges. Then they entered businesses. It became a battle of wills between the people of Beit Sahour and the Israeli army. The soldiers were desperate to get someone to pay; they were even reduced to asking people to pay just one shekel, so they could get a receipt and say, "So and so paid."'

Nidal's point is a simple one, that Beit Sahour's Christian community is very much part of the non-violent Palestinian struggle, and this is echoed in the wider Palestinian Christian community. The current campaign to emerge from the Palestinian Christians takes a different direction from the tax strike and pass card actions, however. Given the propensity of the settlers to insist the land is God-given, a group of theologians and lay people, including Nidal, drafted a theological response, challenging the religious foundations of the settlers and, therefore, the Occupation itself.

'Religion is often abused by politicians and used to justify injustices. It was done in South Africa when the Protestant Church in the Netherlands justified apartheid theologically,' says Nidal, handing me a glossy pamphlet (and thereby landing another blow against the *jihad* on paper). 'The Kairos Palestine Document was launched in December 2009, and it represents the schools of theology in Palestine. So we had Roman Catholics, Greek Catholics, Greek Orthodox, Anglican Lutherans and even Baptists, coming together for the first time to draft this document.'

Getting that crowd in the same room is a feat akin to herding vipers with cooked spaghetti. Coming from a family of preachers and vicars as I do, I know well the potential for schism and splits: I turned my back on it long ago, opting instead for the calm unity of left-wing politics.

'This is a new theology,' continues Nidal. 'The resistance of love. We declare that the Occupation is a sin against God and humanity and that any theology that justifies the Occupation and its injustices is a heresy.'

I might have left religion a long time ago but the roots run deep, and the ringing bell of liberation theology can still turn my head. With my face visibly lighting up, I say, 'Is the object to get this into mainstream church thinking?'

'Yes, we want to make this a mainstream idea and we want to stop the Bible being used to justify the Occupation and the settlers.'

'Are other churches endorsing this idea?'

'Yes, churches from all around the world have endorsed it, even the Protestant Church of the Netherlands. But we call on everyone to join the resistance of love, to target the occupiers to help get rid of their evil. We love our enemy and this is the Lord's teaching. To this end, we ask the world to support the boycott, divestment and sanctions campaign until Occupation ends.'

The Christian Church is calling for the end of the Occupation to save Israelis involved in the Occupation from committing a sin: for all my rationalism and lack of immortal soul, at times like this I wish I had a 'Hallelujah!' to give. I like the concept. I like the theology and I like the idea of calling Netanyahu a heretic, out of love.

*

Today is the last of the three days of our route south of Bethlehem and Al-Khadar and we are walking with Marwan, an old hand at working with international solidarity activists, and Isshaq, a young translator from Ayda refugee camp. We wend our way across the countryside, stopping for water at farmhouses, picking oranges and rescuing tortoises that neither know nor care they are in danger. We don't do it for the praise and adulation: 'It's all part of the job, ma'am,' we say, and walk on.

On the approach to Bethlehem, the wire and electronic fencing of the countryside Barrier gives way to the concrete urban Barrier, and the most intensely graffitied route we have come across. 'In my programme for Internationals I bring them here and get them to paint a message of solidarity on the Wall,' says Marwan.

I reply with that most English of lies and say, 'Oh, how lovely.' In fact, the Barrier is covered in asinine, cliché-ridden shite: 'Love conquers w(all)', 'Walls can never crush the human spirit', 'One Wall, two prisons', 'When freedom is outlawed, only outlaws are free.'

'Oh, bloody hell,' I groan quietly, and whisper to Phil, 'It's like Hallmark-does-graffiti.' It is, therefore, an utterly joyous delight to find the words, 'Netanyahu is a cunt,' sprayed in foot-high blue letters. Some may find it infantile, crude and aggressive but fuck it, he's a heretic. There is another piece of graffiti that is easily my favourite. We follow the Barrier to a Muslim cemetery where the gravestones are overlooked by cameras and watch-towers, and camouflage netting is hung across windows. We walk through it to a road that leads downhill and under a large wooden arch: the entrance to the Ayda refugee camp. Over the arch is an enormous metal key, the most potent of symbols for the refugees (many families still have the keys of their homes in Jaffa or Haifa after fleeing from them in 1948). We walk under the key and the arch, past the cramped homes and alleys, and past the arts centre that runs an outdoor film festival – it paints a section of the Barrier white to project on to, then paints over it again when the festival is at an end. We go past the stone masons and goods yards, where the men stand in tracksuit bottoms, vests and sandals; past the wasteland, past the sheep grazing on rubbish, and kids playing. There, on a long and high stretch of the Barrier written in massive, white letters are two words: 'OPEN SESAME.'

Isshaq, it transpires, studied in England and speaks brilliant colloquial English with the kind of London accent that could feature in a bad Radio 4 comedy sketch about poor people. Walking through the hilltop town of Beit Jala, he proclaims, 'Oh, man, this is a seriously dodgy area.'

'Why's that?'

'Well, 'cos the Wall is not finished here and the crossroad goes in and out, so there are a lot of drug dealers up here, innit.'

By comparison I seem to have turned into Bertie Wooster: 'Good Lord, where's the bloody thing gawn? Phil, we seem to have run out of bally wall.'

The hill road joins the main highway, which flows north into Jerusalem and south to the Dead Sea. As a result, it has a large checkpoint filtering the traffic. Just beyond the point where these two roads merge, the Barrier restarts. It just begins. A tall cantilevered concrete wall begins and it feels as if you can simply choose right there which side you might wish to live on.

'I am not too cool about this,' says Isshaq, walking in the shade of the Barrier on the Israeli side. 'I got a bad feeling about this, man, I'm telling you.'

'It will be fine. I have walked along here before and the Israelis will not stop us,' insists the older Marwan, who promptly walks into a sign forbidding pedestrians.

Back on the Palestinian side, the ground returns to the cement lava flows where concrete has been poured for Barrier foundations. Homes perch above us on the other side of the gully but offer no shadow, and the sun is hard and bright as we stumble over rubble, rubbish and refuse, wandering by old armchairs, tyres, boxes and an odd assortment of discarded children's toys – plastic dinosaurs and toy sheep – scattered bleach bottles, burnt coils of wire and a dead dog.

Gradually, the homes recede, the slopes crumble and a cityscape emerges – Al-Khadar – a panorama of white apartments decked with black water tanks, minarets and a football stadium. Slowly this falls into our view and then from it.

A small plain now spreads beneath the Barrier, fields and crops dot the land, vines twist in perversely neat rows and olive trees line the descending terraces. From the path, we watch the Barrier curve out in front of us in a long arc and then swing away. Running alongside it is a ledge of dried mud and bursts of sprouting shrubs, and we suddenly notice that the Barrier has changed. Gone are the dull grey slabs and in their place are panels of moulded brick, held in place with metal uprights: a concrete version of a wooden garden fence. Only taller, and with a watchtower in the middle. Not a lot, but some thought has gone into aesthetics, as the bricks are a pale ceramic pink colour, with a double course of grey ones running through the middle of the Barrier.

'Is this the middle-class version of the Wall?' calls Phil.

'It's like cladding.'

'It could be the Lakeside version of the Wall.'

'Or posh festival fencing.'

'Barratt Wall?'

'Ikea Wall?'

Ikea is perhaps the closest description, not in style but in reputation, as the Barrier suddenly stops again. It appears to have run out of panels. The Barrier simply ends, unfinished, with just a couple of drainage tubes tied onto the final metal upright. I poke my head around the final panel, looking round the corner onto the Israeli road, tempted to call out, in a neighbourly fashion, 'Yoohoo, anyone in?' It is an odd sense of trespass, this urge to call. 'Hello, Israel, I'm returning the jump leads I borrowed ...'

A boy-with-donkey rides from the Israeli road onto the Palestinian track, as if none of this matters. Stepping around the end panel, my sense of trepidation gives way to a strange feeling: relief. The Barrier has finished and it is a relief not to have it. Yes, it is only for this section and it will start again at some point down the road, but it is a feeling of relief all the same. As this feeling grows, we start to play, nipping from one side to the other, back and forth in one step, singing: 'I'm in the West Bank, now I'm in Israel. I'm in the West Bank, now I'm ...' (Actually, the Barrier here crosses the Green Line so we play, 'I'm in the West Bank, now I'm in the West Bank. I'm in the West Bank, now I'm in the West Bank ...' but you get the point.)

The foundations for the continuation of the Barrier, however, look set, judging by the clear trail that marks its way across the hills: this is the route the Barrier will take.

'It's a depressing thought that this is only a temporary gap,' I mutter.

'But, being positive about it, this is only temporary Wall,' says Phil.

The break in the Barrier here runs along the boundaries of the Gush Etzion settlement block – the oldest of the settlements in the West Bank, and one which Israel believes is 'in the consensus', meaning that in any final-status deal with the Palestinians, Gush Etzion is not for negotiation, it stays over the Green Line and will become part of Israel proper. Numerous court cases brought against the Israeli government have halted construction work on the Barrier, but this time it is not only the Palestinians who object; many settlers do, too. Some object on ecological grounds that it damages the environment, and some fear the Barrier is a border, a stop on their dream of *Eretz Israel*, of claiming all the land God promised.

Tonight there is to be a settler demonstration in Gush Etzion, called by the 'Woman in Green', the people trying to settle the old military base in Beit Sahour. Their leader is Nadia Matar and the organisation got its nickname from the colour of the hats they wore when demonstrating against the peace process.

I have been on a lot of demonstrations over the years, from 'Stop the Invasion of Afghanistan' to 'Start the Invasion of Jersey'; demos of over a million people for 'Stop the War'; and demos where there was no one but myself calling to 'Ban Surrealism'. I have been on silent, candlelit vigils outside the Home Office, and I have demonstrated to 'Stop Star Wars Missile Defence' at a US base in Yorkshire where police on quad bikes chased fellow demonstrators dressed as Princess Leia and Chewbacca across the moors. I can sniff out a weird demo at 150 metres, and this settler demo kinks my nostrils from a mile back.

The protest is being held at the edge of the settlement block by the side of a roundabout, which doesn't seem the ideal place to speak truth unto power, unless the power you are fighting is the roundabout. Equally odd is the theme of the protest; that of demanding tough action on Palestinians who throw stones AND for the end to Barack Obama's settlement freeze on building in the West Bank. Thus, one issue is very local and the other international; the causes seem ill matched, like CND demonstrating to ban nuclear weapons and airguns. It is dark save for the flashing blue police lights, and about a hundred people have gathered, buttoned up against the cold, waving banners at the passing traffic. The slogans declare, 'Barack Hussein Obama: No, you can't!' and 'Don't tread on me', though my favourite is, 'Stop the Obama *Intifada*', an attention-grabbing phrase that links the US president with violent uprising and suicide bombings. To be fair, this is rhetoric and no one in the crowd genuinely thinks the president of the United States is wearing a Semtex belt, of that I am – fairly – certain.

On a patch of gravel next to the roundabout and just by the petrol station, a neat line of white plastic chairs has been laid out for the guest speakers. It creates a formal area for the speakers 'platform', but this is more by way of an affectation as the event is basically a bunch of wing nuts shouting in a parking lot. The adults listen to the speakers while the settler youth hang back in the road, periodically being moved on by the police. Walking among the protestors there are a few mutterings around me, and I pick out the word *goyim*, 'non-Jew' and, while I chat to one settler, some of the youth on the road shout, 'Speak in Hebrew, this is *Eretz Israel*!' but they are reprimanded quickly and there are certainly friendly faces here. Watching all this are the police, who have made it clear this is supposed to be a static demonstration with no marching.

As the other speeches finish, Nadia Matar addresses the crowd. In her sixties protest-singer hat and scarf, she certainly looks the part of a rabble-rouser. The crowd hold her dearly, too: settlers I spoke to talked of her as 'brilliant and courageous', and of how, 'Israel needs leaders like her'. She is not tall, but stands defiantly in the light of the blue flashing lights and demands that the crowd ignore the police and march. The settler youth do not need any encouragement; they slip the leash, surge into the road and set off from the roundabout. The crowd follow Nadia as she briskly sets off after them, waving her flag and singing. The police seem wrong-footed and scurry to herd those nearest back onto the pavement. The bulk of the marching settlers have spread across the road, though, while the youth at the forefront are running, screaming and shouting. Downhill they go, in the centre of a road into on-coming traffic, while Nadia calmly sings behind them.

'Aren't you worried about the kids?' I ask as she stomps after them.

'No. Among them is the future prime minister of Israel.'

Soldiers belatedly give chase but it is a lacklustre effort as kids from the back of the march have run forward and overtaken the squaddies to join the mini-mob bellowing into the path of Israeli drivers. Many of these drivers simply turn tail and drive off in the opposite direction at the sight of the kids looming from the darkness, obviously unaware they are fleeing from a future prime minister. Eventually the soldiers catch up with the kids up and herd them back.

Watching the Woman in Green lead a bunch of children charging down the middle of an unlit road in the middle of the night into on-coming traffic, it occurs to me that here is a woman who is her own metaphor.

Nadia Matar says good night to some final stragglers and starts folding plastic chairs to load them onto a van.

'Would now be a good time to talk?' I ask.

'OK, sure,' she says, and we sail past the highpoint of our relationship without either of us noticing. 'I don't know how biased this will be. English media men I'm always wary of, because Britain is turning into a Muslim country. They are talking very soon of having a Muslim prime minister ...'

Actually I would love Britain to have a Muslim prime minister just so I could say to her, 'It's great – you should try it here,' but her words pour out in a cascade and there is little chance of me catching her as she lurches onwards. In fact, to get a feel of the sheer torrent of her words, try reading out loud what she says next in twenty seconds. Take a breath and ... go!

'The real war is not about settlements, the real war is a war of Islam against the Judeo-Christian civilisations ... We are on the front line defending you in London ... When I am here, I am working for you and I don't really care if you like that or not because I know God is on our side. I don't need your support but you should know if, God forbid, something happens to Israel e.g. the Palestinian state is created, the next step is the destruction of Israel. The next step is the Islamisation of London. Your wife will not be allowed to go out with her ... her ... things over her head ...'

Listening to her is like riding the rapids of half-baked half-truths, untruths and an improvised stream of (barely) consciousness. This is not dialogue or a conversation, this is gestalt therapy without the therapy. At one point, Phil says to her, 'I don't want to censor you but could you make your answers just a little shorter?'

'Yes,' she says, and then repeats what she has just said but twice as quickly. More out of luck than judgement, I manage to speak as she draws breath: 'Tell me about the Barrier,' I say, as I shift into a more comfortable position from which to be spoken at.

'It's called the Separation Wall and it's to separate Jews from their homeland.'

'Are you worried it's a border?'

'Of course. That was my next sentence,' she says admonishingly. 'A border for the creation of the Palestinian state.'

'You're opposed to a Palestinian state?'

'Of course I am opposed to a Palestinian state, in the same way you would be opposed if you had to give half of London away to Al-Qaeda.'

For the first time this trip, I am speechless. After a moment I ask, 'In Beit Sahour, you want settlement there, don't you?'

'I want to keep that hill – Shdema – in Jewish hands. We go back there to make sure the army doesn't leave and we hope one day it will become a Jewish community, yes.'

'Some people will see you and say this woman is just using religion as an excuse to steal land ...'

'Oh, and let's talk about the Muslims using religion to butcher Jews, what about that? Muslims using religion to beat their wives and to cut off the arms of those that steal.'

'The question is not about them, it's about you.'

'The question is always about us!'

Nadia Matar is a taker of land and liberties, but not responsibility. Her constant avoidance leaves only room for bluntness: 'Let's just admit what you are. You are a squatter, aren't you?'

'No. Squatters are those Arabs who came to Sheikh Jarrah,' and in a gasp she heads off once more to talk how the Jewish population fled Jerusalem's Old City during the 1948 Arab-Israeli War, 'after they butchered the Jews and expelled them, they (the Arabs) took over our homes. *They* are the squatters. You are turning all of history around. But you can't do this. Therefore, there is not really a point in discussing this. You have been brainwashed. You have been brainwashed!'

'I get the impression you don't much like Arabs.'

'I don't like journalists who don't learn history and who come and are biased either because they don't know or they don't listen ... We have such a tiny little piece of land, why don't you want us to be here? Why don't you allow us to be in our homeland? Why do you want to kick us out of our homeland? Where do you want us to go? My grandparents were told in Germany, "Dirty Jew, go to Palestine. That's where the Jews belong." Now I am in the land of Israel.'

'I'm not trying to kick you out.'

'This land belongs to me. I came back home and you tell me, "Dirty Jew, go," – where?'

'I didn't call you a dirty Jew.'

'Not you personally … the world.'

According to the Woman in Green, it would appear the UN wants Jews back in Auschwitz, Palestine is under Arab occupation, and that, 'everything is topsy-turvy. We are the owners of this place. Imagine if you own a house and somebody comes and kicks you out of your house and then tells you that have no right to go back to your house.'

Imagine indeed …

Everyone has gone now, save a couple of cops and a huddled helper folding up the last banners in the dark and the cold. Nadia turns from me and sets about picking up the plastic chairs again. Oddly, she cuts a sad figure loading the chairs into her van in an empty lay-by on the side of a roundabout and I instinctively say, 'Can I help you stack the chairs?'

'No, no thank you,' she says, without looking up.

'Are you sure?'

'No, we're fine.'

For many reasons we do not part as friends, not least because Nadia Matar makes it difficult to like her. I think she veers from fantasist to pub bore and back again; in Britain she might be a member of the English Defence League shouting from behind police cordons at plans to build a mosque in Stoke or wherever. But no matter how isolated she looks, Nadia will probably set up her settlement at Beit Sahour, the place she calls Shdema. The army is escorting settlers in already and, once settled, the army will set up buffer zones and watchtowers to protect her religious squatters and future prime ministers. She is being allowed to create 'facts on the ground', because no one, in Israel at least, will stop her.

chapter 21
ALL SMOKE AND
NO MIRRORS

'What's that!'

'Hummer! ...'

' ... a Hummer?'

It's two o' clock in the morning and the house where we are staying, which was raided last night, is woken again. Phil and I are instantly alert to the loud banging and whirring noise.

' ... Get a torch ...'

BANG! BANG! BANG!

' ... Hide the recordings ...'

' ... Check first ...'

' ... it's the back room ...'

' ... both of us ...'

BANG! BANG!

' ... torch! ...'

' ... you ...'

' ... OK, OK ...'

BANG! BANG!

Together we push into the back room holding the torch out, and a figure ghosts into the glare.

'What's happening?'

' ... Mousa? ...'

' ... What the ...'

BANG! BANG!

'Sorry,' says Mousa, standing next to a clanking twin-tub washing machine juddering against the wall. 'It is too late for the final spin?'

The torch beam falls to the floor.

'It's no problem,' I hiss groggily.

'I'll make some tea,' says Phil.

'Mark?' says Mousa, the house's owner.

'Yes?'

'Sorry ...'

'OK.'

' ... but now you really should put some clothes on.'

It is the final stage of the ramble, and we've four days to cover seventy kilometres. This distance passes through settler country and, frankly, I just want the walk over with. I feel like I'm halfway through a Salman Rushdie novel: all I want is to get to the end and say I've done it.

Morning brings nothing but weirdness. The main street in the village of Beit Ummar is full of boys and hardly anyone else; none of them seem older than fourteen, but they swagger and huddle, shouting, waving and whistling for others to join them in the middle of the road. They do, too, and the numbers swell quickly. Soon the main drag is full of anxious bravado and recklessness. The shopkeeper distractedly serves me then returns to the task of locking down the metal shutters.

'The Israelis want our holy sites, so this is a day of rage,' says an old man.

The kids are marching to the watchtower at the entrance of the village. As Phil leaves the shop they spot his camera and surround him, miming for him to photograph them, pulling at his arm. A small crowd tugs at his jacket urging him to come with them; they are about to stone the Israeli army, so obviously they want a memento of the occasion.

'No,' he says, 'I'm not going to do that.'

A wail goes up from the group. One boy slumps, another tuts, and the day of rage starts with a sulk.

We meet today's translator, Yunes, and cram into a taxi just as the army start to tear-gas the other end of the village.

Yunes has a round and mischievous face, and, 'You must not say anything bad about Saddam Hussein,' he proclaims, as he slides into the taxi next to me.

'Yeah, yeah, yeah, I know,' I reply wearily. 'Saddam defied America. Saddam supported the Palestinians. Saddam fired a missile at Israel. Yeah, yeah, yeah.'

'No,' says Yunes in mock outrage. 'It is because Saddam Hussein is my friend.'

At this, the taxi driver turns around smiling, offers his hand and says, 'I am Saddam Hussein.'

'See!' grins Yunes.

I shake Saddam Hussein's hand and say, 'You're looking well, considering.'

'Hello, sir,' he says.

' … and I am sorry for being presumptive, Yunes.'

'Do not apologise. You were right in everything you said about Saddam Hussein. He did defy America and did support the Palestinians …'

'Much more importantly, do you know the directions?' Phil interrupts, diplomatically as ever.

'No. But Saddam Hussein does.'

Actually Saddam Hussein doesn't. He gets confused, confuses everyone else, drives onto a dirt track in the middle of nowhere, declares, 'We are here,' and then, once we are out of the taxi, clears off before anyone can argue. This leaves us three kilometres south of our intended start point.

'Does it matter?' asks Yunes. 'Can't we start the walk here?'

'With him it does,' groans Phil.

'We are going to have to go *back* on ourselves,' I say, looking at the map. 'We have to go three kilometres north, then we'll turn round, walk back to here and go on, south.'

'Do we have to do that?' says Yunes.

'Yes. Yes, we do,' I splutter, 'because if we don't, I will have only walked along *most* of the Wall. Which is not the same as walking *all* of the Wall.'

To which a nearly straight-faced Yunes replies, 'I won't tell anyone.'

Over the next two minutes I calmly explain the ethos of the walk; our agreed *modus operandi*. I swear once or twice and point out that if *the* Saddam Hussein had the same sense of direction as his taxi-driving namesake, then he probably invaded Kuwait by accident and was actually aiming for Yemen. I stomp off along our path pissed off, surly, and determined to enjoy the walk.

'I don't like the Wall being on our left,' says Phil, after some minutes. We are walking north and the Barrier is normally on our right. 'Left is Israel, right is the West Bank. It's like sleeping on the wrong side of the bed.'

What is even odder, however, is the hill in the distance. It sticks out partly because the other hills are green and this one is grey, but mainly because it is on fire. True, this vista is full of fields of barley and bright red poppies, even almond trees and, true, they are all beautiful, but none of it holds our interest quite like the smoke pouring from the mountain. The sight eclipses the entire landscape and is unavoidable from any view, as the wind draws up the rising grey lines of smoke and pulls them into a cloud, then blows the foul reek through the olive groves.

'What is it?' All three of us stop and stare at the hideous, seething mountain.

'Whatever it is, it's not on the map.'

'I have no idea what it is,' says Yunes, 'I have never been this way before.'

We turn and stare at him and defensively he adds, 'I'm a translator, not a guide.'

Shaking his head, Phil says, 'It's a dump! Bloody Saddam Hussein. He's dropped us in the middle of a rubbish dump.' The lane takes us directly to the top of the mountain of burning plastic, rubber and rubbish. The smoke is so sickening we have to leave the path, and descend instead across terraces and rocks to the foothills of the smouldering mound. On its lower slopes two children, no older than ten, are just starting to clamber up the steep, ashen sides. The surface is dappled with a grey and black pallor, and there's only a thin crust on which they scramble. Smoke rises from holes in the cliff-face of the burnt debris, looking like volcanic vents flashing glimpses of the fires below the surface. The grey tendrils of smoke are pulled like twine from within the sides of the mound, twirling and knotting upwards, and still the children climb, keeping upright on the mass burning beneath them, walking around the flames and smoke. One has a small pickaxe and a gardening glove. He scavenges, prodding and pulling at clumps of ash and rubble as small fires pop up around him. He tugs at unseen rewards and moves ever upwards. The younger boy follows, carrying the long-dead carcass of a computer on his shoulder, and keeping carefully to the path of the older lad before he, too, disappears over the ridge and into the cloud of smoke.

'This is hellish,' says Phil, and it is. None of us were quite prepared for this.

Escaping the burning hill as quickly as we can, we cross a valley of barley fields, and trudge up the other side to arrive atop a new hill. Here, set back from the path, is a patch of ground charred black with scorch-marks and thick crusts of withered plastics. Computer frames and shards of broken glass decorate its surface. Sitting to one side on a rock is a man with soot smudges over his face and black overalls tied round his waist, calmly smoking a cigarette.

'*Salam.*'

'*Salam.*'

Yunes quickly explains who we are and where we are from, and we all shake hands. Yunes joins the man in a cigarette and asks about the smoking mountain. The fellow sits hunched and crossed-legged, draws on the cigarette and nods, 'People burn things that contain scrap metal, like cables for their copper, and they come here to do it in secret.'

'Why up here?'

'It is very close to the Wall and far from Palestinian National Authority eyes. It is not allowed to burn things here.' He's thin and dirty and although content to talk, he appears a little distracted.

'Who does the burning?'

'Dealers, merchants – they buy cables or tyres or sometimes cars, you know, useless ones or old cars; they get them from Israel, bring them here and burn them.'

'How do they get the cars in from Israel?'

'Oh, stand by the checkpoint and you'll see Israelis selling cars there, and some Palestinian dealers have permits to go into Israel, too. They buy cars and bring them back here.'

Two more young boys, their faces covered in soot, wait at a polite distance as if instructed. The man on the rock throws them half a glance and though he is open and polite, he seems mindful of them.

'So what do you do here? Do you do the burning?' I ask.

'No, I don't burn. I get the scraps they have left,' he says, with a wave of his hand. 'They take the big stuff and I take the scraps they cannot be bothered with.' Opening his rucksack he reveals the day's haul: a nest of twisted wire and other metal knick-knacks.

'How much do you get for that?'

'Twenty-four shekels a kilo,' he says. About £4.

'How much can you get in a day?'

'Two or three kilos.'

'You must catch a lot of smoke and fumes,' I say.

'I have seven kids and they have to live. I will do whatever is needed, smoke or no smoke.'

With that he gets up, slings his bag over his shoulder and, as he is going in our direction, walks with us. Yunes and I set off first and our new friend lags slightly behind. It is Phil who catches him wave again to the boys, directing them to skirt the lane and follow us from the fields.

'Ask him if those are his kids,' Phil whispers, and I do.

'Yes,' he says, and there is a pause. It is long rather than awkward.

'Do they work with you in the smoke?' I ask eventually.

He nods. 'They join me sometimes when they are not at school, just for a couple of hours.'

The lane from the hills to the outskirts of the village of Idhna is neatly lined with stacks of stripped-out computers; piles of their plastic casings lean against a low stone wall. The man in the black overalls is called Bassem and he walks with us, his children now alongside him, no longer banished from our presence.

'Before the Wall you could work in Israel and make money,' he says. 'Now it depends on permissions and I have not worked in Israel for six months.'

'What work did you do?'

'Picking lemons and grapefruits and oranges, but if someone offered me a permit to work on construction, I worked on construction.'

'When you got your permit,' I ask, 'did you pay for it?'

'Yes, of course.'

This is no innocuous enquiry about administrative charges. Israeli companies often use Palestinian sub-contractors, agents or gang masters to organise Palestinian workers. The agents charge the workers up to half their wages for the permits and as no one officially crosses the checkpoint without a permit, the workers pay. I had met an organiser from the Palestinian General Federation of Trade Unions a few weeks previously, and he'd told me, 'The agents are a serious problem; they can charge up to fifty per cent commission. There are no rights or holidays or work clothes provided by the factories because they don't employ the workers; they employ the agent. The money goes to the agents and then the workers get paid after the commission ... The Palestinian Authorities are trying to make agents illegal but they are very powerful.' Further proving his point, yesterday I had had a cup of tea with a builder employed in Gush Etzion. He had showed me his permit and explained, 'I pay 1,500 shekels a month for this permit and that leaves me 1,800 shekels to take home.'

'When do you pay the commission?' I asked.

'It is taken out of my money before I am paid.'

So I ask Bassem, 'When you got your permit, how much did you pay for it?'

'It depends on how many days a month I worked, but between 1,300 to 1,500 shekels.'

'About forty per cent of your wages?' I ask.

'Yes. People have to do it; they have no other choice.'

'Where was the agent from?'

'He is a Palestinian living in the West Bank. He employs fifty to sixty people so he gets a lot of money ... We have no other choice but we know this is stealing, legal stealing.'

Bassem invites us for tea with his family. The kids drag plastic chairs into the garden, someone arrives with a kettle full of hot tea, someone else arrives with a tray of glasses, and the youngest is paraded and we all clap her cleverness as she walks, waving a toy in her fist. Bassem shows us the chickpeas growing in the small garden and his even smaller workshed, a long cupboard at the side of the house, full of sacks and buckets where he separates the different types of metal: copper, iron, zinc, aluminium and brass. On the floor of this shed, a blackened board holds a tangle of metal rings, components, wires, springs, sprockets, bolts, nuts and bits of foil for him to separate and pick out later. He offers to show us the next step of the scrap-metal food chain – the dealers – and he leads us into Wadi ar Risha, where scrap-metal merchants, one after the other, line what is essentially a country lane. Lorries and trucks bounce up and down it, pulling in and out of yards, some heading for the fiery hill.

'He will be going to burn,' says Bassem, pointing at a van with tall sides. He then points to a line of coaches stripped down to the frame: no windows, tyres, seats or even engine, just the chassis and frame; a coach graveyard. 'This guy does cars and coaches,' he says, and then, pointing across the street, 'This guy does a lot of copper.'

When it is time for Bassem to go, we say farewell and he leaves us in the middle of the noisy lane, in the corridor of scrap metal merchants. One yard has long, thick iron pipes sprawled on the ground; another, industrial water tanks laid side by side; while the next is packed with cars. The air is thick with the noise of grinders, cutters and hammers. Compressed-gas bottles stand on trolleys, dangling their tubes and decked with gauges and regulators. JCBs drive at piles of metal, mounds of gutters, folded panels, beaten sheets, frames, stands, bedsteads, iron grids, pipes and wire while young men wearing gloves wrench at snagged edges.

Other yards are stacked with broken white fridges and cookers, or dull black pipes and fittings. Every yard has a system of sorting boxes: bins and skips for each different type of metal. A massive truck lumbers down the road with hollow clanks and echoes coming from its empty container, ready to be loaded. Through the gates of another yard we see a group of men sitting under a barn roof breaking open gearboxes and tearing at drive shafts. The youngish owner shouts hello and comes to talk to us by the roadside.

'What do you do in your yard?' I ask him.

'Car engines. We break them up and the rubbish left over we burn on the hill,' he says, nodding at the smoking mountain in the distance.

'Do you ever worry about the health risks?'

He laughs and growls the words, 'Pure cancer!'

Another lorry trundles past, creaking and rattling.

'Is burning cables and cars legal in Israel?'

He chuckles, 'It's illegal whether it is in Israel or Palestine; that is why we burn in secret.'

I nod at the hill. 'It's not a secret.' Just then I see a car speed past with another car, of equal size, strapped to its roof. The top car's engine is out and the wheels are off, but apart from that, the bottom car is doing a two's up and driving down the lane. No one pays any attention so I presume this is normal and, once I have stopped gawping, the scarp-yard owner carries on: 'The burning is at one or two o' clock in the morning and it is always done next to the Barrier, where the Palestinian police cannot reach it. We put one or two people to watch the roads and if the police do, by chance, come by, we put the flames out and everyone runs away.'

As he finishes another car drives by, this time with two teenage boys lying on the bonnet and covering the windscreen. They lie straight out and rigid, arms by their sides, laughing wildly as the driver leans his body out of the side window to see where he is going.

The ramble heads south. It is night by the time we come off the Barrier and come to a village. Yunes has spent the past hour tirelessly detailing how exhausted he is, and Phil kindly listens to him for me while I map-read in the dark.

'Do you know where we are?'

'I think I might do.'

'Good, I will phone Saddam Hussein to come and pick us up.'

Fortunately, I am lost. We enter the village and almost immediately someone asks us to take tea with them: the night sky is out and yet a complete stranger offers us hospitality. Sitting outside his house in the cool air, the man of the house fetches chairs, the children fetch tea and Yunes smiles, happy now that he is sitting down with a hot glass of black, sweet tea in his hand. Our host is middle-aged and his wife has come to sit with us, in the type of floral housecoat my grandmother would wear, and a *hijab*.

After explaining who we are, I turn to the husband and say, 'Do you mind if I ask where you work?'

'Oh, he works, he works in Israel,' his wife says.

'That's good; many don't have jobs. Construction?'

'Yes, I am a builder.'

'Did you have to pay for your permit?' I ask, slipping into the old conversations of the morning.

'No,' he says. 'I am lucky as I work for a Palestinian who is a good man and does not charge for the permits.'

'Oh, that is good. And unusual.'

'Yes,' he agrees.

'Ask him what time he gets up to leave for work,' says his wife.

I know it's a loaded question, but still ask, 'What time do you get up for work.'

'One thirty a.m.,' he answers glumly.

'He has to get up at one thirty because there are no buses,' his wife bursts out. 'So he has to get a taxi service with the other men and they get picked up in turn and taken to the checkpoint, so they can start queuing to get through in time to start work at eight o' clock. When he gets home he is tired, he has no time for the children; he has no time for me. This Wall is ruining us.'

After tea, the family help organise a taxi to take us back to Beit Ummar. Silence reigns on the drive. Oncoming headlights rise and fall in the cab, throwing light onto us, only for it to slide away moments later. Yunes has been smoking a cigarette out of the window, but as he rolls it back up he turns to me and says, 'I support non-violent resistance now. But it was not always the way. I used to think that only violence will free us. It hasn't and that is why I am trying to see if non-violence will work. I am trying it. But let me tell you something important: even those people who have always believed in non-violence, there is not one of them who at some point has not felt the rage in their heart, the rage that says, "Do to them what they have done to us." Not one.'

The road back into Beit Ummar is covered with burnt tyres and stones. The fourteen-year-old boys are still out roaming the main street, shouting at each other. Everyone expects the army to raid the village tonight, and the atmosphere is tense. Queuing to buy fresh falafels fished straight from the pan of bubbling oil, one of the lads who had attempted to drag Phil off this morning spots his camera again and runs over, 'You missed it. You missed it all!'

chapter 22
THE MAN WHO
DREW THE BARRIER

A former government minister involved in the construction of the Barrier, had indicated he would be available to take me on a tour of the Barrier and do an interview for a fee of $5,000. This seemed a bit steep. For that money you could book Uri Geller for the whole evening and still have change for a tribute band. The former minister's offer was abandoned after I had indicated which orifice I would like to pay the money into.

The 'tour' industry is a growth area in Israel and the West Bank: guided trips conducted by experts, ex-experts, *soi-disant* gurus and ideologues. Politicians and UN staff do them, the religious right do several, and the Israeli left have a tour of house destructions. I've been on a few, too: I've toured *kibbutzim*, colleges and police outposts; I even toured a reconstruction of a thirties wooden settlement fort, though the tour guide there was oddly defensive (I thank you), and ended up saying, 'Look, don't quote me on the facts; I might have got some of the history wrong'; a sentence that had particular resonance, I thought.

Another tour I do is with the commander of the Israel Border Police, the infamous MAGAV. Nava has excelled herself in arranging this interview and trip around the Barrier, and comes with us for the day.

The commander is an enormous, muscle-bound chap with the straightforward air of expectant authority: when we drive up to a massive steel military gate that does not open when ordered to, he simply gets out of the Land Rover and gives the huge doors a couple of hefty kicks, in the same way my father would hit the TV as if this might repair the problem. For the commander, the Barrier is something to show off, and he drives us round it, taking us for tea on the roof of a police station so we can appreciate it, too.

Turning to one of the military watchtowers along the Barrier he tells us, 'We have the place totally covered; the cameras on one of these can see everything from six kilometres away.'

I bite back the urge to say, 'We know we've been photographed by one.'

This is clearly the commander's first outing with 'the media', and he gets a little carried away, going severely off-script in a hitherto unfamiliar spirit of openness. As we drive past a check-point, he suddenly barks an impromptu command at us: 'Come into the checkpoint. You'll see for yourself how efficient this is. Bring your camera.'

With that, he jumps out of the army van and jogs, completely unannounced, into the Zaytoun checkpoint. The sudden arrival of their boss sends security guards scuttling in wide-eyed anxiety. They instinctively run behind the commander, caught between shock, obeisance and the impulse to stop Phil and me pointing cameras everywhere, while we trail in his wake, attempting to wear the looks of, 'We're on the guest list: Commander plus two.'

Leading us through the turnstiles, the commander turns to us and booms, 'Film whatever you like!'

Having been detained numerous times for doing exactly this, we need no further invitation and film everything that doesn't move and a little of what does. We even go into the inner sanctum: a bomb-proof room full of computers, metal detector screens and biometric readers.

'Go ahead and film. It is OK,' he says as the staff all stare at him, their eyes saying, 'But ... but ... but!'

The commander then orders us out of the room again and goes over to stand by the conveyor belt of the bag scanner, next to two worried-looking Palestinian boys who are clutching a large cardboard box. 'Look at the bomb! Come look at the bomb!' he guffaws, pointing into the box. Inside are two cowering rabbits, which had just gone through the metal detector. 'This is the bomb!' he laughs heartily. The officers laugh but the boys look terrified. Then, with his trademark abruptness, the commander shouts, 'Come on!' and leads us back down a corridor to the exit.

Back in the van he slouches in his seat, cheerfully chatting, shouting occasional instructions to the driver and making pronouncements: 'We've killed the terror,' he says, gesturing out of the window towards the Barrier.

I put to him an assertion I had heard several times on the walk: 'We've met a lot of people along our walk who have said that it was not the Barrier that stopped the suicide bombs; that the Second *Intifada* either burnt itself out or was crushed militarily.'

'The reason the *Intifada* failed was because we finally decided to fight it,' the commander replies easily. 'We started fighting the Palestinian military, Operation Defensive Shield. It was a combination of the two, fighting and searching for terrorists inside the Judea and Samaria area [the West Bank], and building the security fence. A combination of the whole thing; and the fence is part of it.'

We bounce along the military road. Phil is in the front, filming, the army translator and Nava are at the very back of the van while the commander and I occupy the middle seats.

'If it was up to me, the whole thing would be concrete,' he continues.

'The Barrier?'

'Yes, the whole thing would be concrete and I said this, but it was too expensive.'

Only some five per cent of the Barrier is concrete wall; the rest is a standardised formation of wire, electric fence and military road.

'Why did you want the Barrier concrete?' I ask.

'When you have a fence that is not concrete but wire, you can see through it, and this creates a lot of tension.' I notice Phil stiffen as the commander says this. 'When you have a fence, a child sits there and gets many thoughts in his head. But when there is a wall, you know the other side is there but you don't *care* what is on the other side. You don't see it, you don't know it; you don't care. Ah,' he says, and turned to the driver, 'we are going up the hills.'

With that he is on to another topic, pointing and declaiming.

Later, when the tour has finished and we are sitting in a tiny café in the East Jerusalem back streets, Phil fiddles with his goatee, grimaces and says, 'You know what I thought was the most chilling moment of all today?'

'I don't know.'

'Look, he is a policeman; this is his job and this is what he does, that is not the problem. But when he said he wished the whole Wall was concrete; that was chilling. He is saying, he *believes*, that if we don't see each other there will not be a problem. You think you can make a problem disappear because you do not see it?'

The tour with the commander some days ago is but a prelude to the main event: today's tour is special because our tour guide is Danny Tirza, the man who drew the map of the Barrier and, in his own words, 'was the one who designed the route'.

It is his route we have been following all these weeks; each footfall we have taken is tied to this one man who plotted the Barrier's course, it is he who wove it in and out of the West Bank taking land and depositing settlers safe on the Israeli side. On a daily basis, we encounter the impact of his decisions and climb the track he drew.

Over his twenty-five years serving in the Israeli Defence Force, Tirza reached the rank of colonel and was part of technical staff for the famed and failed peace talks with Arafat and Barak. It was his job as the Barrier's route master that brought him both prominence and notoriety. Today, in a pair of wraparound shades and a black suit, Tirza looks like a salesman trying to look like a secret service man. Despite being ex-army he's not the classic outdoors type at all, if anything he is the classic indoors type. But he is amiable enough and the charge for today's tour is $5,000 cheaper than the ex-minister's.

I start by asking him, 'If you're not working for the government and are not in the army any more, why do you do the tour?'

'Because no one is showing the government's point of view,' he explains. 'There are extremists from the right wing against the Wall who do tours, and then the left wing put the Palestinians' case, but you cannot hear the government's viewpoint.'

Today Danny is both tour guide and driver, and he takes Phil and me through the traffic to a hillside at the edge of the Gilo settlement in East Jerusalem, a settlement built on land illegally annexed by the Israelis. To the UN and the rest of the world Gilo is an illegal settlement. To Danny and the Israeli authorities, it's a suburb of Jerusalem.

We get out of the car and he takes up position on a terrace overlooking the valley below. He straightens his suit jacket, tugging at creases, then he leans on the terrace's white railing. In front of us, on the other side of the Barrier, is Ayda refugee camp in one direction, and Beit Jala in the other.

'I will start with a story. I like stories,' he says, and he begins factually. He tells of how the Second *Intifada* was characterised by wave after wave of Palestinian suicide bombers attacking Israel with cruel and bloody impact, how the public mood in Israel shifted towards some kind of barrier and, how the then prime minister Sharon procrastinated, fearful that any decision to draw a line would have political fall-out. He emphasises the public frustration at the government who appeared to be standing by while the suicide bombers kept coming. 'Then, one morning in Gilo,' he continues, 'the place we now stand, a suicide bomber crossed the short distance between the refugee camp and here. Each morning, thousands of illegal workers came across to work in Israel, so it was easy for him to cross, get to the main street and get on bus number 31. It was full of children and he blew himself up just in front of the school. Nineteen children were murdered and sixty-two people were wounded.'

Danny was called to the prime minister's office that evening, along with the police and other army officers. 'He shouted at us, "I gave you so much money, I gave you so many policemen – how can something like this happen?" I asked him, "Please come and see with your own eyes." So the next morning we were here. Thousands of illegal workers were coming from the West Bank to Jerusalem and he saw it for himself. I asked him, "What are your orders? If you don't let us build something on the ground, we cannot stop it."'

Accordig to Tirza, two weeks later, the government took the decision to build a barrier.

'That was the moment when I got the mission to design the exact route of the security fence,' says Tirza. It is a compelling, moving story, but while there is no shortage of horrific incidents that could have triggered the final decision to build a barrier, the one Danny relates doesn't appear to have happened. There are two possible attacks that come near to his description but they occurred after April 2002, when the decision to build the Barrier was made. Perhaps he got confused or misremembered, or just rounded off the edges of the facts to fit the tale.

We drive over to the next location for his tour, near the checkpoint into Bethlehem, and stand on a slip road next to the Barrier. Here the concrete is nine metres high and in the middle of it is an approximately seven-metre-high steel gate, which hangs on large industrial casters and slides open by rolling along an overhanging girder.

'I'll start with a story ...' says Danny. It transpires that this gate is a special gate. 'It is opened only three times a year, for the traditional nativity parades that Christians have. There is one day for Catholics, another day for the Orthodox, another day for the Armenians – we let those patriarchs go to Bethlehem in their traditional way.'

I obviously don't display enough enthusiasm for the point he is making so Danny says it again: 'This gate is opened only three times a year and is closed the rest of the time ... We are not changing any religious traditions by building this security fence.' He stands back, smiling, gesturing to the Barrier as if to say, 'Look at the special Advent calendar door we gave them.' I realise that he wants to demonstrate how considerate Israel is by showing off one

door open for three days in a barrier that will surround an entire
population all year round.

'The other story here is the checkpoints. You know that at first
we built checkpoints on the main roads.' He shakes his head. 'You
cannot check people in the street, it's humiliating.'

'So is the checkpoint designed for dignity?' I point away from
the Christian gate to the massive checkpoint behind me.

'This checkpoint was not only designed for dignity but service.
It works very well. It is built so that at rush hour, approximately
3,000 people can cross at this checkpoint in an hour.'

'And how long does it take for people to get through
individually?'

'At rush hour, I think you wait in the queue for fifteen
minutes, and then it takes five minutes to cross. It'll take you
twenty minutes to cross from one side to the other.'

When I have crossed checkpoints, it has taken anywhere
between forty minutes to an hour and forty minutes, and that is
not during the 'rush hour'. In 2008, there were sixty-one checkpoint closures when no one could cross; shut down completely
for either security reasons or Jewish holidays. And I have witnessed
the checkpoints at 3 a.m., like the one at Qalqilya, when men
arrive just to get a place in the queue for when the checkpoint
opens at 5 a.m. I stood in the smoke and smells of the food stalls
that have erupted around the checkpoint as hundreds of workers
rush for a place in line. Did I really not see these things?

In the back of Danny Tirza's car, on the way to the final location for his tour, he reveals that we share an unusual kinship: 'I
have walked the whole route on foot,' he tells me. It is a strange
connection to have with him, that we are both members of a select
group who Walk the Wall; he's the only person I know of who has
walked the entire proposed route. The thought softens my attitude to him and I reproach myself. Knowing he'd walked where
I'd walked, I wonder why Tirza has not seen what I have seen.
Perhaps he's more concerned with self-justification – he has, after
all, had demonstrations outside his home; letters in the press

against him; and the Barrier has been ordered to be re-routed four times by the Supreme Court under his 'watch'.

Our final journey to the third location is slightly longer, and with time on our hands, I start to ask about the Green Line.

'International condemnation of the Barrier is largely based on the fact that it crosses over the Green Line,' I say.

'But what is the Green Line? It is not a law, it is not an agreement, it is not a border; it is nothing.'

Nothing? Not quite. The International Court of Justice finds the Barrier illegal because it crosses the Green Line. The international community (including the British government) finds the settlements illegal because they are over the Green Line. The Green Line demarks where Israel should stop, even if it does not mark where Palestine should begin. The Green Line is not 'nothing'. Neither is Tirza's statement that it is. For the Barrier's cartographer to say the Green Line is nothing goes some way at least to explaining why the Barrier roves over it so readily.

Tirza glances at me with the distracted exasperation of Dixons' customer services and explains why it does not matter that the Barrier is over the line: 'When we have peace, we will build a new border that will be agreed between the sides. A border is something that is agreed. We will take the fence back to the place where it should be.' He insists that the Palestinian land captured by the Barrier and placed on the Israeli side remains Palestinian: 'We are not changing the status of the land. That the fence is built here doesn't mean that the area is not part of the West Bank.'

Except that, in practice, it does. I have seen settlements that have been built on the land taken by the Barrier. How can that land remain unchanged when someone else has built a house upon it? All along the West Bank I have seen farmers unable to get to their land because of the Barrier: technically it might currently be their land but its status has changed. After all, if someone takes your newspaper and craps on it, is it still your newspaper when they hand it back?

Perhaps I should have expected this. The Israeli Supreme Court accused Tirza of misleading the High Court in his testimony and instead designing the line not on security grounds but for land. But even so I am fascinated by how his vision of the Barrier is so radically different from my experience. It is not that he is a fantasist; frankly, he hasn't the imagination. But as he sits in the driver's seat in his wrapround shades that are too young for him, he cuts a figure that is not quite of this world.

We stand under an arbour on a hill for the final part of the tour, overlooking East Jerusalem, a city he tells me belongs to the Jews. While he gets his maps out and before he starts a new story, I say, 'When I walked the Barrier, I encountered a lot of incidents that very simply took away people's dignity.'

'I don't think it's taking people's dignity.' So I ask about At Tira. He remembers the village instantly.

'I built that tunnel under the road,' he says, referring to the tunnel the schoolchildren have to walk through to get to school. 'It is very complicated there.'

'But the children share that tunnel with drain water and sewage.'

'No, there is a step there. You have seen it?' he says, seeming to register for the first time my experiences during the walk.

'Yes.'

'It's like a box and there is a step that, if you walk on it, the water goes down and ...' He appears to try to visualise the tunnel, wanting to remember which side the ledge appears on. He gestures that the sewage will flow one way and then holds out his hand where the step, his step, should be. Placing it in his mind. 'I tried as hard as I could to get all the details, but this was a very big project ... even down to the detail of this step.' It is a moment of doubt, the only moment of doubt I have seen from him throughout his tour and, like the steel door in the Barrier that is opened only at Christmas, it serves well to highlight the rest of the edifice.

Tirza gets out his maps and continues, by now condemned by the petty planning of his step. He is seemingly unaware that his effort to alleviate the children's experience while forcing them to share a tunnel with human shit is nothing but an admission that he knows how wrong it is.

chapter 23
THE ROAD TO BEIT YATIR

When Michael Mankin gets out of the taxi in a quiet, out-of-the-way Palestinian village, the first thing that's obvious is that he's taken off his *kippah*. He looks around, consciously straightens, then unconsciously hunches again. His half-smile turns into a half-tick which lasts about the same time. There's only one other car in the square and some old men sitting by a shop, but Michael can't wait to get out of it.

On the edge of the village, the fields open onto the hills. With a shrug of his shoulders he looks around, then carefully descends the short rocky way onto the track.

'When you look at that,' I say to him, 'you can take a deep breath and understand why people call it God's country.'

'I don't see it,' says Michael.

'You don't see the beauty?'

'I can't see it.' Michael is shorter than me and like much of the human race, skinnier, too. He has the stubble beard of an artist, the glasses of an accountant and the green hooded anorak of a careful shopper. 'How can I explain it ...' he says, in an Americanised accent. 'Look, even if [as an Israeli] you've campaigned for years against the Occupation, I go into that village and I look for ... well, what I see is a potential threat and I know that is awful but that is what I see. It is awful but understandable. I am not upset with myself. But it is not a comfortable feeling and that is an understatement.'

He begins to garble a bit, stopping and starting like a cut-price Woody Allen. It's tempting to ask if he'd find it easier to talk lying on a couch.

Michael Mankin was drafted into the Israeli army when he was nineteen, became an officer, served in the Nablus area and left the army at twenty-three. 'I had a good time in the army, I enjoyed it. There were aspects I didn't like, like shooting people, but I liked the camaraderie and the outdoors and feeling macho.'

'Did patriotism play a part in you becoming an officer?'

'No, it was probably more because of girls,' he says, with a nerdy giggle.

Michael is an activist in Breaking the Silence, the group of veterans from the Israeli army who collect and publish testimonies from soldiers. Each publication is on a theme, like Hebron, the Second *Intifada* and Operation Cast Lead. The aim is to show the reality of serving in an occupying army and what Israel is asking of its young men and women by conscripting them. The publication of these testimonies has caused considerable shock and consternation in Israel: Operation Cast Lead, for example, was the Israeli assault on Gaza that involved the use of banned white phosphorous on a civilian population. One soldier's testimony read, 'You feel like an infantile little kid with a magnifying glass looking at ants, burning them,' and in a publication on Hebron, a soldier spoke of protecting settlers who graffitied Palestinian homes with things like, 'Arabs Out' or, 'Death to the Arabs' and drew a Star of David, 'which to me is like a swastika when they draw it like that'.

A serving soldier comparing the Star of David to a swastika is probably one of many testimonies that led to Israeli legislation being proposed to cut off EU funding to groups like Breaking the Silence.

Michael might have a slightly nerdy, nervy manner but he has a compelling honesty. As we settle into a pace along the fields, and Michael replaces his *kippah*, I ask him, 'What exactly happened when you got out of the taxi back there?'

'I took off my *kippah* because I don't want them to identify me with the Occupation or settlers or military. The settlers can be violent here, and I don't want my identity to make someone afraid of me.'

'But something else happened ...'

'Look, you go in a place like that and you immediately make assessments of the situation. You saw there was a car that drove in and parked at the side; there were two guys in their twenties. We're not talking about kids, we're not talking about shop owners. Nor the ones who were sitting fifty metres back with their beards; they were fine. The little kids were OK. But the twenty-year-olds, they are potentially dangerous.'

'Is this how the army trains you to assess these situations?'

'Yes, although I am not sure I wouldn't do it if I wasn't trained. Which is frustrating for me. But on the other hand there is a threat, and this is where it gets complex: it is a fact Israelis have been killed by Palestinians. I have been shot at, I have had stones thrown at me; it is not a pleasant experience. I have had friends who were killed and wounded and so on, as have most Israelis of my generation, and that is all there in the mix. All of this went through my mind the second I got out of the taxi.'

The Barrier looks half-finished here, just a fence and a ditch, and running in front of it is a white railing of the type you see at racetracks. I quietly rename this place Hebron Downs just as an elderly gentleman trots into view on the back of a donkey. Michael snatches his *kippah* from his head, stuffs it into his pocket and greets the gentleman in Arabic as he draws near. This is by no means the first time Michael has been back in the West Bank since his time in the army, Breaking the Silence organise tours for everyone from foreign diplomats to Rabbis for Human Rights, but his reaction here is curious.

'Michael, why do you come out here?' There is a pause. A very long pause. Even cricket fans would think, 'This is dragging on.'

Before us is a long, single track through the middle of a field that seems to go on for miles. 'I feel comfortable here,' he sighs.

'This view of the road here, this landscape, is where I came of age and it is what I am used to.'

'You served in this area?'

'Not here but like here.'

'It's a familiar emotional map?' I offer.

'Yes, and because I am more in control of that emotional map, I make better decisions. I can be nice to people.'

'What I don't understand is how you want to be here, but don't see how wonderful it all looks.'

'I can't see it,' he says, simply. 'I mean, I can see it but I can't walk it.'

'I understand our cultures and background are important in this, that I'm standing here as a confused liberal whining, "But look at the view"…'

'Well, actually, it is a terrible view if you look at it. You don't have anywhere to hide, it is all empty. First of all you notice that guy.' He points to another old man on a donkey in the distance. 'The army would say, "What is he doing there? The village is down there! Threat!" Then this is a problematic area because there's nowhere to hide and that hill looks like a rough climb. Then there's a wadi here and a wadi there, so where do you want to put your troops? Because "they" are going to want to cross this fence here,' he says, pointing at the Barrier. '"They" want to get into Israel and we need to make sure they don't, so you need to place your people here and place your people there … so that is what I see. Yes, it is pretty, but it is not what I see.'

'There are lots of ways to see this view.'

'Yes,' Michael replies.

'I see a barrier and behind it red roofs. Red tiles mean it is Israeli but they are behind the Green Line so they're not settlers, but are near settlements. I see that side has pine trees and this side has olives, and I know settlers plant pines because they grow quickly. I see the grass on the other side of the fence is literally greener, which means they have greater access to water or can afford more fertiliser.'

'Yeah, there are lots of ways to see this,' he says, but with the sun going down, the most important view is of the map, which is not a good view at all. We need to get off the hills before dark, Michael needs to get to Jerusalem, and we have come too far into the countryside to get onto West Bank roads easily. On the Israeli side, just over the Barrier, is Road 354 – temptingly close, but there's no checkpoint for another ten kilometres.

'Ah, the army is here,' says Michael, spotting a jeep pull up by the fence. The layout is odd. An access road runs from Israel into the West Bank to a large quarry and trucks merrily rumble up and down it, filling up and departing. But for some reason, there is virtually no Barrier here and the army would be fools if they've not kept the receipt, as the military road suddenly ends, the electric fence ends, the ditch ends, the barbed wire ends. All that is left of the Barrier is a line of concrete bollards, the type used to direct traffic flows, no more than a metre high.

'*Ahlan*,' Michael shouts 'hello' in Arabic, then says, 'Oops, better use the right language. *Shalom*!' The soldiers stay in the jeep with the engine running but they shout a dialogue with Michael, then, with a wave, drive off.

'What did they say?'

'They asked us not to climb over the fence,' he says smiling.

'They must have assessed us as non-threatening.'

'Well, I use the word "brother" a lot. It's army slang, "How are you, brother," "Thanks, brother," so that helps.'

'They must have me down as too old to be threatening ... But now they are out of sight ...'

'Yeah?'

' ... we could cross.'

'Yes, we could.'

We straddle the concrete Barrier, walk into Israel and get a taxi.

The following day is a good spring morning; the breeze nudges the cloud along and the sun is warm. Four of us stride the ridgeway decked in hats: a fishing hat circa The Stone Roses for Zohar; Phil has on his straw cowboy hat; I've a red trucker's cap; and Isshaq a baseball hat.

Walking the hilltop, clapping along to Zohar's football songs, we could well be mistaken for a stag night that has got horribly lost. Isshaq is the young translator we walked with in Bethlehem and Beit Sahour, and Zohar is the ex-soldier who trespassed with us onto the Barrier and into the arms of military detention. As he is currently singing about how much he hates right-wing religious settlers while walking past a settlement, it's fair to say he is a man with boundary issues. Clutching a football scarf, he bellows a chant in Hebrew complete with shouts, shrieks, moans and clapping, all of which could double up as a passable impersonation of a flamenco dancer giving birth. Then he translates in a rapid monotone: '"I am from Katamon / and I have a song to sing / Come on and give me more, and give me more / And we will never stop marching / Because I will never stop marching / With the hammer and the sickle / the *Internationale* with a red shirt / and the hatred of the menorah ..." The menorah, by the way, is the symbol of the fascists.'

'Wow,' I say, impressed.

'What about you, Isshaq, who do you follow?'

'It's Manchester United, innit.'

'Oh, no, you Palestinians!' Zohar cries in exasperation. 'Always the big clubs!'

'Yeah, but they're the best,' Isshaq laughs.

Although the route is all on the Palestinian side of the Barrier, we move in and out of settler municipal areas, Area B (Palestinian partial control), Area C (Israeli total control) and a couple of Palestinian villages, so it is good to have both Hebrew and Arabic speakers to cover all eventualities. And if the walk gets dull, I might force them to sing a Paul McCartney song about peace and coexistence, out of bored cruelty.

'We have come prepared,' I say to them. 'If the Palestinians get upset you point at him' – I gesture at Zohar – 'and say, "He's a Jew!" and if the settlers go mad, he gets to point at you' – I point at Isshaq – 'and say, "He's an Arab!"'

'And what about you?' asks Zohar. 'Who gets to point at you?'

'Oh, I'm "Arts and Crafts", love. Exempt from fighting and, in the event of a hostage situation, I'm the one that does the pleading.'

With only this southern border to complete, the ramble is coming to an end. From the settlement of Eshkolot to the final checkpoint and the end of the Barrier, it's about twenty-eight kilometres. Today's aim is to get to Shani checkpoint, which is twenty kilometres of hilly terrain, leaving us a short walk for the last day, and on schedule.

With the finish in sight and no interviews to do or itinerary to organise, this is a day to concentrate on the walking. The hilltops are full of scrub and shrub and the earth here is dry and scruffy with white jagged boulders that sit between tangled thorn bushes and the odd tortoise, sometimes leaving a track only wide enough to walk one foot in front of the other. From the valley below springs a blanket of grasses that spills up the side of the slopes, stopping abruptly a third of the way up to form a line of green, a tidemark of grass around the hills.

Zohar and Isshaq have fallen behind, eager to find out more about each other.

'So do you see many Palestinians?' Isshaq asks Zohar.

'No, only on demos and protests, really. The first Palestinians I really met were at a peace conference. We met and talked, found out about each other, became friends and once that was done, we could have the political arguments.'

They walk and chat together for most of the morning; of politics, religion, football and ice cream, instinctively compensating for the lack of contact the Barrier has brought. I walk ahead of the group, further into the hills. The sight of these has gripped my heart from the first day until these last ones. Looking at this much space unwind before you is a joyous thing, and there is something to marvel at in the scale and the distance, a feeling of insignificance, of being a mere speck in a geological expanse and, at the same time, feeling an overwhelming urge to explore all before you. The hills offer a promise of freedom as they roll on beyond human gaze and over the horizon. It's a view that is full of yearning.

Lunch is a communal affair, stopping in a glade of eucalyptus trees, surrounded by daisies, soft red poppies, and purple irises with white and yellow dashes on their petal tongues.

Lying in the dappled sunlight by the Barrier is the usual (discarded) red sign: MORTAL DANGER: MILITARY ZONE. ANY PERSON WHO PASSES OR DAMAGES THIS FENCE ENDANGERS HIS LIFE. I walk over and pick it up.

'A souvenir?' asks Phil.

'A memento, really.'

'What will you do with it when you get it home?' asks Zohar.

'Put it up on the wall and tell boastful stories about it, I suspect.'

'Could you not tell the boastful story, anyway?'

'I could,' I say.

'He will,' adds Phil.

The walk is good with the exception of an encounter with a shepherd and his seven dogs. We politely say hello to a shepherd, and he politely says hello back, when his seven dogs go mad and we find ourselves surrounded by seething lumps of teeth and drool. We laugh and play it down and so does the shepherd, and then he fucks off! He simply walks away, leaving us with a pack of dogs that appear to have shunned water in favour of White Lightning. Clutching a red sign warning of MORTAL DANGER in one hand and a retractable walking stick in the other, I think, *This is like being a judge for the Crufts Best in Rabies category*, but what actually comes out of my mouth is a minimalist beat poem revolving around the words, 'off', 'mutt' and 'fuck'. Then, with the sudden contrariness of a drunk, the dogs lose interest and slink back to terrifying the sheep.

The rest of the afternoon is spent wandering dry river beds, happy to follow the dusty bends of the river corridor and the coursing curves of rocks worn smooth by water. We edge around fields of rustling barley that are growing up the lower slopes and using every bit of available land with moisture in it. We search for tracks, clambering on boulders to keep off the crops. I cling on to the red sign and we tramp the hills, one foot after the other, past clumps of thorn, shrubs and scree, walking in silence now, happy to hear only our breath and the crunching rhythm of our boots, concentrating on the pace, swapping an occasional glance or a moment to take some water. As the temperature starts to drop and the sky turns a darker blue, we come over the brow of a hill and in front of us is the watchtower of Shani checkpoint.

From the vantage point of the roadside we stare back at the land we have travelled over, searching for the landmarks of our route, watching the fat yellow sun drop down in a purple sky, staring into ripe colours and dazzled by the haze. We blink into the glow until with speeding haste the sun dips beyond the horizon and night comes.

An army Hummer arrives with its headlights on full. 'OK?' says a soldier to Zohar as they draw up beside us.

'Yes, all it fine. We have been out walking.'

'Are you sure you are OK; you don't need anything?' they ask him in Hebrew, looking at us.

'Fine, everything is good, these guys are from Britain.'

'And what is this?' asks the soldier in English, through the opened door of the Hummer.

'What?'

'That board; that sign you are holding. What is that?'

'Ah, I am very glad you asked that,' I say chirpily. 'I was walking along and found this littering the place and I thought the Israeli army must be unaware of this or they would have picked it up, so I brought it up here hoping to catch you so you can tidy up after yourselves.' And I hand him the sign.

'I'll keep this,' he says.

'Good. Make sure you recycle it.'

He shuts the door and drives off down the dark road. At that point, tired, wind-blown, slightly sunburnt and even devoid of a memento, I realise I have had a perfect walk.

On our last day in the West Bank, we ramble the remaining five kilometres to reach the very end of the Barrier. We have Walked the Wall. Tomorrow we fly home: tickets are booked, families are waiting and I will call my mother to tell her she has bought yards of yellow ribbon in vain.

The roundabout at the Beit Yatir checkpoint is our final stopping point. This is our finish line and, as we approach it, Phil stops, taps my shoulder and we hug each other. We have rambled the entire length of the constructed Barrier, some 450 kilometres of it, and we have walked on the foundations of some of the unfinished route, too. Despite spats, sulks and too often sleeping in the same room, breathing each other's old air, we have finished friends. This is our champagne and confetti moment. There should be some way to celebrate, a ribbon to run through, a certificate and medal to collect; I wish I had considered this and brought along something to celebrate with: Kendal Mint Cake or a bottle of fizzy pop, something, anything to mark the end of our journey.

With their usual impeccable timing, the Israeli military provide it. We finish the walk as we had started: in the arms of security.

'Hey! Hey! You!' a soldier shouts. He's wearing shades and with a machine gun slung around his neck, he beckons me with his hand. Feeling belligerent and having no further need to negotiate, I shout back, 'No, *you* come here!' and beckon him with my hand. He cocks his head, fetches a senior officer and they both start waving their arms in the air like a pair of armed tic-tac men offering odds.

'We should go over,' says Phil.

As we start towards them I find myself shouting across the concourse, 'Do you know how far I've bloody walked! I've walked the entire length of this bloody thing and you lot have shouted and told us off the entire bloody way.'

'Who are you and what are you doing here?' says the security man.

'My name is Mark Thomas. I have just walked the entire length of this Barrier and I'm writing a book about it.'

'ID.'

'Why? We have done nothing wrong.'

'I have to check you are who you say you are. You cannot film with your camera.'

'Yes, we can. That's rubbish. All along here people have told us that we are not allowed to do this and not allowed to do that, and most of the time it's been made up or completely wrong. We can film. We can walk. Here's my international press card. Now if you've finished, I'll have it back and we'll be off. We're walking this way and we are filming.'

The guard hands the card back, shakes my hand and says, 'Have a good day.'

As we walk off, my outburst still ringing in our ears and the eyes of the security still upon us, I whisper to Phil, 'Put the camera down, mate. I don't fancy trying to get away with that twice.'

We walk the last few steps to the finish, duck our heads and stroll on, job done.

There is one more thing to do before going home and that is to sit on a drain inspection point with a member of the Christian Peace-maker Team. Frankly, that's all I am fit for, as I'm possessed by tired-ness and end-of-term elation. I share the concrete manhole with Janet, who is small, retired, Scottish and calmly tenacious. The morning sun feels good and takes the edge off the chill, in fact, I wouldn't mind sitting here for a while and if anyone had a cup of tea on the go... At the top of the hill in front of us, a lane runs between the illegal Israeli settlement of Ma'on and the even more illegal outpost of Havat Ma'on, then on down the hillside to the concrete manhole where I sit with Janet. In 2002, one of the settlers from Havat Ma'on was arrested for taking part in an attempt to blow up a Palestinian school, which pretty much defines the ethos of the place.

'The children from the villages on the other side of the hill have to walk between the settlement and the outpost to get to the school here in At Tuwani,' explains Janet, sitting cross-legged on the concrete. 'The children have been subjected to attacks from the settlers, with rocks thrown at them, death threats …'

'How old are the children?'

'Between six and thirteen. In 2004, after four years of this, the Christian Peacemaker Team was asked to escort the children to school.'

'To protect the kids with an international presence, presumably?'

'Yes, but twice they were attacked by the settlers. Serious attacks with clubs and chains and serious injuries, broken bones, hospital-isation. The ensuing publicity forced the army to say they would escort the children as long as the internationals didn't accompany them because they said we were a provocation to the settlers.'

To sum up: settlers stone six-year-olds. Israeli army does not raid settlement to drag these settlers to jail. Settlers continue to stone children for four years. Faith group and children are attacked by settlers. Army blames faith group.

Janet's own kids have grown up, so she now lives in At Tuwani for much of her time, sharing a home with other members of the team. I rather like the fact that a retired Scot chooses to spend her time working with this village, but I have to ask, 'If the army provide the escort now, why are we here?'

'Well,' says Janet, getting out a pair of binoculars, 'sometimes the army don't turn up or they only escort them part of the way. So we monitor the army and if the jeep doesn't come we have a number to call. There have already been a couple of stonings this year.' Janet looks through the binoculars. 'Sometimes you peer into these for ages and they're there right in front of you.' She looks down, taps her watch and mutters, 'Come on, kids.'

They emerge on cue from behind the pine trees up on the hill. Gambolling would be the best way to describe their entrance: twenty kids gambol down the lane. Two boys sprint ahead in a race, others play, giggle, chat and tig their way down. A game of grass darts breaks out, kids flinging sticky darts from wild barley, twisting to avoid them, throwing, feinting and laughing. A girl runs with her *hijab* covered in darts, laughing as she plucks and pulls at them, then turns to reuse them on her opponent. Driving slowly behind them is an army jeep with its headlights on.

A painful thought occurs to me. The children's walk today under military escort is as good as that walk gets. There is no 'perfect stroll' to school under this Occupation. I've just watched the best it would ever be. So how can my walk ever be 'perfect'? It can't. It could never have been. The entire notion of finding a perfect walk on the West Bank is folly. How could my experience be perfect when so many people are denied access to their land because of their race? How could I ever hope to experience the freedom walking brings when so many have so little of it? How could I wander in a reverie on the back of others' misery? The shame of my stupidity numbs me. The walk yesterday could never have been about experiencing freedom: it was a good day because nothing happened. It was a freak event; it was one day in fifty-one of them. It was a 'perfect walk' because the Occupation forgot to intervene; my enjoyment was entirely dependent on the random whim of the Israeli authorities and military law. Yunes our translator was right: no one knows if the views and the fields will be here tomorrow. Samia the Ramallah rambler was right: these walks are to escape the reality of the Occupation; they can never be moments of true freedom. How can escapism be freedom? These walks can only be moments of reprieve. I wince at how stupid I have been.

epilogue

Nava the Israeli fixer raises her glass. 'Congratulations. Well done and much success.'

'Thank you,' I say and lift my glass to hers.

'Wait. The toast is not finished. I have spoken with you every day. I answer your calls every day; I came out of a step class to answer a question for you. I am with my family on Shabbat and I answer the call and get the army to release you. I even wake up wondering why you have not called. So this is the toast. Well done. Now go home, don't call me and let me sleep!' She lifts her glass in the air, we clink, and Phil adds, 'You're not the only one thinking that.'

This is our last night before flying home, and I am happy to owe Nava a meal for securing our release from the clutches of the military, among so many other things.

'Where would you like to eat?' she had said. 'I know a place that does good Middle Eastern food.'

'No, no more hummus.'

'Pizza,' says Phil.

'Italian.'

'OK, I know a place,' she had replied.

The place is in East Jerusalem, not far from Sheikh Jarrah and the families facing eviction, just up the road from the journo haunt of the American Colony hotel and in the middle of the NGO and diplomat area. The room is full of foreign accents and half-heard conversations about reports, funding and office politics.

Sitting in a corner by a brickwork wall and in candlelight, Phil chats away to one of the folk from the Ecumenical Accompaniment Programme who has come over for a drink.

'I have been to this place before,' I say to Nava.

'Really? It's a nice place, yes?'

'Yes. It was on my first day in East Jerusalem, during the recce before the first walk. I rushed from Jerusalem to Bethlehem and back. I saw illegal outposts, I met leftie campaigners, talked to human-rights folk, and bumped into Mordechai Vanunu, the nuclear whistleblower. I met Ray Dolphin from the UN, and went to Sheik Jarrah all on my first night. I was flabbergasted. Totally bewildered, and Ray brought me here for a meal at the end of it all.'

'You came here to recover from your culture shock.'

'And just when I thought the day couldn't get any weirder, Tony Blair's wife walked in for her dinner.'

'Wow!'

'Just there,' I say, pointing to a table through an arch. 'All I remember thinking was, "If I can get through the tiramisu before her husband walks in everything will be OK."' It is an evening for remembering, for talking about falling off hills, missed meetings, maps and mishaps, a time to say thank you and propose honest toasts. But over coffee, Nava says to me, 'You know your problem?'

'Will it stop you if I do?'

'Not really. Your problem is you didn't meet Israelis.'

'That's not true,' I say defensively. 'I spoke to loads of Israelis and you often helped arrange it.'

'Sure you spoke to some Israelis. You spoke to political activists at one end of the spectrum, and the settlers and soldiers at the other end. But there is all the rest of Israel in the middle that you didn't see. You only saw soldiers, settlers and the activists.'

'That's true, but that is who is out there by the Barrier: soldiers, settlers and activists. The rest of Israel isn't there. They don't live there and it barely intrudes on their consciousness.'

'Of course it doesn't. Seventy per cent of Israelis live on the coast, in places like Tel Aviv …'

'With their croissants and small dogs …'

' … and they want a nice life. They don't want to live next to the Occupation and the Wall.'

'You know, when I first started the walk I thought, "Do Israelis know what is happening here?" Because the hardship of living under occupation is so great that I thought, "If Israelis knew about this they would not allow it."'

'But, Mark, most Israelis don't *want* to know. That is the truth. Most Israelis don't know and if they do they don't care. You only spoke with the crazies ...' (when I had wanted to meet one particular settler leader, Nava had arranged the interview and had said, 'OK, enough crazies now or you want me to get you some more?') '... and the crazies do not represent all Israelis, all Israel is not like them.'

'But that is not good enough. It is no good saying, "We're not like them," if no one takes responsibility for them. The settlers are de facto government policy: they build and expand into the West Bank unless stopped. All the Israelis, the ones I didn't meet, have failed to stop the settlers and take control of them. And until they do, Israel will allow the settlers to create facts on the ground.'

Nava and I have talked throughout the walk and although it was not her job to defend Israel's actions, she does passionately want me to understand. 'During the Second *Intifada* people were terrified,' she says. 'A bomb went off near where I live; it was in a coffee shop. When my girlfriends and I would go out, instead of saying "Which coffee shop shall we meet in?" we would say, "Where do you want to die?" You understand? We joke but it is frightening.'

'I can understand people were terrified and I can understand public fear became the political motor to put the Barrier up, but what will get it down?'

'I don't know. Do you know what I tell my friends? I say all of this Occupation and the Wall has to end, because we are better than this.' She holds my attention with her intensity and repeats the words, 'We are better than this.'

I started this walk thinking that a barrier like this is an admission of failure; after all, a military structure 723 kilometres long can hardly be described as a ringing endorsement of a political process. But it is far more than a symbol of failure. From the commander of the Border Patrol to settlers in Ariel, most people I have met say the Barrier is to stop suicide bombers. But when questioned further, they know they can never prevent them. So many people cross the Barrier illegally already that if a suicide bomber wanted to cross they probably will. True, the process will have been made more difficult for them, but if someone wants to blow themselves up and everyone else around them, they will have transgressed enough boundaries already not to allow a merely physical one to get in their way. For Israel, the Barrier is a *trompe l'oeil*, a trick of the eye; it gives the illusion of safety and the illusion of security, with no effort to end the Occupation or strive for peace.

'You know why this Barrier is so stupid for Israel?' I say to Nava, knowing full well that she does. 'It *allows* Israel to turn its back on the problem, literally for those on the coast, and pretend it is not there. The Barrier is mile after mile after mile of self-delusion.'

The more I think about it, the more the layers of irony begin to pile up: as Israelis turn their back on the West Bank, so the rest of the world starts to be evermore drawn to it. As Israel turns further from the Middle East, looking instead to the West, so the calls for boycotts on Israel grow even louder from Europe.

This Barrier does not only isolate the West Bank.

Tiredness gets the better of us in the restaurant and we leave while the place is still full, and before Cherie Blair pops in for a nightcap. Outside we say our final goodbyes and promise to keep in touch. Phil and I are staying in East Jerusalem before flying home tomorrow, and the hotel has the harp music playing when we walk in past the overgrown plants and scruffy easy chairs. It is a comforting sound. Genuinely. I am glad for its Celtic ambient plinking playing over the sound system outside my bedroom door. A slit of light shines into my hotel room from outside, cutting through a gap in the blinds, and the small sounds of the street come in, too: a car on the road, a shout, and something falling over. I lie awake, remembering random moments of the ramble: the posters of the dead decorating the streets, wild asparagus, bullet-proof cars, the green light from the mosque at Zububa, cigarette smoke in the back of the Hummer while under near-arrest, orange groves, tortoises, poppies, hot sweet black tea in glasses and of, course, the hills.

Three days later, I am standing in front of parents and teachers and I ask them a question. I am at my daughter's primary school so some of these people are friends, some are nodding acquaintances in the playground, and then there is the head teacher I have known since I was ten when, as a young teacher, she taught me. It is what you might call a home crowd.

Holding up the microphone I ask, 'What ...' and pause, waiting for them to give their full attention. 'What is the collective noun for sea cucumbers? Question seven.'

'What?' shouts one of the dads, who is something in the City.

Slowly I repeat the question. The Parent Teacher Association quiz night is in various stages of inebriation, most of it friendly, some awkward; the growing lack of coordination is highlighted by the child-sized tables and chairs the adults are seated at. A couple of mischievous mums are flirting with a teacher; dads who have not been seen all year have turned up in stripy yuppie shirts braying about the wine; and the school secretary has complained that I don't ever ask questions that she knows the answer to. For years I worked as a stand-up comic and would take a crowd of late-night drunks any day of the week over this audience: at least you can tell the club drunks to shut the fuck up without them complaining about it in the playground for the rest of the year.

'Where would you find Vulgaria?'

'Wha' ...?' goes the man from the City, but I am there before him and chip in with the repeat, 'WHERE ... would you find Vulgaria?' Folk look at each other and shrug, a couple gasp, 'Oh, oh, oh, I know!' then clap their hands over their mouths to whisper the answer.

I walk to the CD player, announcing, 'And now the music round!' There's a Johnny Cash question and an Arabic version of 'Rock the Casbah' to come tonight.

It feels good to be home.

In the break my wife Jenny comes over and squeezes my hand, then, turning to friends, grins and says, 'It's all right, I've told him if there are any questions about Israeli human rights abuse, he'll have me to answer to.'

Familiar faces queue at the bar, which is a Formica table in front of the cubbyhole holding sports equipment and stacked chairs. Everyone brings something for the buffet: home-made salads, bowls of lentils and spinach things, cooked meats, piles of chicken wings and quiches; others bring supermarket pies and cheeses, joking, 'I made it all myself.' Everyone helps themselves and chats to whoever they are next to in the queue. People are kind here. Some who know about the ramble come up and say, 'Glad to have you home,' Or, 'Good to see you safe.'

'Bet you're glad to see the family,' says another, and a few ask, 'How was it?', keen for an answer but desperate for a short one, because they know me. The dad from the City leans in and says, 'Terrorists. Had to stop 'em, eh?' with brash certainty before sailing past, leaving behind him a wake of aftershave and swapped looks.

I still don't know if the Barrier succeeds in its officially declared aims. Did it stop the suicide bombers of the Second *Intifada*? There are different schools of thought. Palestinians say the suicide bombers stopped because the Second *Intifada* burnt itself out, while the Israelis, who might share a similar view, phrase it differently; that the military were sent in to get the terrorists in Jenin, and that is what stopped them. Then there are those who say that it did stop the bombs, as the number of attacks decreased as the Wall was built. I don't know one way or the other. This barrier of wire and concrete is a blunt instrument of complex desires but, unfold them, and this wall, this fence, this military barrier, is the continuation of the conflict in concrete and wire form. It imposes a de facto border, creating a one-sided 'solution' achieved not through negotiation but through subjugation. It claims security but grabs land, which settlers then build upon. It is no mere protective shield but a military entity which, if completed – with the Two Fingers in the north and the El corridor in Jerusalem – has the added intent on destroying a possible Palestinian state.

I set out wondering how a people can find their freedom and a country can protect its citizens from suicide bombs. And I did find an answer of sorts: *not* with a barrier, which degrades, steals, humiliates, violates and impoverishes. If Israel is lucky, the growing campaigns of non-violent resistance will flourish. If Israel is lucky, ordinary men and women across the world will realise that it is not politicians and the UN that are the real international community, but us. Everyone from trade unions to faith groups, from the Women's Institute to the Lib Dems, will realise that this cannot be ignored any more and that this Occupation is one of the biggest moral issues of our age. The Boycott, Divestment and Sanctions call has come from Palestinian civic society and, if Israel is lucky, this call will be heeded and more and more people around the world will support the non-violent boycotts, divestment, legal challenges and direct action. If Israel is lucky, the Barrier will come down quickly and the Occupation will end. If not, I fear Israel will find the Barrier does not deter suicide bombers but, instead, simply breeds the hatred from which they spring.

Out in the school's hall, a dad in corduroy, clutching a paper plate loaded with Ritz crackers and stilton and a glass of slopping red, innocently makes the most offensive comment possible.

'It must have been awful out there,' he says with a face of concern. I reply in a flash of clarity. Very calmly, I put my hand on his shoulder and say, 'No, it wasn't, it really wasn't. It was great.

I mean, really, really *great*. It was one of the best things I have ever done.'

And it was. In time I come to think that actually it didn't matter about the 'perfect walk', as Phil and I rambled in the best sense of the word. We walked in areas we should not have been in but carried on regardless; we assumed we could walk anywhere and did so unless told not to; and sometimes we ignored that and carried on anyway, until we were stopped.

And that, my friends, is proper rambling.

acknowledgements

Above all thanks goes to Phil Stebbing for talking the talk and walking the walk. Special thanks goes to Susan McNicholas who I am extremely lucky to have as a researcher and friend. And Conor, Rian and Orla for their endless patience. Special thanks also goes to Ed Smith agent, friend and Colonel Tom Parker figure. Of course thanks to Nava, Lydia and Abed.

To all the walkers and talkers. Daoud, Fadhi, Geoff, Hakim, Hindi, Jakob, Jamal Marwan, Martine, Matt, Michael, Mohammad from Jayyus, Othman, Mousa, Ray, Richard, Sami, the Shepherds, Yunes, Taysir, Wael, Yunice, Zohar. Especially to Mustafa, Mohammad from Qalquilya, Isshaq, Fred and Itamar who went above and beyond all possible expectations. Salem, Shalom and WTF! The Khouriya family guest house at Jifna, The Freedom Theatre, Cinema Jenin, Al Komajti, the Alcazar hotel in Wadi Al Joz, Green Olive Tours, Abu Hanta, Haj Sami and all those who put us up and let us sleep on their floors.

Thanks to Yasmin Khan, John Hillary and all at War on Want, Jews for Justice for Palestinians, Israeli Committee against House Demolition and Linda, IMET 2000 and Professor Colin Green, Palestinian Solidarity Campaign, Stop the Wall, Abdefattah Abusrour, Tony Pletts, Jeni Dixon, Ashifa Farooq, Donna Baranski-Walker, Amanda Telfer, Haaver Ellingsen, Nick Hildyard, John McGhee and all the support from the Regional and National Fire Brigade Union, Combatants of Peace, Veronica Pasteur and Fairtrade Foundation, Atif, Zaytoun, Felix Gonzales, Mark Brown and friends, Alternative Information Centre, Dror Etkes, B'Tselem Ecumenical Accompaniment Programme, International Solidarity Movement, everyone who helped from the Christian Peacemaker Team, Ecumenical Accompaniment Programme, Machon Watch, The Red Crescent. And Frank.

Keren, Bipasha and Nicky. Mike and Martin and Janet at Roast Beef Productions. Amy at Phil Mac's. Jake, Liz, Ali, Sarah and Rae at Ebury Press.

As usual thanks to JL, CB and IJ ...No! You're the best!

appendix

FULL TEXT OF THE Boycott, Divestment and Sanctions CALL IN 2005

Palestinian Civil Society
Calls for Boycott, Divestment and Sanctions against Israel until
it Complies with International Law and Universal Principles of
Human Rights
9 July 2005

One year after the historic Advisory Opinion of the International Court of Justice (ICJ) which found Israel's Wall built on occupied Palestinian territory to be illegal; Israel continues its construction of the colonial Wall with total disregard to the Court's decision. Thirty-eight years into Israel's occupation of the Palestinian West Bank (including East Jerusalem), Gaza Strip and the Syrian Golan Heights, Israel continues to expand Jewish colonies. It has unilaterally annexed/occupied East Jerusalem and the Golan Heights and is now *de facto* annexing large parts of the West Bank by means of the Wall. Israel is also preparing – in the shadow of its planned redeployment from the Gaza Strip – to build and expand colonies in the West Bank. Fifty-seven years after the state of Israel was built mainly on land ethnically cleansed of its Palestinian owners, a majority of Palestinians are refugees, most of whom are stateless. Moreover, Israel's entrenched system of racial discrimination against its own Arab-Palestinian citizens remains intact.

In light of Israel's persistent violations of international law; and given that, since 1948, hundreds of UN resolutions have condemned Israel's colonial and discriminatory policies as illegal and called for immediate, adequate and effective remedies; and given that all forms of international intervention and peace-making have until now failed to convince or force Israel to comply with humanitarian law, to respect fundamental human rights and to end its occupation and oppression of the people of Palestine; and in view of the fact that people of conscience in the international community have historically shouldered the moral responsibility to fight injustice, as exemplified in the struggle to abolish apartheid in South Africa through diverse forms of boycott, divestment and sanctions; and inspired by the struggle of South Africans against apartheid and in the spirit of international solidarity, moral consistency and resistance to injustice and oppression; we, representatives of Palestinian civil society, call upon international civil society organisations and people of conscience all over the world to impose broad boycotts and implement divestment initiatives against Israel similar to those applied to South Africa in the apartheid era. We appeal to you to pressure your respective states to impose embargoes and sanctions against Israel. We also invite conscientious Israelis to support this Call, for the sake of justice and genuine peace.

These non-violent punitive measures should be maintained until Israel meets its obligation to recognise the Palestinian people's inalienable right to self-determination and fully complies with the precepts of international law by:

1) Ending its occupation and colonisation of all Arab lands and dismantling the Wall;
2) Recognising the fundamental rights of the Arab-Palestinian citizens of Israel to full equality; and
3) Respecting, protecting and promoting the rights of Palestinian refugees to return to their homes and properties as stipulated in UN resolution 194.

Endorsed by:

The Palestinian political parties, unions, associations, coalitions and organisations below represent the three integral parts of the people of Palestine: Palestinian refugees, Palestinians under occupation and Palestinian citizens of Israel.

Unions, Associations, Campaigns
- Council of National and Islamic Forces in Palestine (Coordinating body for the major political parties in the Occupied Palestinian Territory)
- Palestinian Independent Commission for Citizen's Rights (PICCR)
- Union of Arab Community Based Associations (ITTIJAH), Haifa
- Forum of Palestinian NGOs in Lebanon
- Palestinian General Federation of Trade Unions (PGFTU)
- General Union of Palestinian Women (GUPW)
- General Union of Palestinian Teachers (GUPT)
- Federation of Unions of Palestinian Universities' Professors and Employees
- Consortium of Professional Associations
- Union of Palestinian Medical Relief Committees (UPMRC)
- Health Work Committees – West Bank
- Union of Agricultural Work Committees (UAWC)
- Union of Palestinian Agricultural Relief Committees (PARC)
- Union of Health Work Committees – Gaza (UHWC)
- Union of Palestinian Farmers
- Occupied Palestine and Syrian Golan Heights Advocacy Initiative (OPGAI)
- General Union of Disabled Palestinians

- Palestinian Federation of Women's Action Committees (PFWAC)
- Palestinian Campaign for the Academic and Cultural Boycott of Israel (PACBI)
- Palestinian Grassroots Anti-Apartheid Wall Campaign
- Union of Teachers of Private Schools
- Union of Women's Work Committees, Tulkarem (UWWC)
- Dentists' Association – Jerusalem Center
- Palestinian Engineers Association
- Lawyers' Association
- Network for the Eradication of Illiteracy and Adult Education, Ramallah
- Coordinating Committee of Rehabilitation Centers – West Bank
- Coalition of Lebanese Civil Society Organisations (150 organisations)
- Solidarity for Palestinian Human Rights (SPHR), Network of Student-based Canadian University Associations

Refugee Rights Associations/Organisations
Al-Ard Committees for the Defense of the Right of Return, Syria
Al-Awda Charitable Society, Beit Jala
Al Awda – Palestine Right-to-Return Coalition, U.S.A
Al-Awda Toronto
Aidun Group – Lebanon
Aidun Group – Syria
Alrowwad Cultural and Theatre Training Center, Ayda refugee camp
Association for the Defense of the Rights of the Internally Displaced (ADRID), Nazareth
BADIL Resource Center for Palestinian Residency and Refugee Rights, Bethlehem
Committee for Definite Return, Syria
Committee for the Defense of Palestinian Refugee Rights, Nablus
Consortium of the Displaced Inhabitants of Destroyed Palestinian Villages and Towns
Filastinuna – Commission for the Defense of the Right of Return, Syria
Handala Center, al-Azza (Beit Jibreen) refugee camp, Bethlehem
High Committee for the Defense of the Right of Return, Jordan
(including personal endorsement of 71 members of parliament, political parties and unions in Jordan)
High National Committee for the Defense of the Right of Return, Ramallah
International Right of Return Congress (RORC)
Jermana Youth Forum for the Defense of the Right of Return, Syria
Laji Center, Ayda camp, Bethlehem

Local Committee for Rehabilitation, Qalandia refugee camp, Jerusalem
Local Committee for Rehabilitation of the Disabled, Deheishe refugee
    camp, Bethlehem
Palestinian National Committee for the Defense of the Right of Return, Syria
Palestinian Return Association, Syria
Palestinian Return Forum, Syria
Palestine Right-of-Return Coalition (Palestine, Arab host countries,
    Europe, North America)
Palestine Right-of-Return Confederation-Europe (Austria, Denmark,
    France, Germany, Italy, Netherlands, Norway, Poland, Sweden)
Palestinian Youth Forum for the Right of Return, Syria
PLO Popular Committees – West Bank refugee camps
PLO Popular Committees – Gaza Strip refugee camps
Popular Committee – al-'Azza (Beit Jibreen) refugee camp, Bethlehem
Popular Committee – Deheishe refugee camp, Bethlehem
Shaml – Palestinian Diaspora and Refugee Center, Ramallah
Union of Women's Activity Centers – West Bank Refugee Camps
Union of Youth Activity Centers – Palestine Refugee Camps, West Bank
    and Gaza
Women's Activity Center – Deheishe refugee camp, Bethlehem
Yafa Cultural Center, Balata refugee camp, Nablus

Organisations
Abna' al-Balad Society, Nablus
Addameer Center for Human Rights, Gaza
Addameer Prisoners' Support and Human Rights Association, Ramallah
Alanqa' Cultural Association, Hebron
Al-Awda Palestinian Folklore Society, Hebron
Al-Doha Children's Cultural Center, Bethlehem
Al-Huda Islamic Center, Bethlehem
Al-Jeel al-Jadid Society, Haifa
Al-Karameh Cultural Society, Um al-Fahm
Al-Maghazi Cultural Center, Gaza
Al-Marsad Al-Arabi, occupied Syrian Golan Heights
Al-Mezan Center for Human Rights, Gaza
Al-Nahda Cultural Forum, Hebron
Al-Taghrid Society for Culture and Arts, Gaza
Alternative Tourism Group, Beit Sahour (ATG)
Al-Wafa' Charitable Society, Gaza
Applied Research Institute Jerusalem (ARIJ)
Arab Association for Human Rights, Nazareth (HRA)
Arab Center for Agricultural Development (ACAD)
Arab Center for Agricultural Development – Gaza
Arab Educational Institute – Open Windows (affiliated with Pax Christie
    International)

Arab Orthodox Charitable Society – Beit Sahour
Arab Orthodox Charity – Beit Jala
Arab Orthodox Club – Beit Jala
Arab Orthodox Club – Beit Sahour
Arab Students' Collective, University of Toronto
Arab Thought Forum, Jerusalem (AFT)
Association for Cultural Exchange Hebron – France
Association Najdeh, Lebanon
Authority for Environmental Quality, Jenin
Bader Society for Development and Reconstruction, Gaza
Canadian Palestine Foundation of Quebec, Montreal
Center for the Defense of Freedoms, Ramallah
Center for Science and Culture, Gaza
Chamber of Commerce and Industry, Ramallah – Al-Bireh District
Child Development and Entertainment Center, Tulkarem
Committee for Popular Participation, Tulkarem
Defense for Children International – Palestine Section, Ramallah (DCI/PS)
El-Funoun Palestinian Popular Dance Troupe
Ensan Center for Democracy and Human Rights, Bethlehem
Environmental Education Center, Bethlehem
FARAH – Palestinian Center for Children, Syria
Ghassan Kanafani Society for Development, Gaza
Ghassan Kanafani Forum, Syria
Gaza Community Mental Health Program, Gaza (GCMHP)
Golan for Development, occupied Syrian Golan Heights
Halhoul Cultural Forum, Hebron
Himayeh Society for Human Rights, Um al-Fahm
Holy Land Trust – Bethlehem
Home of Saint Nicholas for Old Ages – Beit Jala
Human Rights Protection Center, Lebanon
In'ash al-Usrah Society, Ramallah
International Center of Bethlehem (Dar An-Nadweh)
Islah Charitable Society-Bethlehem
Jafra Youth Center, Syria
Jander Center, al-Azza (Beit Jibreen) refugee camp, Bethlehem
Jerusalem Center for Women, Jerusalem (JCW)
Jerusalem Legal Aid and Human Rights Center (JLAC)
Khalil Al Sakakini Cultural Center, Ramallah
Land Research Center, Jerusalem (LRC)
Liberated Prisoners' Society, Palestine
Local Committee for Social Development, Nablus
Local Committee for the Rehabilitation of the Disabled, Nablus
MA'AN TV Network, Bethlehem
Medical Aid for Palestine, Canada

MIFTAH – Palestinian Initiative for the Promotion of Global Dialogue
    and Democracy, Ramallah
Muwatin – The Palestinian Institute for the Study of Democracy
National Forum of Martyr's Families, Palestine
Near East Council of Churches Committee for Refugee Work – Gaza Area
Network of Christian Organisations – Bethlehem (NCOB)
Palestinian Council for Justice and Peace, Jerusalem
Palestinian Counseling Center, Jerusalem (PCC)
Palestinian Democratic Youth Union, Lebanon
Palestinian Farmers' Society, Gaza
Palestinian Hydrology Group for Water and Environment Resources
    Development – Gaza
Palestinian Prisoners' Society-West Bank
Palestinian Society for Consumer Protection, Gaza
Palestinian University Students' Forum for Peace and Democracy, Hebron
Palestinian Women's Struggle Committees
Palestinian Working Women Society for Development (PWWSD)
Popular Art Centre, Al-Bireh
Prisoner's Friends Association – Ansar Al-Sajeen, Majd al-Krum
Public Aid Association, Gaza
Ramallah Center for Human Rights Studies
Saint Afram Association – Bethlehem
Saint Vincent De Paule – Beit Jala
Senior Citizen Society – Beit Jala
Social Development Center, Nablus
Society for Self-Development, Hebron
Society for Social Work, Tulkarem
Society for Voluntary Work and Culture, Um al-Fahm
Society of Friends of Prisoners and Detainees, Um al-Fahm
Sumoud-Political Prisoners Solidarity Group, Toronto
Tamer Institute for Community Education, Ramallah
TCC – Teacher's Creativity Center, Ramallah
Wi'am Center, Bethlehem
Women's Affairs Technical Committee, Ramallah and Gaza (WATC)
Women's Studies Center, Jerusalem (WSC)
Women's Center for Legal Aid and Counseling, Jerusalem (WCLAC)
Yafa for Education and Culture, Nablus
Yazour Charitable Society, Nablus
YMCA – East Jerusalem
Youth Cooperation Forum, Hebron
YWCA – Palestine
Zakat Committee – al-Khader, Bethlehen
Zakat Committee – Deheishe camp, Bethlehem

notes

1   UN figures according to the latest published route.
2   The 'Green Line' refers to the 1949 Armistice line, the demarcation line separating Israel from its neighbours following the 1948 Arab–Israeli War.
3   Since 1967 successive Israeli governments have encouraged Israeli citizens to live in settlements in the Occupied West Bank by offering land and financial incentives. The international community regards the settlements as contrary to international law. There are over 200 Israeli settlements in the West Bank, housing over 300,000 Israelis, not including East Jerusalem, and along with the roads and buffer zones around them, they now take up at least forty per cent of West Bank land. The settlers are subject to Israeli law and Palestinians are not allowed to enter settlements without permission.
4   Israel's internationally recognised borders as set out in its ceasefire agreements after the 1948 Arab–Israeli War. During the 1968 Six Day War, Israel captured territories over the Green Line including the West Bank and East Jerusalem. The international community deems these areas 'Occupied Territories', whereas Israel calls them 'Disputed Territories'.
5   About a fifth of the West Bank, mostly in the Jordan Valley, is designated a 'closed military area'. Once you add this to the settlements and the Israeli declared 'nature reserves', it turns out that ninety-four per cent of the West Bank's fertile, water-rich Jordan Valley is off limits to Palestinians. Source: Save the Children, Jordan Valley Fact Sheet, October 2009.
6   The Oslo Accords in the early nineties divided the West Bank into three temporary administrative zones – Area A under Palestinian control, Area B under joint Israeli and Palestinian Control and Area C under the full control of the Israelis for security and planning, with the provision of basic services supplied by the Palestinian Authority. This division was meant to be an interim measure while final status negotiations took place between the two sides, and a deal reached on the transfer of power from the Israeli Civil Authority to the Palestinian Authority. It never happened. Source: United Nations.
7   Approximately sixty-one per cent of the West Bank, including ninety per cent of the Jordan Valley, falls within Area C. Israeli government figures show that between January 2000 and September 2007, over ninety-four per cent of building permit applications in Area C submitted by Palestinians were refused; 1,600 Palestinian buildings were demolished and a further 5,000 demolition orders issued. Source: United Nations Office for the Coordination of Occupied Palestinian Territory, 'Lack of Permit' Demolitions and Resultant Displacement in Area C, May 2008.

8 Between the end of the 1948 Arab–Israeli War and the Six Day War in 1967, the West Bank and East Jerusalem were under Jordanian rule as set out in the 1949 Armistice agreement.

9 'Legal Consequences of the Construction of a Wall in the Occupied Palestinian Territory,' International Court of Justice. http://www.icj-cij.org/docket/index.php?p1=3&p2=4&code=mwp&case=131&k=5a'.

10 If charged, Yaya would have been put on trial in a military court, contrary to international law. There are currently 350 children in Israeli prisons, often in 'prolonged periods of solitary confinement, in inhumane and degrading conditions'. Their families are often unable to get the permits for access into Israel to visit them. Israel treats its own population as minors until eighteen, whereas Palestinian children are charged as adults from sixteen years old. Most offences are for stone throwing, which carries a maximum twenty-year sentence. Nearly all convictions are as a result of a 'confession'. Sources: United Nations Committee on the Rights of the Child and Defence for Children International.

11 Source: Five Years after the International Court of Justice Advisory Opinion: A Summary of the Humanitarian Impact of the Barrier July 2009, UN OCHA OPT.

12 Source: Israeli Settlements and International Law, Israeli Ministry of Foreign Affairs http://www.mfa.gov.il/MFA/Peace+Process/Guide+to+the+Peace+Process/Israeli+Settlements+and+International+Law.htm.

13 ibid.

14 ibid.

15 Excluding East Jerusalem, which amounts to approximately 210,000 more settlers.

16 Michael Sfard took the case of the five villages caught in the Alfei Menashe bubble to court, where it was ruled that the Barrier should be rerouted to re-include three of the five original villages back into the West Bank. Arab ar Ramadin, however, remains on the Israeli side of the Barrier, and its children now have to travel by bus every day to get to school. The round trip is thirty-two kilometres, despite the school being two kilometres to the south of Arab ar Ramadin on the West Bank side of the Barrier.

17 Quoted in article, 'Forcible Removal of Arabs gaining support in Israel' *The Times*, 24 August 1988.

18 Source: http://www.haaretz.com/news/benjamin-netanyahu-israel-to-retain-key-west-bank-settlement-in-any-peace-deal-1.262417.

19 Source: *Haaretz* News: 'The painful cost to Israel of its settler adventure, 20/07/09.

20 Source: Peace Now website.

21 Source: Amnesty International, Troubled Waters. Palestinians denied fair access to water, 2009.

22 Source: PBS, 'Now with Bill Moyers' 6 June 2003.

23 Source: http://www.haaretz.com/news/high-court-controversial-settlement-neighborhood-to-remain-in-place-1.228883.

24 In 2009, the Israeli Supreme Court ruled that the general closure of the road to Palestinians was illegal. In May 2010 the road was partially reopened although with two new checkpoints controlling access to the road, and a third controlling access into East Jerusalem, for which they requisitioned more than 170 *dunums* of private Palestinian land. Although Palestinians can now drive on the road, they can't access Ramallah from it, so the impact of its opening is minimal, 'improving mainly the vehicular movement between the villages'. Source: OCHA, West Bank Movement and Access Update June 2010.

25 This is Area C so there is no building work allowed without a permit.

26 Although Route 443 now has some limited access on part of it, it is not the only road Palestinians cannot access freely. More than 300 kilometres of roads in the West Bank are off-limits or restricted to Palestinians. Source: B'Tselem.

27 During Israel's creation in 1948 and the 1967 Six Day War more than half of Palestinians living in pre-1948 Palestine were displaced, one of the largest displaced populations in the world. There has been dispute over what actually happened in 1948. Palestinians accuse the Israelis of widespread ethnic cleansing whereas the Israelis claim the Arab population left of its own accord to avoid a war started by its Arab neighbours. It is perhaps no surprise that Palestinians refer to the creation of Israel as the 'Nakba', the catastrophe, and the right of return for these refugees has proven to be a major stumbling block to peace.

28 A trade worth between £10m and £30m a year. Although it is UK 'policy' that no British arms should be used in the Occupied Territories, they 'almost certainly' were during the offensive in Gaza in 2008. Source: House of Commons Committees on Arms Export Control.

29 So far, over sixty Palestinians have lost their homes and another 500 are at immediate risk. Source: OCHA.

30 The Boycott, Divestment and Sanctions (BDS) campaign is modelled on the sanctions campaign against South African apartheid in the 1980s, and was officially launched in 2005 by a plethora of groups representing Palestinian civic society, collectively known as the Boycott, Divestment and Sanctions Campaign National Committee (BNC). These groups represent a range of people from teachers to farmers, political parties to trade unions, refugees to students, as well as associations and campaigns. The BDS campaign urges non-violent punitive measures to be brought against Israel until the military occupation ends, colonised land is returned, and Israel dismantles the Barrier.